"[An] illuminating but unconventional new biography of Abraham Lincoln. . . . [Brookhiser] succeeds brilliantly in giving us a new and original perspective on Lincoln's statesmanship. His prose is spare and robust (the author has been schooled by Lincoln) and even readers who know little of Lincoln will find the treatment entirely readable, enjoyable, and persuasive."

—*New Criterion*

"As he has before . . . he clearly demonstrates—in decided contrast to so many of his comrades on the right—that he takes history seriously. And here, providing us with a close historical reading of Lincoln's speeches, notes, and correspondence, he enables us to not only better understand, but also (and even more effectively than he did in his previous biographical studies) to actually 'feel' his subject's battles both with his antagonists and with history itself."

—HARVEY KAYE, *Daily Beast*

"Drawing on Lincoln's official papers, speeches, and private letters, the book makes clear how he looked back to the Declaration of Independence and the Constitution's Preamble to resolve the great contradiction that the Founders couldn't—slavery's existence in a nation where all are created equal and have unalienable rights."

—*Pittsburgh Tribune-Review*

"An unconventional new biography of Lincoln. . . . Brookhiser quotes many of Lincoln's speeches and letters to demonstrate how he was influenced by the Founders in his struggle with the great issues of his time, slavery, and civil war."

—*Seattle Times*

"A compact, profound, and utterly absorbing new life of Abraham Lincoln. . . . With searchlight intensity, it dazzlingly illuminates the great president's evolving views of slavery and the extraordinary speeches in which he unfolded that vision, molding the American mind on the central conflict in American history and resolving, at heroic and tragic cost to the nation and himself, the contradiction that the Founding Fathers themselves could not resolve."

—*City Journal*

"Irresistible pacing, exciting, and accessible, [*Founders' Son*] is a unique and essential insight into this pivotal figure from American history."

—*San Francisco Book Review*

"A pithy biography of the man who not only ended slavery in America, but also distilled the Founders' legacy. Astonishingly, Brookhiser has added to the massive Lincoln literature a book that is both distinct and important."

—*Commentary*

"Working mainly from Lincoln's speeches, Brookhiser carefully examines the full range, from his early talks as Lincoln began his career to the famous ones of the Lincoln-Douglas debates and those of his presidency. . . . There is much to admire in *Founders' Son*."

—*American Scholar*

"Brookhiser excels in describing Lincoln's political fights over government banks and in parsing his presidency in wartime—specifically, his detailed account of the complex evolution of the president's views on slavery."

—*Publishers Weekly*

"Lincoln knew that history was both past and prologue, and he sought to appropriate the earlier age properly to guide the nation successfully through the Civil War. This highly accessible read will appeal most to readers who desire to learn more about Lincoln and especially the ideas, dogmas, and dreams that moved him to his public career and life in the White House."

—*Library Journal*

"[Brookhiser's] discussion of the second inaugural is genuinely moving and instructive. The narrative always smoothly returns, though, to the Founders and Lincoln's unceasing attempt to divine their intentions and to examine the institutions they built and the opportunity they created for someone like him to thrive. For years now, Brookhiser has helped bring the Founders back to life, precisely Lincoln's purpose as the president contemplated for his country a new birth of freedom, 'the old freedom' they envisioned in 1776 but couldn't quite perfect."

—*Kirkus Reviews*

"Lincoln was not a conventional politician, and neither is Richard Brookhiser a conventional historian, nor, fittingly, is *Founders' Son* a conventional biography. For the sixteenth president, as Brookhiser dazzlingly argues, ideas *mattered*—but never so much as when translated into action. Throughout Lincoln's life, the Founders served as his touchstones, their ideals his lodestars, and he dedicated himself to completing the task they had left unfinished; the destruction of slavery, that Damoclean Sword menacing the Republic since its creation, would be both his monument and his tomb. *Founders' Son* is an ingenious intellectual biography, a work of the highest order written by one of our most creative historians about the most brilliant of our presidents."

—ALEXANDER ROSE, author of *Washington's Spies:*
The Story of America's First Spy Ring

"In his first inaugural, Abraham Lincoln spoke of the 'mystic chords of memory' that bound those about to fight a civil war over the meaning of union and liberty to those who had built a system of government on them during and after the Revolution. Distinguished historian Richard Brookhiser strikes those chords in *Founders' Son*. In doing so, he reveals Lincoln to be not only a student of the past, but a leader with the mind and courage to redeem America's first 'birth of freedom' with a new one, sealed in blood."

—HENRY LOUIS GATES, JR., Alphonse Fletcher
University Professor, Harvard University

"Abraham Lincoln is the most written-about man in American history, yet Richard Brookhiser, a historian and writer of extraordinary talent, has written an analysis that is lively, incisive, novel—and brilliant. This book reminds us of Lincoln's reverence for the Founders, his 'stubborn concern for first principles' and—ultimately—the often-overlooked reverence for the Almighty God that guided him in America's darkest hours."

—JOHN BOEHNER, Speaker of the House

FOUNDERS'
SON

❦

A LIFE *of* ABRAHAM LINCOLN

RICHARD BROOKHISER

BASIC BOOKS

A Member of the Perseus Books Group

NEW YORK

Copyright © 2014 by Richard Brookhiser

Published by Basic Books
A Member of the Perseus Books Group
First paperback edition published in 2016 by Basic Books

Books published by Basic Books are available at special discounts for bulk purchases in the United States by corporations, institutions, and other organizations. For more information, please contact the Special Markets Department at the Perseus Books Group, 2300 Chestnut Street, Suite 200, Philadelphia, PA 19103, or call (800) 810-4145, ext. 5000, or e-mail special.markets@perseusbooks.com.

Designed by Linda Mark
Text set in 11.5 pt Fairfield LT by the Perseus Books Group

Library of Congress Cataloging-in-Publication Data
Brookhiser, Richard.
    Founders' son : a life of Abraham Lincoln / Richard Brookhiser.
       pages cm
    Includes bibliographical references and index.
    ISBN 978-0-465-03294-5 (hardcover)—ISBN 978-0-465-05686-6 (e-book)
 1. Lincoln, Abraham, 1809–1865. 2. Presidents—United States—Biography.
 3. United States—Politics and government—1861–1865. I. Title.
    E457.45.B76 2014
    973.7092—dc23
    [B]
                                                           2014021173
    ISBN: 978-0-465-04001-8 (paperback)

10 9 8 7 6 5 4 3 2 1

For
Elizabeth Altham and her students

Contents

NOTE ON SPELLING
AND USAGE

Nineteenth-century rules for spelling and punctuation differed somewhat from ours, and the uneducated followed no rules at all; even Lincoln made a few characteristic mistakes throughout his life (he liked double consonants—*verry*). I have corrected and modernized everything I have quoted, except for italics used for emphasis (mostly by Lincoln, and by Parson Weems).

INTRODUCTION: TWO OLD MEN, ONE YOUNG MAN

W HEN ABRAHAM LINCOLN WAS A YOUNG MAN IN HIS twenties, the last of the founding fathers—the men who won the Revolution and made the Constitution—finally died. As their number dwindled, attentive people hastened to record their thoughts about America, its prospects and its problems, before they passed.

In November 1831, the last surviving signer of the Declaration of Independence, Charles Carroll, age ninety-four, was visited by Alexis de Tocqueville, a young Frenchman touring America to study its institutions. Carroll, a wealthy planter from the state of Maryland, reminded his guest of an English aristocrat—genial, gracious, proud ("he holds himself very erect," Tocqueville noted). Carroll was especially proud of the glory days of American independence and of his own role in proclaiming it. In the concluding sentence of the Declaration, the signers had pledged their lives, fortunes, and sacred honor to support

1

it; Carroll let Tocqueville know that the fortune he had pledged had been "the most considerable" in America. ("There go a few millions," another signer commented, with gallows humor, as Carroll signed the revolutionary document.)

The Revolution had been won, and Carroll kept his millions. Now, however, he fretted about the nation he had made, for America was becoming too democratic for his tastes. He mourned "the old aristocratic institutions" of Maryland, by which he meant property qualifications for voting, which had been abolished in 1810. (Before then, a Marylander had to own fifty acres of land to vote—no problem for Carroll, who owned 13,000.) He feared even more changes. "A mere Democracy," he warned Tocqueville as the visit ended, "is but a mob"—willful, possibly violent. Fortunately, America had a safety valve: "Every year we can push our innovators out West." This was Carroll's vision of the frontier: as a dumping ground for democrats. Carroll died in 1832.

In February 1835, the last surviving signer of the Constitution, James Madison, played host to another curious traveler, Harriet Martineau, an English writer making her own study of the United States. Madison, an eighty-three-year-old Virginian, was a grander figure than Carroll, for he was a former president as well as the signer of a founding document. Physically he had aged harder than Carroll—rheumatism confined him to a favorite chair in his bedroom—but his mind and his conversation sparkled: Martineau, clearly enchanted with him, called him "wonderful," "lively," "playful." Madison's upbeat temperament suited his politics, for unlike Carroll, he had no fear of democracy. He was a democratic politician par excellence; he and his best friend, Thomas Jefferson, had founded a political party (first called the Republican Party, then the Democratic) that had dominated American politics for over thirty years. "Madison," as Martineau put it, "reposed cheerfully, gaily . . . on his faith in the people's power of wise self-government."

He had a concern of his own about the state of the nation, however, and that was slavery. Like Carroll, Madison was a planter and a slave owner. He had grown up with the institution, knew its evils from the inside, and discussed them frankly with Martineau. Slavery kept owners in a state of perpetual fear. It degraded slaves' minds, even when it did not brutalize them physically (he cited promiscuity and cruelty to animals as bad habits encouraged by lives of bondage).

How could the country free itself of the evil? Ideally, Madison believed, slaves should be freed (though he had not freed his own). But where then could they go? Free states did not want them—many had stringent laws to keep out black immigrants; Canada, he thought, was too cold for them. Maybe they could be sent back to Africa (Martineau thought that scheme was fantastic: American slaves were Americans; they would not want to leave). Where slavery was concerned, the last of the founders "owned himself to be almost in despair." In 1836 Madison died.

If the dying founders were anxious about their legacy, their heirs were no less troubled to see them go. Fathers should die before their children; it is the order of nature. But then responsibility and anxiety shift to new shoulders.

In January 1838 Abraham Lincoln gave a speech to the Young Men's Lyceum of Springfield, Illinois, on "The Perpetuation of Our Political Institutions." His speech was both a farewell to the founding fathers and a somewhat fearful look ahead.

Lincoln himself was a young man as he delivered it—he would turn twenty-nine in two weeks. No curious foreigner interviewed him; his remarks were printed in the *Sangamo Journal*, a local newspaper.

Illinois was the west that Carroll had spoken of to Tocqueville—almost the frontier of American civilization. Northwestern Illinois had been the scene of an Indian war only six years earlier (Lincoln had served in it). No one would ever mistake Lincoln for an English aristocrat: he was the son of a subsistence farmer and carpenter, and his own property consisted mostly of debts. He had spent his early twenties bouncing from job to job—river boatman, clerk, storekeeper, postmaster, surveyor—until he settled on politics and law, getting himself elected to the state legislature and becoming the law partner of an older officeholder. Socially he belonged to the democratic mass, and the life he had chosen to pursue was climbing the ladders of democratic politics and litigation.

Lincoln was an autodidact—all his schooling amounted to no more than a year in one-room schoolhouses—and he gave an autodidact's speech to the Young Men's Lyceum: well-planned, but stiff and a little fancy, like a brand-new suit. One phrase foreshadowed the Lincoln to come: in his peroration, he said, of the founding fathers, "what invading foemen could *never do*, the silent artillery of time *has done*. . . . They are gone." Lincoln's artillery metaphor had the force and paradox of great poetry: artillery is the loudest thing on a battlefield, as it is the most destructive; but the deadliest artillery of all is noiseless, quieter even than the ticking of a watch. Lincoln's metaphor also had the music of great poetry. It was a three-word variation on the letters *i* and *t*. *Silent*—a long *i*, trailed by a soft final *t*. *Artillery*—a sharp *t*, followed immediately by a short *i*. *Time*, the monosyllable—a sharp *t* with a long moaning *i*. The music underscored the image: *Silent* (ready) *artillery* (aim) *time* (fire—direct hit). For the rest, Lincoln's thoughts and his language were sometimes interesting, sometimes half baked. That was all right; he had years of baking ahead.

The institutions whose perpetuation he discussed at the Lyceum were those of American democratic republicanism: "a system," he told the young men grandly, "conducing more essentially to the ends of civil and religious liberty, than any of which the history of former times tells us." This system was the handiwork of the founding fathers: "a legacy bequeathed us" by "hardy, brave and patriotic" ancestors.

How was the legacy doing in 1838? Lincoln was worried; though he had not read Carroll's or Madison's last thoughts, some of his worries echoed theirs. He had a lot to say about mobs—an "increasing disregard for law," he argued, "pervades the country," a point he illustrated by describing recent lynchings in Mississippi, Missouri, and Illinois. If mobs raged unchecked, the people, disgusted, might turn to a Napoleon, a dictator, to tame them. He had a little to say about slavery:

the man the Illinois mob had lynched—in Alton, a town only sixty miles southwest of Springfield—had been the editor of a crusading antislavery newspaper.

But the backdrop for Lincoln's talk—its framing anxiety—was the passing of the founding fathers and the void they left. The men who had built the country had been personally committed to its success, but now that they were gone, that commitment would inevitably weaken. "I do not mean to say, that the scenes of the [American] revolution are now or ever will be entirely forgotten; but that like every thing else, they must fade upon the memory of the world, and grow more and more dim by the lapse of time." History would tell the story of the founding fathers' great deeds, but now that they had died, it could no longer be living history. "They were the pillars of the temple of liberty; and now, that they have crumbled away, that temple must fall, unless we, their descendants, supply their places with other pillars."

In 1838 Lincoln had a not-quite-thirty-year career ahead of him; much of it would be preoccupied with the founding fathers—their intentions and their institutions, and how to fulfill and perpetuate them. As a lawmaker and a lawyer, he worked within the systems they had left behind. As a politician, he wanted to wrap himself in their aura. As a poet and a visionary, he drew on them for rhetoric and inspiration.

But Lincoln invoked the founding fathers not just to do his jobs, win elections, or speak well, but also to solve America's problems. His perceptions of those problems would change over the years, but in the climax of his career, from 1854, when the repeal of the Missouri Compromise "aroused him," as he put it, "as he had never been before," through 1865, the end of his presidency and the Civil War, he tried to solve the problem of slavery—James Madison's—by solving the problem of democracy—Charles Carroll's.

America had been a continent of slaveholders since colonial times, and the founding fathers had accepted the evil fact (reluctantly, Lincoln said). But, he would argue, they had hoped slavery would one day die out, and they had taken steps to contain it (ending the slave trade,

forbidding slavery in the Northwest Territory). They had left words expressing their repugnance: the first self-evident truth in the Declaration
of Independence was that "all men are created equal." They had also
left silences: even though the Constitution protected slavery in several
ways, it never named it (so that, Lincoln said, there should be no trace
of slavery "on the face of the great charter of liberty" after slavery had
finally vanished).

But how could an institution as deeply rooted as American slavery
ever be made to vanish, even over the very long haul? (At different
times Lincoln envisioned end-dates as remote as 1893, 1900, or deep
into the twentieth century.) The forum of democratic politics posed a
danger—and offered an opportunity. If Americans embraced slavery, or
even became indifferent to it, then it would spread nationwide (Lincoln
would fear it was doing just that in the 1850s). If a minority of Americans, having lost an election, simply left the country, as happened in
1861, they could take slavery with them—and cripple the very notion
of republican government on their way out. (What good is a form of
government that cannot maintain itself?) But if Lincoln could convince
enough Americans that slavery was a blight and persuade them to vote
their convictions, then slavery would be contained. If he could convince
enough of them that the Union was worth fighting for, then it could be
saved—and slavery extinguished sooner than 1893.

Lincoln's most important allies in these efforts were the founding
fathers. They were dead. "They *were* a forest of giant oaks," Lincoln
told the young men of Springfield, "but the all resistless hurricane has
swept over them." But Lincoln called them back to life for his purposes.
Their principles, he maintained were his; his solutions were theirs. He
summoned the past to save the present. (To make the founding fathers
effectual allies, he first had to edit them a bit—to use the past, he had to
save it from aspects of itself.) Lincoln turned the founding fathers into
his fathers—and the fathers of a revitalized American liberty to come.

For Lincoln, the road to the future always began in the past—America's, and his. As a boy he admired George Washington as a champion

of liberty. As a young man he found in Thomas Paine lessons about religion, which he ultimately abandoned, and about how to win arguments, which he retained for the rest of his life. At the height of his career he embraced Thomas Jefferson's Declaration of Independence as a statement of principle (an "apple of gold," he called it, quoting the Bible) and the Preamble to the Constitution, which named the people as the beneficiaries and guardians of freedom.

The life of a man so preoccupied with symbolic fatherhood naturally makes us curious about his relationship with his actual, flesh-and-blood father. What did Abraham Lincoln owe Thomas Lincoln (1778–1851)? Not a lot, Abraham himself would say when he talked about his origins, which was seldom. But the son owed Thomas more than he ever admitted. Some women also had a profound effect on him—though not his lovers, except for one who died. Some of the most potent women in Lincoln's life were widows, beginning with his stepmother; some were figures of his imagination (and some of these imaginary women were black).

There were many problems for Lincoln in his efforts to use the founding fathers. Not least was the fact that other politicians and writers used them too, for very different purposes of their own. Maybe the founders were models of moral virtue, with no application to modern political problems. "Give us his *private virtues*," wrote Parson Weems in his *Life of Washington*, which Lincoln read. "It was to those *old-fashioned* virtues that our hero owed everything. . . . Private life is always *real life*." Or maybe the problems that Lincoln found so pressing were not problems at all, and the founders were the source and bulwark of an ideal status quo. "Why cannot this government endure divided into free and slave states, as our fathers made it?" asked Stephen Douglas, a senator and an old rival of Lincoln's.

Or maybe—a minority view, but it had advocates—the founding fathers were mistaken or evil. Perhaps the Declaration's assertion that all men are created equal was not a self-evident truth, but "fundamentally wrong," as Alexander Stephens, a former congressman and a friend of

Lincoln's, put it. Or perhaps the Constitution, instead of securing the blessings of liberty, as the Preamble boasted, secured the institution of slavery and made thereby "a covenant with death, and with Hell," as abolitionist William Lloyd Garrison said. Maybe no faith need be kept with the men who had written, signed, and implemented such wrong-headed documents.

Lincoln spent years contending with rival visions of the founding fathers. He contended successfully—and legitimately. For all the times he squeezed the evidence or hurried over the record, he was more right about the founders than wrong—and more right about them than any of his contentious contemporaries.

But the main problem for Lincoln in his dealings with the founding fathers, as he (unwittingly) neared the end of his life, was that they were not quite enough for him. Their systems and their ideals would survive the Civil War, but the strain was unbearable, horrors upon horrors. By the end the father Who stood above all others was God the Father—and for Lincoln, His all-encompassing superintendence raised the further problem that, though He perhaps listened, He rarely spoke. It was lonely—soul-destroyingly lonely—to be left with a Father who left you so alone.

This book is not a full-dress biography of Lincoln, or a history of his times. It is not about Lincoln's marriage, or how the Battle of Gettysburg was won, though it will touch on these and many other points. It is the history of a career, and the unfolding of the ideas that animated it.

Because Lincoln was a politician in a democracy, he had to present his ideas to the public; a history of his career is in large part a history of his rhetoric. Rhetoric is how democratic politicians point with pride and view with alarm; how they sketch their visions and justify their deals. It is one of the most important ways by which they earn their reputations, win elections, and wield power. There is a lot of Lincoln's writing in this book—jotted down notes, state papers, private letters that were written for public consumption. There is even more of his speaking—orations before huge open-air crowds, stories told in small rooms. Because

Lincoln was both self-taught and multitalented, he drew on a variety of models and genres: humor, logic, poetry; fart jokes, Euclid, Byron. He went from mocking the Bible as a youngster to channeling it as a prematurely old man. But time and again he came back to the founders, the men who most inspired him.

This book is also a history of the afterlife of those great Americans, his predecessors—how their words and their reputations percolated into the nineteenth century, in great debates and in the frontier reading of a curious boy. Other books on Lincoln have noted his interest in the founding fathers and how he looked back to them, but here, for the first time, a historian of the founding looks ahead to Lincoln.

This book, finally, is training—in thinking, feeling, and acting. The founding fathers were world-historical figures; so was Abraham Lincoln. If we study how Lincoln engaged with them, we can learn how to engage with them, and him, ourselves.

PART
ONE

1809–1830: Youth

WHEN LINCOLN WAS A CHILD HE LEARNED TWO UNSETTLING
things about his family tree, one for each branch of it.

His paternal grandfather, also called Abraham Lincoln, was killed
when he was forty-two years old. This Lincoln, a Virginian, had been
a captain in the militia during the Revolution, helping to build frontier
forts. As the war wound down, he moved with his family to Kentucky.
One day in 1786 he was in his field with his three young sons when
an Indian shot him from the cover of the trees. One boy ran for help;
another, the eldest, ran for a gun. The Indian ran for seven-year-old
Thomas, the youngest, but the eldest brother managed to shoot and kill
him before he carried Thomas off.

When Thomas grew up he told the story so often that it became a
"legend" to his own son, Abraham, who said it was "imprinted on my
mind and memory." In the speech to the Young Men's Lyceum, Lincoln
would say that veterans of the Revolution had supplied a "living history"
of the war in every American family. The repository of living history in

his family was no Revolutionary War veteran, but a survivor of frontier violence. That long ago shootout, as sudden and arbitrary as it was brutal, almost erased the future: if Thomas Lincoln had been killed along with the first Abraham Lincoln, there would have been no second.

Lincoln's mother, Nancy, whom Thomas Lincoln married in Kentucky in 1806, was a Hanks, another family of transplanted Virginians. The recurring shadow in the Hanks family was illegitimacy. Nancy Hanks was born eight years before her mother, Lucey, married. The shadow covered a second generation: years after Nancy died, old neighbors accused her of adultery, assigning Abraham's paternity to various men besides Thomas Lincoln. Dennis Hanks, one of Abraham's cousins, would bluster to an inquiring biographer that "the stories going about, charging wrong or indecency [or] prostitution" in the Hanks family were false. But since Dennis Hanks had been born out of wedlock himself, he protested too much. Abraham Lincoln almost never mentioned the family stain, but he was aware of it.

The near-death of Abraham Lincoln's father almost canceled his existence; the mores of the Hanks family clouded his identity.

Lincoln absorbed another life lesson when he was very young, not about himself but about the world. When he was no older than seven, he helped his father, Thomas, plant one of the family's fields. This was a seven-acre patch laid out in cornrows. Abraham's task was to drop pumpkin seeds in the mounds where the corn would grow—"two seeds every other hill and every other row." The next day a cloudburst in the surrounding highlands caused a flood in the valley where the Lincoln farm lay, which swept away pumpkin seeds, corn, soil—everything.

The flood did not sour Lincoln on work. All his life he would preach the value of hard work—not farm work, which he detested, but the labor of self-improvement, for which he had a passion. But his childhood effort, done in a day, wiped out in an hour, showed him that an otherwise-minded cosmos does not always support our efforts.

Thomas Lincoln successively owned three farms in central Kentucky, south of Louisville. He and Nancy had three children—Sarah (born in 1807), Abraham (born in 1809), and Thomas (born in 1812, died after three days). In December 1816 the Lincolns left Kentucky, crossing the Ohio River into southwestern Indiana, where they would live until Abraham was twenty-one.

We know almost nothing about Lincoln's mother. No letters by or about her, no pictures, no trustworthy descriptions survive. Dennis Hanks, who knew the Lincolns in Kentucky and followed them in their later moves, recalled that Nancy Lincoln "learned" her son "to read the Bible." She could not write, not even her name, but she probably told Abraham the stories. One of Dennis Hanks's recollections of the Lincoln family turns on a biblical phrase, and it has the texture of a remembered scene. One day when Nancy was weaving, Abraham abruptly asked her, "Who was the father of Zebedee's children?" (Matthew 27:56 mentions "the mother of Zebedee's children"; Zebedee was the fisherman on the Sea of Galilee whose sons James and John became Apostles. The father of Zebedee's children was, obviously, Zebedee.) Nancy laughed and told her son to scat: "Get out of here you nasty little pup, you." Abraham, said Dennis Hanks, "saw he had got his mother and ran off laughing." A simple riddle like that is just what a bright little boy would think was the funniest thing in the world; Nancy's response is just the reaction a hardworking, affectionate mother might have, caught in the midst of her chores.

In September 1818 Nancy's aunt and uncle, who were neighbors of the Lincolns in Indiana, died. The cause was "milk-sick," a disease carried in the milk of cows that had eaten white snakeroot, a poisonous wild plant. The symptoms were grotesque: coated tongue, changing from white to brown; stomach pain, constipation, vomiting. Death could come in three days. Early in October Nancy Lincoln died of milk-sick, too. Before she passed, she told her children to be good to their father and to each other, and to worship God.

Thomas Lincoln spent a year as a widower, then at the end of 1819 went back to Kentucky looking to remarry. The woman he sought was Sarah Bush Johnston, an old acquaintance a few years his junior, now a widow herself. According to the man who issued their marriage license, the courtship was quick. Thomas told Sarah "that they knew each other from childhood, that he had no wife and she no husband, and that he came all the way to marry her and if she was willing he wanted it done right off." Sarah said she had a few small debts she wanted to pay first. Thomas asked for a list of them, and paid them that night. He returned to Indiana with a new wife and her three children.

Sarah Bush Lincoln is more vivid to history than Nancy Lincoln; she outlived both her husband and her famous stepson, and was interviewed in her old age. Unlike the wicked stepmothers of fairy tales (and real life), she embraced her new family as her own. She made her husband put a wood floor in the family cabin and cut a window in the walls; she mended Abraham's and his sister Sarah's clothes; where there had been the disorganization of death, she brought cleanliness and warmth.

She noticed, as an exceptional woman would, that her stepson was exceptional. Her reminiscences of him as a boy were both observant and admiring. "He didn't like physical labor—was diligent for knowledge— wished to know, and if pains and labor would get it he was sure to get it." He learned by listening: "When old folks were at our house," he was "silent and attentive . . . never speaking or asking questions till they were gone, and then he must understand everything, even to the smallest thing, minutely and exactly. He would then repeat it over to himself again and again, sometimes in one form and then in another, and when it was fixed in his mind to suit him he became easy." He learned, most of all, by reading. "Abe read all the books he could lay his hands on, and when he came across a passage that struck him he would write it down on boards if he had no paper and keep it there till he did get paper. Then he would re-write it, look at it, repeat it."

Lincoln learned to read in school. He had briefly attended two country schools in Kentucky when he was little, and in Indiana he would attend three more. These schools were all short-lived ventures, depending on the presence in the neighborhood of men, generally young, who knew enough to stay ahead of their pupils, and were vigorous enough to keep the older ones in line. One of Lincoln's schoolmasters was surnamed Hazel, which gave rise to jokes about hazelnut switches as pedagogical tools. As Lincoln aged, his attendance was limited by how long he could be spared from farm chores; all told, he spent no more than a year in his various schools. When he was a man he would say that he had not learned much in them, but he did learn to write, to do arithmetic up to the level of cross-multiplication, and to read.

He read a few widely used primers; a few popular classics—*Aesop's Fables*, *Pilgrim's Progress*, *Robinson Crusoe*, selections from the *Arabian Nights*—and a few popular biographies. Reading was the skill that first gave him the power to stretch himself, to go into himself, and to get away from his surroundings. Sarah Bush Lincoln watched over these stirrings with sympathy. "His mind and mine—what little I had," she added too modestly, "seemed to run together."

———

Lincoln's mother died when he was nine years old; he did not meet his stepmother until he was almost eleven. His father, however, was at his side for the first twenty-two years of his life. Thomas Lincoln was the man who provided for him, exploited him, and shaped him, through repulsion and attraction both. Abraham Lincoln served his father, rejected him, and never acknowledged the ways—few but crucial—in which he took after him.

Lincoln's father worked at farming and carpentry all his life. His farming was small scale; the farm where Abraham was born was 300 acres, the first farm in Indiana was 160 acres. Those properties would have entitled Thomas to vote in old Maryland, though someone like Charles Carroll would have barely noticed them. As a carpenter he built his family's houses, and made his family's coffins; sometimes he did carpentry work for others. He never went broke, or left bad debts, and served on a few juries (a sign of respectability, if not prosperity).

One mark of his less-than-middling status was that he never owned a slave, though Kentucky was a slave state. Slavery was one of the reasons he left for Indiana. As a small farmer Thomas Lincoln feared the competition of slave labor, and he would not find it in his new home, which was admitted to the Union as a free state in December 1816, the very month he moved there.

Indiana had been part of the old Northwest Territory of postrevolutionary America, bounded by Pennsylvania, the Ohio and Mississippi rivers, and the Great Lakes. The Northwest Ordinance, the legislation that regulated this wilderness quadrant, had ruled it out of bounds for slavery: "There shall be neither slavery nor involuntary servitude in the said territory, otherwise than in the punishment of crimes." The Northwest Ordinance was older than the Constitution; the one-house Congress of the Articles of Confederation passed it in July 1787, as the Constitutional Convention was in mid-session. After the new Constitution went into effect, the House, the Senate, and President George Washington confirmed the Ordinance in the summer of 1789.

A more immediate reason for Thomas Lincoln's move was challenges to his existing land titles in Kentucky—a problem faced by many Kentuckians besides him. Land ownership in the state was a nightmare of bad surveying and conflicting claims. But the land of the Northwest Territory had been laid out by the federal government, which guaranteed clear possession. As far as both slavery and land were concerned, the Lincolns knew firsthand the power and the consequences of federal legislation for the territories.

Southwestern Indiana was forest when Thomas Lincoln took his family there—dense with trees, draped with wild grape vines, all the intertwined rankness of old-growth North America. As soon as Abraham was big enough to swing an axe, he was put to work, clearing land and splitting rails. Once the fields were cleared he plowed and reaped. He had a spurt of growth around age twelve, which sped his labors. Old friends disagreed about how much shin showed between his socks and his suddenly-too-short pants: one said six inches, one said twelve. People competed to tell tall tales about the tall boy. Whatever the length of his breeches, Lincoln's lifelong look of awkward elongation started before his teens. Luckily for him he was as strong as he was tall, so although everyone smiled at him, no one bullied him. And meanwhile he worked—on his father's farm, and on the farms of neighbors, his services rented out by his father, who pocketed his earnings.

Lincoln told one of these neighbor/employers that his father had taught him how to work, but never learned him to love it. He failed to love it because he was not working for himself. Working for your father on the family farm was one thing; working elsewhere, as a hired tool or draft animal, like a plow or a horse, was something else. It is true that using family members as contract laborers was a common practice, but common practices take different people different ways. Lincoln took it badly. He would make a political philosophy, almost a theology, out of a man's right to own the fruits of his own labor; the seeds of it may have been planted while he was planting or chopping as Thomas Lincoln's unpaid work crew.

What Abraham loved instead of farm work, as his stepmother testified, was reading and learning. His father had mixed feelings about that.

Thomas Lincoln could read a little and sign his name; that was the extent of his literacy. But he wanted more for his son, which is why he sent him to school five times. Each sojourn had to be paid for, in cash or kind, and in his son's labor lost, once Abraham was old enough to work, so there was expense involved. In her interview as an elderly widow, Sarah Bush Lincoln insisted that her husband had joined her in encouraging his son's intellectual efforts: "Mr. Lincoln never made Abe quit reading to do anything if he could avoid it. He would do it himself first." Reading, writing, and arithmetic were useful skills to have, and Thomas wanted his son to have them.

But reading was more than a skill to Abraham: it was a portal to thought and inspiration. The act of reading was also a visible mark of his aspirations. Abraham read everywhere, outdoors as well as at home; he would take a book with him into the fields when he plowed, stopping to read whenever the horse stopped to rest. He did this because, as any devoted reader knows, a book can be all-absorbing. But he also did it to show family and friends what a reader he was. All this was beyond Thomas Lincoln's ken.

Quick wits can make a boy forget his place, and Thomas Lincoln didn't like that, either. If a stranger rode by the Lincoln property when father and son were at the fence, Abraham would horn in with the first question, and sometimes his father smacked him for it. When Abraham asked his mother who was the father of Zebedee's children, she laughed and called him a nasty little pup. When he was pert in the presence of his father, Thomas gave him the back of his hand. (Sarah Bush Lincoln did not recall Abraham horning in on her, perhaps because he felt less competitive with his stepmother.)

Father and son inhabited different mental worlds; certainly Abraham thought so. Years later, when he was running for president, he wrote in a campaign autobiography that his father "never did more in the way of writing than to bunglingly sign his own name." How much scorn still coils in that word *bunglingly*. Scorn, and judgment: *my father could have learned to sign his name properly if he had made the effort; after all, I did.*

Only one remark of Thomas Lincoln's stuck in Abraham's mind enough for him to repeat it in later years: "If you make a bad bargain, hug it the tighter." It is a Delphic remark. It suggests persistence, which Thomas Lincoln had; maybe stubbornness—persisting in small farming, a way of life his son came to dislike. The clearest possible meaning of Thomas Lincoln's dictum seems to be: if you make a bad choice, try to make the best of it. Abraham did not follow this advice where Thomas was concerned; he had not chosen his father and he did not try very hard to make the best of him.

And yet, our fathers give us life, while this father additionally gave Abraham twenty-two years of his company. Something rubbed off.

Thomas Lincoln was a temperate man. In his time and place this was a rare distinction. Early nineteenth-century America was a nation of drunkards; Americans consumed hard liquor at a rate of five gallons per person per year; some working men drank a quart a day. Thomas Lincoln took no part in the national binge; one in-law said he "never was intoxicated in his life." Abraham was as temperate as his father.

The Lincolns were differently built—Abraham (who rose to be 6'4") lean and gawky, Thomas (who stood 5'10") compact and solid. But both of them were powerful, and Thomas proved it when he had to. In Kentucky he fought another reputed strong man in an arranged fight, a challenge match, and beat him, after which "no one else ever tried his manhood." Such contests were a common feature of frontier life, a form of communal hazing; Abraham would undergo them himself, as successfully as his father.

These physical tests came to the Lincolns; neither of them looked for trouble. This, too, was noteworthy in a society of brawling and all-in fighting, which could descend to gouging, biting, and maiming. Probably their sobriety helped keep them peaceable.

But by far the most important quality father and son shared was telling stories and jokes. John Hanks, one of the many Hanks cousins who knew both men, thought Thomas was as good a storyteller as Abraham; Dennis Hanks maintained that Thomas was even better. Maybe one reason Thomas cuffed his son when he spoke up to passersby at the fence was that he was spoiling his father's set-ups. Stories were the only form of entertainment—apart from sermons, trials, and elections—that rural America had, and the only one that was readily available. Church congregations met once or twice a week, sessions of court and political campaigns were much less frequent. Stories were there anytime, if you knew how to tell them. Any tavern, any store, any hearth could spawn them. They passed the news, brought in company, held the darkness at bay.

Abraham Lincoln took to storytelling because he was good at it—he was an excellent mimic, and he developed a great sense of timing—and because he enjoyed the applause he got. It gave him a role in the world, his first and his longest-running. Young Lincoln was bookish and strange-looking; as he aged, he would acquire other unprepossessing traits (shyness around women, depression). But when he opened his mouth to tell a story, he could be the life of any party. He could put his height and his ungainliness to work; being funny-looking makes you even funnier.

Among the staples of his repertoire, after he graduated from riddles about the father of Zebedee's children, were off-color stories (scatological more often than sexual, though he told both kinds). One of his favorite off-color stories—his law partner William Herndon, who wrote it down, said he heard Lincoln tell it "often and often"—incidentally showed how story- and joke-telling worked for him. It was about "the Man of Audacity."

"There was a party once, not far from here," it always began. Among the guests "was one of those men who had audacity . . . quick-witted, cheeky, and self-possessed, never off his guard on any occasion." When supper was ready, the Man of Audacity was asked to carve the turkey. He "whetted his carving knife with the steel and got down to business," but as he began, he "let a fart, a loud fart, so that all the people heard it distinctly." Silence. "However, the audacious man was cool and entirely self-possessed. . . . With a kind of sublime audacity, [he] pulled off his coat, rolled up his sleeves, put his coat deliberately on a chair, spat on his hands, took his position at the head of the table, picked up the carving knife, and whetted it again, never cracking a smile nor moving a muscle of his face." Then "he squared himself and said loudly and distinctly: 'Now, by God, I'll see if I can't cut up this turkey without farting.'"

If you fart, go further with it. If you are funny-looking, be funny. If you make a bad bargain, hug it the tighter.

Storytelling served another function for Lincoln, which he discovered as early as his days in Indiana. In 1826, when he was seventeen, his sister, Sarah, married a neighbor, Aaron Grigsby. She comes to us, still living, in the memory of one of her Grigsby in-laws, forty years after her wedding: "Her good humored laugh I can see now—is as fresh in my mind as if it were yesterday." In 1828, laughing Sarah died in child-birth. Of Lincoln's blood relations, everyone—infant brother, mother, sister—was now gone, except his problematic father. In 1829 he took it out on the Grigsbys, on the occasion of a double wedding of two Grigsby brothers. With the help of friends, he contrived to have the grooms led to each other's beds on the wedding night; he then wrote a satirical account of the mix-up, in pseudo-biblical prose. "So when [the grooms] came near to the house of . . . their father, the messengers came on before them, and gave a shout. And the whole multitude ran out with shouts of joy and music, playing on all kinds of instruments of music, some playing on harps and some on viols and some blowing rams' horns." It is pretty tame stuff, but it amused the neighbors; one claimed decades later that it was still remembered in that part of Indiana, "better than the Bible." There truly was not much in the way of entertainment in rural America.

Mocking the Grigsbys would not bring sister Sarah back—no mock-ery of anyone or anything could do that—but it could distract the trou-bled mind. If life makes a terrible bargain for you, a funny story can push it aside for a time.

———

In 1830, when Abraham was twenty-one, the Lincolns moved once more, to central Illinois. A year later, Abraham and Thomas parted ways.

Abraham had little to do with his father after that; the rest of their story is quickly told. Thomas continued his life of farming. By this time he had bonded with John Johnston, his second wife's youngest son by her first marriage, and, like Thomas, a farmer for life. Even as Sarah Bush Lincoln chose her reading stepson to be her special companion, so Thomas chose his farming stepson to be his. In the 1840s Thomas and Johnston began hitting Abraham up for small amounts of money.

Abraham paid, but came to suspect dementia in his father (who was approaching seventy), and manipulation on the part of his stepbrother.

Shortly after New Year's Day of 1851, Abraham got word that Thomas was dying. He wrote Johnston that he would not be able to come see his father; his own wife was sick (*I have a new family, which has replaced my old one*). He commended his father to God, "who will not turn away from him in any extremity" (*I will, but God won't*). Thomas died soon thereafter.

Lincoln named a horse after his father (Old Tom), and his fourth son (born in 1853). In later years, he thought of putting a tombstone on his father's grave, but he never did.

Two

GEORGE WASHINGTON
AND LIBERTY

T HIS WAS LINCOLN'S FAMILY, WHAT HE GOT FROM IT, AND
what he did not get. But since we never get everything we want
or need, we look for sufficiency in surrogates—adopted families of
friends, mentors, or figures of history and myth. For a boy in early
nineteenth-century America the handiest surrogates, great enough to
be awe-inspiring, near enough to be familiar, were the founding fathers.

Father of his country—*pater patriae*—was an honorific bestowed by
the Roman Senate on Camillus, a general of the fourth century BC, who
earned it by refounding the city after driving out an invasion of Gauls.
Americans revived and pluralized the terms "father" and "founder" to
honor the heroes of the Revolution.

Abraham Lincoln never laid eyes on an actual founding father. The
only one who ever ventured near him was that honorary French founder,
Lafayette. Ardent, guileless, selfless, patriotic, Lafayette loved the country

he had come to fight for during its Revolution, and America loved him back. On a triumphal tour of his second homeland in 1824–1825, the old hero was conveyed hither and yon for public celebrations and celebrity visits. He saw his old friend John Adams in Massachusetts, and his old friend Thomas Jefferson at Monticello. He dined with President John Quincy Adams at the White House, and met Andrew Jackson, hero of New Orleans, in Nashville. In May 1825, the steamboat in which he was traveling struck a rock in the Ohio River and foundered; he abandoned ship and spent a night on the Indiana shore in the pouring rain. He was about fifteen miles from the Lincoln cabin, but the Lincolns were not on his itinerary.

If Lincoln wanted to meet a founding father it had to be in books. The book that made the greatest impression on him was about the greatest of the founders, George Washington.

When Americans used the term "father of his country" in the singular, it always, and only, meant Washington. He had earned it by his long and spectacular career—eight and a half years as commander in chief of the Continental Army during the Revolution, eight years as the first president—and even more by the personal qualities that wove an aura of confident masculinity around him. With a few exceptions—George Mason, who was eight years older; Benjamin Franklin, who seemed older than the hills—Washington was senior to most of his revolutionary colleagues: John Adams was younger by three years, Thomas Jefferson by eleven, James Madison by nineteen; Alexander Hamilton and Lafayette, who were twenty-five years younger, were mere boys next to him. At 6'3½", Washington was generally the tallest man in any gathering, as well as the strongest and most graceful (ladies loved to dance with him). He was always the finest horseman (Jefferson, an excellent rider himself, called him "the best horseman of his age"). Washington offered a republican substitute for the dignity of royalty—a point Washington Irving made jokingly in his 1819 story "Rip Van Winkle," in which Rip's enchanted sleep takes him through the Revolution; when he wakes up, the painted head on the signboard of his favorite tavern wears George

Washington's cocked hat instead of George III's crown. Same head, same first name; new ideal.

One accident of biography confirmed the political nature of Washington's fatherly role: he was childless, possibly sterile. Martha Washington had four children with her first husband, Daniel Parke Custis, who died when she was twenty-six, but none with her second husband, George. There could be no Washington dynasty aspiring to a crown— "no family to build in greatness upon my country's ruins," as Washington himself put it. Instead he was the father of all Americans.

The most popular early biography of Washington was *The Life of Washington,* by Mason Locke Weems, better known as Parson Weems. Lincoln read it when he was a boy.

How he got the book was a story in itself, vouched for by several of his old acquaintances. Lincoln borrowed Weems's *Life* from Josiah Crawford, a Kentuckian who had settled near the Lincolns when they lived in Indiana. Lincoln slept in the loft of his family's cabin; he put the book on a shelf by the window, where it got soaked by rainwater leaking in overnight. Crawford let him keep the damaged volume, but made him pay for it by pulling corn for fodder for two or three days.

Mason Locke Weems was an itinerant minister and book dealer. Although he was an ordained Episcopal clergyman, his income came from hawking books up and down the East Coast. He calculated that a *Life of Washington* would find a market. The hero died in 1799; Weems wrote and self-published a short biography by 1800. He was right about the popularity of his subject; he brought out an expanded version of the *Life* in 1808, which would have been the one Lincoln read.

Weems boasted about his intimacy with his subject. He had exchanged a few letters with Washington—"I have taken upon me to circulate moral and religious books among the people, with which I know Your Excellency, as Father of the People, is not displeased"—and even visited him once at Mount Vernon. From these wisps of contact Weems the biographer made an identity for himself, which he proclaimed on his title page: "Rector of Mount Vernon Parish." But this was sheer fabrication; there was no such

parish, nor was he rector of it. These and many other inventions made
Weems the butt of later Washington biographers.

Yet Weems did some actual research, hunting up old acquaintances
of the great man (causing one academic historian to remark that the
trouble with Weems is that he is not lying all the time). In any case, his
purpose was not archival. He aimed to tell the story of a good and great
man, and to offer it as an example and inspiration.

Lincoln responded to parts of Weems's story, though not to the parts
that have become the most famous.

———

The purpose of Weems's *Life*, announced at the beginning, was to hold
up Washington as a model of virtues: "piety and patriotism," "industry
and honor." Weems began with two chapters on Washington's childhood
and youth, which presented their hero as a model boy.

Lincoln could be comforted by the fact that Washington's education
did not sound much better than his own. Weems said that Washington
had only two schoolmasters, and he insisted that he "never learned a
syllable of Latin" (the mark, in both Washington's lifetime and Lincoln's, of a college student). Lincoln himself would write, in a note for
a biographer, that if anyone "supposed to understand Latin" had appeared in Indiana, he would have been looked on "as a wizard." Lincoln
also learned from Weems that young Washington was strong—he could
throw a stone across the Rappahannock River—and that he did not fight
with other boys. So far their lives were alike.

But Weems's description of the Washington family must have struck
Lincoln as alien. Weems said little about George's mother, Mary, focusing instead on his father, Augustine Washington, and their relationship,
which Weems depicted as an idyll of nurturance.

Weems presented three scenes of paternal instruction.

The first was a lesson in generosity. One autumn Augustine takes
George to an orchard groaning with fruit. Back in the spring, one of

George's cousins had given him an apple, which he had not wanted to share with his siblings, even though, as Augustine reminds him, "I promised you that if you would but do it, God Almighty would give you plenty of apples this fall." George sees the promised bounty and vows never to be stingy again.

The second scene of instruction was the story of the cherry tree, a lesson in honesty that is still remembered today, though the set-up is generally forgotten. Augustine begins by telling George never to tell lies—he even says he would rather see him dead—but then he pivots to explain that a child will become a liar if a parent beats him for every misdeed: "The terrified little creature slips out a *lie!* just to escape the rod." Weems was addressing two audiences, children and parents, telling the former *Don't lie*, telling the latter *Don't be brutal*. Only then do we get the story of the cherry tree—George barking it accidentally with his hatchet, then admitting to his father what he has done: "I can't tell a lie, Pa; you know I can't tell a lie"—whereupon Augustine practices what he has preached: "Run to my arms; glad am I, George, that you killed my tree; for you have paid me for it a thousand fold."

We do not know what Lincoln made of these lessons or of the paternal relationship that accompanied them. Smacked at the fence and hired out to work, he could have envied George and Augustine's bond, or dismissed it as unreal.

The third scene of instruction may have seemed the strangest of all.

This was a lesson about God. One day George sees newly sprouted seedlings in a garden bed that spell out his name: GEORGE WASHINGTON. Baffled, he asks Augustine what it means, and his father begins by teasing him: "It grew there by *chance*, I suppose." When George refuses to believe that, his father admits that he planted the seeds, in order "to introduce you to your *true* Father"—God. "As my son could not believe that *chance* had made and put together so exactly the *letters* of his name . . . then how can he believe, that *chance* could have made and put together all those millions and millions of things that are now so exactly fitted to his good!" Such a good world must have been made by God; George is persuaded.

This was what philosophers and theologians call the argument from design. Its persuasiveness in Weems's telling depended on George's sense that the world was good, and good for him. Yet Lincoln had already had a planting experience that suggested a different lesson. Thomas and Abraham had planted a field with corn and pumpkin seeds, which did not grow up to spell ABRAHAM LINCOLN; instead, a storm or a stormy God wiped them out. This made a very different argument about the design of both the Lincoln family and the world. No wise father; no friendly God.

There was a final lesson about Washington and his father and it pushed Weems's *Life* in a different direction. At the beginning of Chapter Three, when George is still a boy, Augustine dies. The deathbed scene Weems wrote is in a way crueler than the real death of Lincoln's mother: George is staying with cousins when his father sickens, and he returns too late to speak to him.

Then came a shift. As George becomes an adult and a soldier, Weems's book willy-nilly becomes an account of his public career. Augustine suddenly shrinks in importance. "Where George got his military talents," Weems wrote, was a mystery. "Certainly his earthly parents had no hand in it." Both are described as creatures of peace, Augustine an "amiable old gentleman," Mary an anxious natterer: when her son wins the Battle of Trenton, all she can say is, When is he coming home to tend the farm?

Weems did not quite repudiate what he wrote in Chapters One and Two: Washington had already gotten his moral foundation, and Weems decided that his talents as a warrior must have been gifts of Providence. But maybe, Weems suggested, once your family receded, you could make your own way. Washington's only chance of "rising in the world," Weems wrote, was "by his own merit." That must have been encouraging to Lincoln.

But what might he rise to become? Rich? Famous? Or something more? The *Life of Washington* gave an answer to that question, and we know Lincoln took it in, because there came a time when he said what the answer was, and where he had read about it.

———

In February 1861 president-elect Lincoln took a train from his Illinois home to Washington, DC, where he would give his First Inaugural Address. The trip was a political tour, showing the flag as the country fell apart, with stops in six states.

On February 21 he spoke in Trenton, to each house of the New Jersey legislature in turn. He began his address to the state senate by recalling New Jersey's role in the Revolution. Few states, he said, had witnessed so many battles, which was true: New Jersey saw three major ones (Trenton, Princeton, Monmouth) plus a blizzard of small engagements.

"Away back in my childhood," Lincoln went on, " . . . I got hold of a small book, such a one as few of the younger members have ever seen, Weems's *Life of Washington*." He proceeded to tell the senate about an episode in Chapter Nine. Of all the battles Weems described, "none fixed themselves upon my imagination so deeply as the struggle here at Trenton. . . . The crossing of the river; the contest with the Hessians; the great hardships endured at that time, all fixed themselves on my memory."

What else would we expect Lincoln to say? What else would any politician say? He was in Trenton, on the day before Washington's Birthday; Weems's book, so far from being obscure, was still in print. Bring on the clichés.

But Lincoln's remarks did not float in the ether of buncombe; brief though they were, they tracked Weems's account of the battle. He was not speaking in generalities but recovering a reading experience from more than thirty years earlier.

Every feature of the Battle of Trenton that Lincoln summarized—river, Hessians, hardships—was something Weems had described at length. When Weems took Washington across the Delaware, he piled on the details: "Filled with ice . . . darksome night, pelted by an incessant storm of hail and snow . . . the unwelcome roar of ice, loud crashing along the

angry flood . . . five hours of infinite toil and danger . . . *frost-bitten."* These
details—none of them, in this case, imagined by Weems, but historically
accurate—also underlie Lincoln's reference to "great hardships." Weems
gave the Hessians several pages, first as clownish marauders, speaking in
crude German accents, who believed that Americans scalped, skinned,
and ate their prisoners—"Vy! Shure, des Mericans must be de deble"—
then as pitiable prisoners themselves, induced to switch sides by the
merciful treatment they receive: "Poor fellows!" the Americans tell them,
"leave [your] vile employment and come live with us."

But the strongest proof that Lincoln had been molded by Weems's
Life is that the most important lesson he drew in 1861 from the Battle
of Trenton was the very lesson that Weems had presented as the most
important. "I recollect thinking," Lincoln continued, " . . . boy even
though I was, that there must have been something more than common
that those men struggled for . . . something even more [important] than
national independence; . . . something that held out a great promise to
all the people of the world to all time to come."

Weems thought so, too, and he expended his powers, such as they
were, in evoking it. When Washington and his troops, having crossed
the Delaware, began their march on Trenton, they were accompanied,
Weems wrote, by an invisible being, "the weeping GENIUS OF LIB-
ERTY." This was no father figure, but a grieving mother. "Driven from
the rest of the world, she had fled to the wild woods of America, as to
an assured asylum of rest." But tyranny had followed—"the *inhuman
few*, with fleets and armies, had pursued her flight!" Who would fight
for her? *"One little band alone* remained . . . resolved to defend her or
perish." For Weems, the Battle of Trenton was a struggle for the world;
the fate of liberty everywhere depended on it.

When the Americans finally reached Trenton, Weems gave the last
word to Washington. *"All I ask of you,"* he tells his troops as they are
about to charge, *"is, just to remember what you are about to fight for."*

Lincoln remembered. He told the New Jersey Senate that he wanted
to perpetuate liberty and Union "in accordance with the original idea

for which that struggle"—at Trenton and other battles—"was made." Washington and his men had defended liberty, Lincoln and the nation must be ready to defend her again. Washington's task was now his.

———

Lincoln found Washington in Weems, but he also had to save him from Weems, or from those chapters of *The Life of Washington* that had the greatest popular impact. So powerful were Weems's tales of Washington's youth that the Father of his Country became an icon of moral virtues, beyond and above politics. Thanks to Weems, the most famous thing Washington ever said—"I can't tell a lie"—was something he almost certainly never said.

Honesty is a good thing, but it comes in different flavors. Honesty about our feelings is sincerity; honesty about our intentions is candor. But suppose our feelings or intentions are childish or evil? What then do we gain by expressing or avowing them? The most important form of honesty, especially in a leader, is discerning the right course of action and forthrightly pursuing it.

When Lincoln first read Parson Weems, he responded most not to Washington as a good boy but to Washington as a man of action and principle, and he invoked that response again during his own trials decades later. Not that he reread Weems before he spoke to the New Jersey Senate in 1861 (or maybe ever, after he first worked off the price of it for Josiah Crawford). He did not have to; Washington was inside him. As he said in Trenton, "you all know, for you have all been boys, how these early impressions last longer than others." The Battle of Trenton was more useful to Lincoln, as an ambitious boy and as president-elect, than the cherry tree.

Weems set out to describe a model of private virtue, but he also portrayed a champion of liberty. This was how Washington saw himself. His career, from the beginning of the Revolution to his retirement from the presidency, was a decades-long defense of his country from foreign enemies and threatening political problems. He loved life on his farm and thought of it constantly when he was away from it in the field or in office. But he left it whenever duty called. This was the Washington who thrilled Lincoln.

But Lincoln did not own Washington. Washington was everyone's favorite American and everyone had his own take on him. Lincoln would have to pick his way among competing visions of Washington for years to come.

———

There was one other way that Lincoln looked to Washington, glancingly and in secret; so far as we know he only revealed it to one friend, once.

About 1850 Lincoln and his law partner, William Herndon, were in a buggy bound for a county court where they were to argue cases. As they rode along, Lincoln revealed an astonishing thing. His mother, he said apropos of nothing much, was illegitimate. This is what most historians and genealogists now believe: Nancy's mother, Lucey Hanks, did not get married until eight years after Nancy was born. But Nancy's father, Lincoln now told Herndon, was not Lucey's eventual husband, an ordinary farmer like all the other Hankses and Lincolns, but a "well-bred Virginia farmer or planter . . . a broad-minded, unknown Virginian." It was from this man, Lincoln explained, that he derived his brains and ambition—"his better nature and finer qualities"—via heredity. The finer qualities, in other words, came straight from his maternal grandfather, skipping Thomas Lincoln entirely. The fact that these ennobling genes had been transmitted out of wedlock was also a plus, since Lincoln believed that illegitimate children were "sturdier and brighter" than those born in marriage, showing what we might now call hybrid vigor. Lincoln fell silent, Herndon did not press him. Then a chatty old man rode up alongside them, Lincoln told some stories, and the window of revelation closed.

The secret of the noble father is a staple of fiction and fairy tales, and is sometimes found in real life. It might possibly be true of Nancy Hanks, though only Lincoln, among all the people who talked about illegitimacy and his family, ever mentioned it, and why would he know? Children or grandchildren are typically the last people to learn such things. He gave Herndon no details. Who was the father of Lucey Hanks's children?

The well-bred, broad-minded Virginian is a fantasy—a fantasy Lincoln entertained because it explained so much. He was different from everyone around him, his stepmother partly excepted. Certainly he was different from his father (it is interesting that he spun his theories of inheritance and illegitimacy to Herndon about 1850, as his father was failing). He could read about Washington in Weems, but there must also be a more direct connection between them: he was descended from such a man.

George Washington had no children by Martha, which suggests that he was sterile—but maybe it was she who had become infertile, and Washington was capable of having illegitimate children after all. (There are black Americans today who claim to be descendants of George Washington, by a slave named Venus; their actual ancestor is almost certainly George's nephew, Bushrod Washington, who was the son of Venus's owner.) There was another great Virginian, Thomas Jefferson, who had children by his wife and, it was widely believed, by his slave Sally Hemings. Lincoln would forge a moral and political bond with Jefferson that was even more explicit than his connection with Washington. But perhaps there was another bond as well.

Or, if his true maternal grandfather was neither of these great men, then maybe it was some neighbor or acquaintance, a lesser member of the interlocking Virginia gentry, a founder by proximity. By whatever channel, Lincoln himself could be the living history of the Revolution in his family.

It was food for thought, and hungry hearts and restless minds will chew on whatever crusts they can get.

Three

1830–1840: MANHOOD

IN HIS TWENTIES, AFTER SOME YOUTHFUL FUMBLING, LINCOLN found the careers he would pursue for the rest of his life: politics and law. He lost two lovers and made two friends. His successes and his trials would prime him for his next engagement with the founding fathers.

————

In 1830 the Lincoln family moved to central Illinois, near the Sangamon River village of Decatur. This was a different landscape from the tangle of southwestern Indiana—prairie crossed by winding streams that flowed ultimately into the Mississippi.

Illinois had become a state in 1818. The Northwest Ordinance had defined it as a free territory, and pioneers who were weary of slavery moved there for that reason. Edward Coles, an idealistic young Virginian who was a friend and neighbor of Jefferson and Madison, freed his slaves in 1819 and came with them to Illinois, giving each head of a household 160 acres. Other settlers wanted to change the new free state into a slave state, however. (The Northwest Ordinance applied only so long as the areas it covered were still territories: any state, once it was established, could introduce slavery if it chose to do so.) Coles ran for governor in 1822 to keep Illinois free. He won the governorship and the fight to keep Illinois a free state, although tough laws restricting free blacks remained (they could not vote, for example). A county east of Decatur was named after Coles the year the Lincolns arrived; Thomas and Sarah Bush Lincoln moved there in 1831.

That same year Abraham Lincoln turned twenty-two, becoming legally independent of his father. He wanted a physical separation as well, so he moved in the opposite direction, to New Salem, a village down the Sangamon River to the west. He arrived, as he later put it, like a piece of floating driftwood.

River work drew him first. There was a merchant in New Salem, Denton Offut, a typical American type: a promoter, a big talker, a horse whisperer on the side. He wanted some young men to take a flatboat of hogs down the Sangamon to the Illinois River, and so to the Mississippi and New Orleans. Lincoln signed up.

Lincoln had already made one flatboat trip to New Orleans in 1828, when he was still living in Indiana, via the Ohio and the Mississippi. Rivers were the easiest transportation in a vast frontier with a few wretched roads; the Mississippi was the watershed of half a continent, and New Orleans at its mouth was the spigot. It was the fifth-largest city in the United States, with over 40,000 people (New Salem only had one hundred). It was a creole city with a French and Spanish colonial past, only recently overlaid by English speakers; it was also filled with slaves and free Negroes. A rustic like Lincoln had never seen anything like it. It was the only city in the Deep South he would ever see.

Given Lincoln's later history, the men who accompanied him on these trips would look for portents in his youthful reactions. The spectacle of a slave metropolis, with auctions and buyers inspecting the bodies of the merchandise, might be revolting on first acquaintance; to some minds, it might be thrilling. Lincoln's friends testified that the experience had distressed him. But were their recollections authentic? Allen Gentry, who went on the first trip, left only thirdhand testimony, reporting Lincoln's feelings—"Abraham was very angry"—to his son, who told someone else. John Hanks, who went on the second trip, said that Lincoln's "heart bled" in New Orleans. If it did, Hanks did not see it, because he went no farther than St. Louis (though of course Lincoln might have told him what he had seen and felt in New Orleans after they both came home).

The one memory that Lincoln himself ever recorded was that during the first trip the flatboat was attacked by a gang of black thieves— escaped slaves lurking along the riverbank—whom the Illinoisans fought off. Poor white men could have unpleasant interactions with those who were worse off yet.

Lincoln did not stay with the river. For the rest of 1831, he clerked in Offut's store and did odd jobs. He wrestled the local tough guy, one Jack Armstrong, who managed to throw him only by using a trick hold. That was good enough to make Lincoln accepted by Armstrong and all his pals. Like father, like son.

In 1832 Lincoln performed the only military service of his life. An old Sauk chief named Black Hawk, who had fought alongside the British during the War of 1812, led 450 warriors into northwestern Illinois in a forlorn attempt to reclaim their lost homeland (the US government had required the Indians of the Northwest to move beyond the Mississippi). To repel him Illinois called out the militia. Lincoln enlisted for three months. For the first month he served as a captain, elected by his own company, a mark of recognition that pleased him no end (Armstrong was his sergeant).

Lincoln's war was not a very martial experience. Black Hawk was cornered and captured without the participation of Lincoln's unit; he saw no action, and in later years would poke fun at his service. For all that he admired George Washington's manly independence and idealism, he had no inclination to follow him into military life. The benefits he got from the Black Hawk War were of the peacetime sort: it made him better known among his fellow militiamen, and he earned some money at a time when he was broke.

One grim memory stayed with him, of a morning when he came upon five men who had just been killed in a skirmish and scalped. "Every man had a round red spot on top of his head, about as big as a dollar," he recalled later. Blood seemed to be everywhere. "The red sunlight seemed to paint everything all over." Lincoln's unit buried the corpses. This made an impression on the grandson of the first Abraham Lincoln.

———

Back to New Salem, and the quest for work. Lincoln became a partner in a general store, which failed in a few months, leaving him saddled with debt (he would refer to it as "the national debt"; it took him almost a decade to pay it off). In 1833 he managed to be appointed village postmaster—this brought him some income, not much work, and the opportunity to read everyone else's newspapers. He learned surveying, and was also appointed deputy surveyor for the county (some of the roads he laid out are still in use).

There were some educated men in New Salem, and Lincoln sought them out: a few college graduates, and a village ne'er-do-well who spent his time fishing and quoting Shakespeare and Burns. He kept reading, and reading in public. A New Salemite saw him one day sitting atop a wood pile with a book in his hand. "What are you studying?" he asked. "Law," said Lincoln. "Great God Almighty!" exclaimed the neighbor. Since there were no law schools then, novices typically learned by studying and working in the offices of established lawyers. It was possible to teach oneself and be accepted into the profession, but that was the hard way to go about it.

Lincoln argued small cases as an amateur advocate before the local justice of the peace, and he would ride, sometimes walk, to Springfield, a town a dozen miles away, to borrow books from John Stuart, a lawyer he had met in the Black Hawk War. Both the justice of the peace and the lawyer, like the neighbor at the wood pile, found him odd, even amusing at first—"he was the most uncouth looking young man I ever saw," said Stuart's partner—but when he spoke, they were impressed with his intelligence.

———

Lincoln impressed his friends with his grief. His woe began with a romance. Ann Rutledge was the daughter of New Salem's tavern-keeper, eighteen years old when Lincoln first saw her, and a beauty—"straight as an arrow, and as quick as a flash," is how she appeared in the mind of one neighbor thirty years later. She was engaged to a local storekeeper, but in 1832 he left town (he said) to tend to family business back East. He was gone for months, then a year, then two. Lincoln, as postmaster, could keep track of the gradual withering of the couple's correspondence. As the fiancé's absence lengthened, Abraham and Ann became engaged themselves.

When and how she would have broken the news to her first fiancé will never be known, for in August 1835 she got "brain fever," presumably typhoid—the symptoms were delirium, diarrhea, and fever. When she died Lincoln was crushed. "Lincoln told me that he felt like committing suicide often," one friend remembered. "He was fearfully wrought up," said the daughter of another friend. "My father had to lock him up and keep guard over him for some two weeks I think."

The weather seemed to give him particular pain. "One day when it was raining," his landlady at the time recalled, "[he said] he could not bear the idea of its raining on her grave." A comrade from the Black Hawk War remembered him saying the same thing: "I can never be reconciled," Lincoln told him, "to have snow, rains and storms to beat on her grave." Illinois had had the wettest spring and summer in the young state's experience; it had rained continuously for four and half months. Lincoln knew the destructive power of rain from his boyhood. Dead Ann would not wash away—graves hold bodies more securely than fields hold seed. But rain dramatized her obliteration.

Ann was the third young woman in Lincoln's life to die—mother, sister, now fiancée. Anyone in his situation would be grief-stricken. But he now showed the special grief of the depressed. Those who have never been depressed can scarcely comprehend it. Depression is not a mood that comes and goes, but a climate, a permanent backdrop, your most faithful friend. Consider Lincoln's sensitivity to the rain. Rain falls on everyone, just and unjust, living and dead, depressed and not depressed. But the depressed feel that it is addressed specially to them.

Lincoln's depression would flow on throughout his life, noted by friends of long standing and by acquaintances alike. The most famous description would come from his last law partner, William Herndon: "His melancholy dripped from him as he walked." Work, once he settled into his adult careers, could block it from view; so could his endless flow of stories and jokes, which continued as before. Humor was his distraction, his safety valve, his protective screen (it hid his sorrow from others and from himself). But melancholy never forsook him.

About this time—the mid-1830s—he told one friend that he never carried a pocket knife. Every man carried a pocket knife in those days, to cut things, to trim things, to whittle and waste the time. But Lincoln said he "never dare" do it. Lest he find some other use for it.

————

After tragedy, farce. One of the ladies of New Salem had an unmarried sister in Kentucky, Mary Owens, who came to Illinois for a long visit in 1836. She was attractive, educated, and feisty. Lincoln began a courtship that sputtered on for a year. Perhaps he felt it was too much too soon, perhaps he felt pressured into it by matchmaking friends. The letters he wrote Mary, when they were apart, were arias of hesitation. In one he threw the burden of deciding their future on her: "What I do wish is that our further acquaintance shall depend upon yourself." Not surprisingly, she decided to have no further acquaintance. "I thought him lacking in smaller attentions," was how she put it (to say nothing of larger ones).

After it was all over, Lincoln summed up his second experiment in courtship in a letter to a married woman friend. He made a series of crude jibes about Mary's weight, her skin, and her bad teeth, as if her looks had given him cold feet. It is a cringe-making performance; the funny man was trying to be funny, but his timing and delivery were all off. By the end of the letter, Lincoln finally put the blame for the failed relationship where it belonged. "Others have been made fools of by the girls, but this can never be with truth said of me. I most emphatically in this instance made a fool of myself."

Maybe he had done them both a favor; if he did not love Mary Owens, she would not die.

———

By the time Lincoln had lost Ann and driven off Mary, he had taken the first steps in the careers that he would pursue for the rest of his life—he had become a state legislator and the junior partner in a two-man law firm.

Lincoln made his first run for office in 1832, for the Illinois House of Representatives, the lower house of the General Assembly, or state legislature. The Black Hawk War kept him away from the hustings for most of the campaign; when he was able to appear before audiences, he was cheered by Jack Armstrong's posse. Because he had no reputation in the county as a whole, he lost his bid, though he managed to win 277 out of 300 votes in greater New Salem. In 1834, when his service as a postmaster and a surveyor had made him more widely known, he won handily. He came into the legislature as a protégé of John Stuart, his Black Hawk War comrade and lender of law books.

In his very first races Lincoln employed a technique he would use ever after: poor-mouthing himself. "If the good people in their wisdom shall see fit to keep me in the background," he said in declaring his first candidacy, "I have been too familiar with disappointments to be very much chagrined." This sounds like beginning a campaign with a concession speech: poor Abe! The modesty, however, was tactical; Lincoln was creating a role, a persona, the rube/boob, which served the same function in his political rhetoric as his odd appearance did in his joke-telling. *I am an unprepossessing man of humble origins.* Both the humorist and the politician warm up the audience by softening it up. *But I will hold your attention anyway*, was the implicit offer of the humorist. *I will persuade, or lead, or inspire you*, was that of the politician. Lincoln admitted his infirmities to make way for his strengths. The technique would not have worked, of course, if he had no strengths.

The fact that the rube/boob persona worked at all was a tribute to the democratization of American life. The founding fathers were austere republicans who rejected monarchy and aristocratic orders. But they thought of themselves as "natural" aristocrats—the expression was Jefferson's—proud of their talents. Almost all of them were wealthy men, or at least well off. George Washington, the first president, never learned Latin, but he was a Virginia planter; so were the third, fourth, and fifth presidents, Jefferson, Madison, and James Monroe. The other founding president, John Adams, was a Harvard-educated lawyer. Settlers in new states like Illinois were not unimpressed by such credentials, but they also liked leaders who were more like themselves.

Why had Lincoln chosen politics in the first place? Other paths were closed to him—he hated farming, and the failure of the store in 1833 showed he had no head for business. Politics was more inviting: in a newish, growing state, it was fluid, with fewer barriers to entry than in settled communities. And Lincoln might be suited to it: he was smart, and he liked thinking and talking on his feet. Finally, he was ambitious. "Every man is said to have his peculiar ambition," he admitted in his first campaign statement. His ambition was to be "truly esteemed of my fellow men, by rendering myself worthy of their esteem." That was a trifle stiff, a bit faux-marbled, but it showed the bent of his hopes. His own nature, perhaps with an assist from reading Parson Weems, had raised his sights.

————

Politics was a rowdy game in 1830s Illinois. At one meeting Lincoln picked up a heckler and tossed him aside. Candidates and their supporters rumbled in taverns and the open air. John Stuart fought another politician, Stephen Douglas, in a grocery—a store that sold liquor by the drink—when both men were running for Congress. When they stopped, exhausted, Stuart ordered a barrel of whiskey for all the spectators. Sometimes pistols were pulled, though they were seldom fired.

There were real issues in the commotion, along with mere animal spirits. The first American two-party system had pitted the Federalists of Washington, Adams, and Alexander Hamilton against the Republicans of Jefferson and Madison. Federalists wanted a strong federal government run by a self-confident leadership class. Republicans stood for small government and the common man, however uncommon Jefferson and Madison were. This system had vanished when Lincoln was a child—the Federalist Party disappeared after opposing the War of 1812. In the election of 1824 four Republicans fought among themselves to succeed Monroe, the last founder president: Andrew Jackson, John Quincy Adams, William Crawford, and Henry Clay. Jackson narrowly lost that contest to Adams, but he came back to win in 1828 and 1832, and to become the catalyst and polarizer of a new party system.

The Jacksonians called themselves Democrats. They, too, embraced small government and the common man, like their Republican forebears, but they were also identified with Jackson's contentious personality. Jackson—victor of the Battle of New Orleans—was the second former general to become president, after George Washington, but their temperaments could not have been more different. Washington had been an icon of self-control. Parson Weems got this right: "In him," Weems wrote, the "noble quality" of courage was always the "ready servant" of his reason. Jackson, by contrast, was a fighter, willful and tempestuous. He had killed a man in a duel, and he had brawled with one of his colonels in a frontier hotel with pistols and swords.

Harriet Martineau, the English traveler who visited Madison on her tour of the United States, met President Jackson in Washington, DC, at a characteristic moment. Early in 1835 a madman fired two pistols at him on the steps of the Capitol (both misfired and Jackson was unhurt).

In Martineau's opinion, "the president's misconduct" over the weeks that followed "was the most virulent and protracted." Jackson told everyone who would listen that a hostile senator had plotted to kill him. Jackson's conspiracy theory was fantastic: the shooter was a crazy loner who blamed Jackson for keeping him from the British throne. Martineau was embarrassed for the president's paranoid credulity, and worried for the country. Jackson's tendency to personalize everything, she said, would sow a "poisonous crop of folly." Decades later Lincoln would come to view Jackson more favorably, but Old Hickory in his heyday seemed to be a dangerous man.

By the mid-1830s Jackson's enemies were calling themselves Whigs, borrowing the name from eighteenth-century English politics, when Whigs were the opponents of royal power. Similarly, American Whigs opposed King Andrew and his overbearing ways.

Lincoln became a Whig—a decision with long consequences, for Illinois was a solidly Democratic state. In twenty years it would never vote for a Whig presidential candidate, never elect a Whig senator, and almost never send more than one Whig representative at a time to the House. (Illinois would elect a Whig governor—once.) Central Illinois, where Lincoln lived, was the state's lone Whig stronghold. Locally, Lincoln had done the prudent thing; statewide, he had tied himself to perennial losers. Whig minority status would test his mettle, but whatever it gave by way of instruction, it would not give much by way of victory.

————

Democrats and Whigs became national omnibus parties contesting a variety of issues, especially after Jackson retired in 1837. The first issue to absorb Lincoln was internal improvements, particularly canals.

Rivers were nature's infrastructure, but suppose man could improve them, or dig his own waterways? The model for all American canal builders was the Erie Canal, which when completed in 1825 ran across New York State, linking the Great Lakes to the Hudson River, and so to the Atlantic Ocean. The produce of the old Northwest could flow through New York, without making long detours down the St. Lawrence or the Mississippi. Upstate New York flourished, and New York City was confirmed as the nation's greatest port.

The Erie Canal made a hero of DeWitt Clinton, the New York Republican who had planned and completed it—and not just in his home state: Clinton County in Illinois was named for him in 1824, and DeWitt County would be added in 1839.

Lincoln knew about river transportation firsthand, and he knew the problems with Illinois' rivers. The Sangamon was a tangle of meanders and switchbacks. Canal-building would be a way to earn the esteem of his fellow men. He told a friend he intended to be the "DeWitt Clinton of Illinois."

All American politicians supported canals. They differed only about whether the federal government should pay for them. Democrats, true to their Republican antecedents, tended to think not; Whigs thought so. But both parties agreed that states could do as they liked. New York State had raised the money for the Erie Canal itself, and reaped the benefits. Surely Illinois could follow its lead.

But what canals should it dig? The most obvious project would be to link the Illinois River (which flowed into the Mississippi) with Lake Michigan at the old trading post of Chicago; the great north-south pathway of the Mississippi would then intersect with the new east-west artery of the Great Lakes and the Erie Canal. But Illinois was a large, broad state, half as wide as it was long; great expanses of it were dozens, even a hundred miles distant from Lake Michigan or the Mississippi. Any program of state-subsidized transportation would have to be a system of trade-offs, giving something to everyone.

The system that Lincoln ended up supporting—it was known locally simply as "the System"—would have covered the state with canals and the very latest form of infrastructure, railroads. The first American railroad, the Baltimore and Ohio, had been chartered in 1827; Charles Carroll laid the cornerstone the following year. In 1837 Illinois proposed to borrow $8.5 million to dig the Illinois and Michigan canal; $400,000 to improve navigation in five rivers; $10 million to build two major rail-roads and six spurs; and $200,000 for miscellaneous projects in places that had not benefited from any of the above.

One side effect of adopting the System was to move the state capital—and, incidentally, Lincoln himself. Since 1819 the capital had been in Vandalia, a town in southern Illinois. But if the whole state was about to be developed, then a more central location was de-sirable. Lincoln and eight fellow legislators from Sangamon County lobbied for Springfield (the nine politicians were known as the Long Nine—their combined height was 54 feet). They succeeded, and the capital moved there in 1837.

Lincoln moved along with it and moved up in the world. Springfield was no village, but a town of 1,500, and growing. Lincoln became John Stuart's law partner; he would no longer be a pettifogger arguing before a country justice of the peace, but a bona fide lawyer.

In Springfield he also met two of the most important men in his life. Joshua Speed was Lincoln's first Springfield landlord, renting him a room on the second floor of a general store he managed. Space was so tight, Lincoln and Speed shared a bed for four years. For a time Speed became Lincoln's best friend, maybe the only true friend he ever had. They were soul-mates—intelligent, sensitive, and depressed.

William Herndon, younger than Lincoln by nine years, was a clerk in Speed's store; for two years he would sleep in the same room as Lin-coln and Speed, in a separate bed. He was not Lincoln's soul-mate—he was far less temperamental—but he became his disciple. Herndon fell in love with Lincoln—the love of admiration and devotion. He would become his law partner and his almost-Boswell, the author of the best book on Lincoln that was never quite written.

The System, however, ended in catastrophe. Becoming the next DeWitt Clinton was harder than Lincoln had thought. New York had started from a stronger financial base than Illinois—it was already a prosperous state when it began digging the Erie Canal—and it pursued a more coherent goal: its canal was one project, not a dozen.

The System was also battered by a national economic storm. In 1829 Andrew Jackson declared war on the Second Bank of the United States, the national bank that regulated the money supply. Jackson hated it because he believed it was a tool of the rich and the Whigs, and by 1836 he had succeeded in destroying it. But when the bank went down, credit dried up nationwide, especially for grandiose projects like the System. In January 1840 the law authorizing the System was repealed, with only 105 miles of canal dug and 26 miles of track laid. The System, Lincoln wrote Stuart glumly, was "put down in a lump."

The collapse of the System hobbled Illinois for a time. But the state was growing so rapidly that it soon recovered; the canal to Lake Michigan and the most important railroads all got built eventually. Young, healthy communities can afford to roll the dice.

The demise of the System would hobble Lincoln's career, too—he stayed loyal to it to the bitter end, vainly urging the legislature "to save something . . . from the general wreck"—but he eventually found other issues. Good politicians know how to move on, sooner or later.

In passing, Lincoln touched on what was then a marginal issue for him—slavery. The 1830s saw the emergence of an American movement to abolish it. Older critics of slavery, such as the Quakers, were joined by a more aggressive breed of polemicists. William Lloyd Garrison's new Boston weekly, *The Liberator*, set the tone: "Tell a man whose house is on fire, to give a moderate alarm; tell him to moderately rescue his wife from the hands of the ravisher; tell the mother to gradually extricate her babe from the fire into which it has fallen—but urge me not to use moderation in a cause like the present."

For all their fervor, abolitionists remained a tiny minority. Democrats and Whigs were both national parties with slaveholders in their ranks; abolition threatened to upend the economy and society of half the country and annul the Constitution's protections of slavery. (Each slave was counted as three-fifths of a freeman in apportioning seats in the House of Representatives—Article I, Section 2—and slaves escaping to free states had to be returned to owners who sought them—Article IV, Section 2.) Although Illinois was a free state, most Illinoisans had little love for Negroes, free or enslaved. In January 1837 the legislature voted overwhelmingly in support of a motion condemning "abolition societies."

At the tail end of the session in March, Lincoln and Dan Stone, another lawmaker from Sangamon County, entered a brief Protest on Slavery into the record. Although the two men agreed with their colleagues in disapproving of abolitionists, they declared "that the institution of slavery is founded on both injustice and bad policy." And while they acknowledged that Congress could not "interfere" with slavery in the states where it existed, they pointed out that it could abolish it in the District of Columbia, which it governed directly. Even so, they went on, Congress should not act "unless at the request of the people of the District."

Why go to this trouble on an issue of minor importance—Lincoln was then far more concerned with the System—and for no practical effect? (No one else in the legislature joined Lincoln and Stone in their Protest.) The arguments of the Protest showed some characteristic features of Lincoln's mind. He respected both legal punctilio—hence the parsing of Congress's powers—and public opinion—Congress should be guided by the District's voters. He also had a stubborn concern for first principles—hence the abstract statement about slavery's injustice. The Protest resembled the course of his own education—it was careful, incremental, and self-directed. He worked up his own thoughts, and he would not forget anything once he had thought it.

If there had been no Civil War from which to look back on it, Lincoln's 1837 Protest would be legislative trivia, mere lint. But perhaps most principles are lint until they are challenged.

Four

Thomas Paine,
Laughter, and Reason

L INCOLN'S TWENTIES PASSED AS THOSE OF MOST PEOPLE DO, in loving and working (he was less lucky than average in the first, luckier in the second). Meanwhile he continued to educate himself. In this decade he encountered Thomas Paine—an eccentric founding father who gave him provisional answers to some big questions, and who encouraged him in certain styles of thinking and writing. Paine taught him—for a while at least—to laugh at Christianity, and he showed him, to his lifelong benefit, how to use laughter in winning arguments.

———

Paine sits a little uneasily among the founding fathers. He never had serious political or military responsibilities—he was secretary of a congressional committee for two years during the Revolution, a glorified clerk. He led a peripatetic life: born in England in 1737, he migrated first to America in 1772 on the eve of our revolution, then to France in 1792 in the midst of its, going wherever the winds of change were stirring. In 1802 he returned to the United States, and he died in Greenwich Village the year Lincoln was born.

It was Paine's writing that gave him his eminence as an American patriot. His pamphlet *Common Sense*, calling for American independence, appeared in January 1776, half a year before Congress declared it. *Common Sense* made a sensation, selling 150,000 copies (in a country of 3 million, that was the equivalent of selling 15 million today). *The American Crisis* was the name Paine gave a series of essays commenting on the progress of the war. The first appeared in the grim December of 1776, a week before the Battle of Trenton; its first paragraph ("These are the times that try men's souls . . . ") is the most stirring lede in the history of journalism, the republican equivalent of King Harry's speech before the Battle of Agincourt in *Henry V*—Shakespeare in prose.

Paine almost unmade his reputation by his writing, too. *The Age of Reason*, a book-length attack on Christianity published in the mid-1790s, raised up a swarm of enemies, including a number of his fellow founders. Benjamin Rush, signer of the Declaration, refused to meet him after he returned to America, and Samuel Adams, another signer, wrote him a chiding letter about his religious views: "When I heard that you had turned your mind to a defense of infidelity [i.e., irreligion] I felt myself much astonished, and more grieved." Only Thomas Jefferson stayed loyal to him, welcoming Paine to the White House.

But Paine's works, both patriotic and anti-Christian, stayed in print. Parson Weems included *The Age of Reason* in the stock of books he sold, though he recommended buying it with a Christian antidote. Lincoln first read Paine in New Salem.

Son of a Quaker father and an Anglican mother, Paine was exposed to both faiths when he was a boy. But in *The Age of Reason* he said that his disenchantment with Christianity began when he was seven or eight years old. Some family member had given a home reading of a sermon on substitutionary atonement—the doctrine that Christ died for our sins. In the Christian notion, the sins of Adam and Eve (which infected all their descendants) were so egregious that they and all men thereafter must die. But Jesus offered His death on the cross to God, His Father, as payment for their offenses. When the sermon ended, young Paine went outside, "and as I was going down the garden steps (for I perfectly recollect the spot) I revolted at the recollection of what I had heard, and thought to myself that it was making God Almighty act like a passionate man that killed his son when he could not revenge himself any other way; and as I was sure a man would be hanged that did such a thing, I could not see for what purpose they preached such sermons."

Paine declared his own mature credo at the beginning of *The Age of Reason*: he believed "in one God, and no more," but considered all existing religions "human inventions set up to terrify and enslave mankind." Paine made some cracks at Islam, and more at Judaism, but he aimed most of his fire at Christianity. He employed three sorts of arguments, each centered on the Bible.

He made much of the contradictions scattered throughout the bible (he always lowercased it). The Books of Ezra and Nehemiah list, tribe by tribe, the Jews who returned to Jerusalem after the Babylonian captivity; but the lists disagree with each other, and their enumerations do not add up. "These writers," Paine wrote, "may do well enough for bible-makers, but not for anything where truth and exactness is necessary." The four gospel accounts of Jesus' ancestry, crucifixion, and resurrection differ on points large and small. If the authors had given such inconsistent evidence in court, said Paine, "they would have been in danger of having their ears cropped for perjury, and would have justly deserved it." Paine was not the first man to notice these inconsistencies: Christian and anti-Christian polemicists had been explaining or deriding them for centuries. But Paine's catalog of contradictions was well-tailored to impress or anger a nation of Bible-readers; it was literalism standing on its head.

Another characteristic line of attack for Paine was to arraign the Bible for indecency. He was ever on the lookout for naughty bits, and inviting his readers to snigger at them. He described Ruth wooing her future husband, Boaz, as a "country girl creeping slyly to bed" with him. "Pretty stuff indeed to be called the word of God!" He called the Song of Solomon "amorous and foolish," Ecclesiastes the reflections "of a worn out debauchee." He explained Mary Magdalene's presence at Jesus' empty tomb by her being "upon the stroll"—that is, trolling for tricks. The story of Jesus' birth struck him as "blasphemously obscene. . . . Were any girl, that is now with child, to say, and even to swear to it, that she was gotten with child by a ghost, and that an angel told her so, would she be believed?" Not by Paine.

Paine's erotic history was as unhappy as Lincoln's. He married twice, at ages twenty-two and thirty-four. His first wife died in childbirth after they had been together less than a year, and he separated from his second after three years, possibly for reason of impotence. There are no accounts of him having lovers. He liked arguing politics with the guys in coffeehouses and taverns. Nothing wrong with that; it was a common male pastime in all of Paine's homelands. But sexuality, especially female sexuality, seems to have alarmed him, in the Bible as in life.

Violence in the Bible—Paine's third target—disgusted him. Israel's wars with its many enemies in the Old Testament struck him as "horrid . . . a military history of rapine and murder." Claiming that God had ordered and approved this bloodshed was "blasphemy." But what most rankled Paine was what had disturbed him at age seven or eight: the notion that Jesus, God's Son, would offer Himself as a sacrifice in payment for man's sins, and that God, His Father, would accept it. It seemed both irrational—Wasn't God powerful enough to pardon sins without such a transaction?—and sadistic—How could crucifying an innocent man benefit others? "The Christian story of God the Father putting his son to death . . . cannot be told by a parent to a child; and to tell him that it was done to make mankind happier and better is making the story still worse, as if mankind could be improved by the example of murder."

Paine's alternative to Christianity was a religion of reason (hence the title of his book). God's word was to be found not in any scripture, but in creation itself; the way to read it was by using our reason—"the choicest gift of God to man." Applying our minds to the world around us would show us how the universe worked, and how we should behave. Paine's God says, "I have made an earth for man to dwell upon. . . . LEARN FROM MY MUNIFICENCE TO ALL, TO BE KIND TO EACH OTHER." Paine, though he would not capitalize the "b" of "Bible," capitalized this sentence.

———

The Age of Reason defied everything Lincoln had been taught about religion as a child. Thomas Lincoln belonged to the Baptist church, which was growing rapidly in turn-of-the-nineteenth-century America; he had joined a congregation in Indiana and had even served as a church trustee. Abraham Lincoln attended services as a boy, and afterward, he would repeat the sermons he had heard to other children as a performance, generally a humorous one. But his stepmother noticed some aloofness on his part: "Abe had no particular religion. . . . He never talked about it."

After Lincoln moved to Illinois, he read Paine and other anti-Christian authors whose works circulated even in rural America: Voltaire and another Frenchman, Constantin de Volney, whose book *The Ruins* was a meditation on the transience of all empires and religions. But Paine was the American skeptic, who spoke with an American voice.

Books can both express thoughts we already have and stimulate us to have new ones. Whether because of his reading, or because he was no longer living with churchgoing parents, Lincoln in Illinois started talking about religion.

James Matheny heard him doing it in Springfield. Nine years younger than Lincoln, Matheny clerked in various government offices there. Springfield had a small downtown, making it easy for anyone to call on anyone else. Matheny remembered that when he and his fellow clerks had "nothing to do," Lincoln, who was by then John Stuart's junior law partner, would drop by, "pick up the Bible, read a passage, and then comment on it—show its falsity and its follies on the grounds of reason." Matheny gave as an instance Lincoln calling Christ "a bastard." Contradictions of the Bible, the test of reason, Jesus' illegitimacy—it sounds like a Thomas Paine triple play.

Lincoln's biblical exegeses were in part an act, a performance. He was older than Matheny and the other clerks; although he had never been to college, when he picked up the Bible he was taking the role of an upperclassman scandalizing the freshmen. Christ's bastardy would also have had a special meaning for Lincoln, which he did not share with the gaping clerks: if Jesus was an ordinary illegitimate child, then the Holy Family was a lot like the Hanks family. It made the Bible less awesome, and the Hankses less deplorable.

Lincoln did more than just talk about religion. When he was still living in New Salem, he wrote a Paine-ite pamphlet explaining that the Bible was not God's word, and Jesus was not His Son. He read it aloud to friends during the slack hours of his postmaster's job, and spoke of getting it printed—until Samuel Hill, an older man who owned one of the village's stores, took the manuscript and burned it.

Lincoln was already seeking political office. Paine's views had injured even his considerable reputation as a patriot; writing up similar views would have snuffed Lincoln's reputation before it was made. So Hill did the young man a good turn. The story of the burned pamphlet became a topic for local gossip even so; Hill's son heard old folks mention it "hundreds of times." In 1846 when Lincoln was running for Congress, Peter Cartwright, his Democratic opponent and a Methodist minister, started a whispering campaign about his irreligion. Lincoln had to issue a statement denying that he had ever been "an open scoffer" at Christianity. Shocking (and titillating) a roomful of clerks could qualify as private scoffing. Publishing a pamphlet would certainly have been open scoffing, but Lincoln, thanks to Hill, had been spared that blunder.

Paine was the first founder Lincoln encountered writing in his own voice. Washington appeared in Weems's *Life* in the third person; Weems included some of his authentic sayings and writings, but many of the words Weems assigned Washington were made up. Paine wrote for himself.

Paine also wrote surpassingly well. Weems told good stories—we still remember the cherry tree, two centuries later—but he told them in runaway sentences, never using five words when he could use twenty. Washington's own prose was grave and a little stiff, like the man himself. Paine had the punch of an editorial writer, with the clarity and speed of a good reporter.

This made Paine important to Lincoln the future writer and speaker. Lincoln already knew how to tell stories; Paine showed him how to make and win arguments.

Paine's knack for ridicule made him particularly useful to Lincoln, who already had the knack himself. Paine could nail down his points with similes that fixed them in the memory. He called the Book of Jeremiah "a medley of unconnected anecdotes"—then added, "as if the various and contradictory accounts that are to be found in a bundle of newspapers . . . were put together without date, order, or explanation." Paine could turn ideas he did not like into slapstick, by means of speed and concreteness. Christians, he wrote, accepted "the amphibious idea of a man-god; the corporeal idea of the death of a god; the mythological idea of a family of gods; and the christian system of arithmetic, that three is one, and one is three."

At his funniest Paine used the *reductio ad absurdum*, taking an idea and pushing it until the consequences become ludicrous. Paine's bugaboo, the story of Christ dying for our sins, became this when placed in an astronomical context: "Are we to suppose that every world, in the boundless creation, had an Eve, an apple, a serpent, and a redeemer? In this case, the person who is irreverently called the Son of God . . . would have nothing else to do than to travel from world to world, in an endless succession of death, with scarcely a momentary interval of life."

It took Lincoln a while to master these techniques—humor and seriousness can be an unstable mix—but as a mature debater and speechmaker he would use them all. In the 1850s, he would argue that his rivals had become too casual about slavery: they "cease speaking of it as in any way wrong, [they] regard slavery as one of the common matters of property, and speak of negroes as we do of our horses and cattle." The first two phrases defined the problem; the simile of the third planted it on the family farm. When rivals accused him of being in favor of race mixing, he protested that just because he did not want a black woman for a slave did not mean he desired her for a wife. "I need not have her for either. I can just leave her alone." Here he demolished an argument with concreteness, cutting through lurid fears with a plain personal reaction. As president, he defended onerous wartime measures with the *reductio ad absurdum*: Americans were no more likely to maintain them in peacetime than a sick man would "persist in feeding upon . . . emetics" once he became well. All these techniques are related to the stretching and teasing of good storytelling—to the Man of Audacity milking his own embarrassment. But Paine and the older Lincoln used them to poke holes in the arguments of their enemies.

They are common techniques that Lincoln could have picked up in many places. Jonathan Swift was a master of this kind of mockery, and *Gulliver's Travels* was a classic that was in print all during Lincoln's life. We could easily call Lincoln's exercises in this style of humor Swiftian— except for one thing. There is no indication that Lincoln ever read Swift, or even mentioned him, Gulliver or Lilliput. Paine was the mocking humorist he did read.

––––

Lincoln would retain traces of Paine's style for much of his life, but there was a barrier between him and the author of *The Age of Reason* that prevented him from becoming a full-fledged Paine-ite. That was Paine's optimism.

Paine believed that studying the world would demonstrate God's "MUNIFICENCE" (all caps) because he believed that the world was a good place. "Do we not see a fair creation prepared to receive us the instant we were born—a world furnished to our hands that cost us nothing? Is it we that light up the sun; that pour down the rain; and fill the earth with abundance? Whether we sleep or wake, the vast machinery of the universe still goes on." Paine is like Augustine Washington in Weems's *Life* teaching young George about God's bounty.

Paine is half right. The world is a good place—except when it's not. What of the many coughs and rattles in the machinery of the universe— floods, famines, droughts, plagues, eruptions, earthquakes? What of the one-on-one disasters and retail catastrophes that fill every life—the death of Paine's first wife? The deaths of Nancy Lincoln, Sarah Grigsby, and Ann Rutledge? Paine, from conviction or temperament, heroism or stupidity, looked the other way. Lincoln could not.

As with the world, so with fathers. Paine's outrage over the substitutionary atonement sprang from his horror at the notion that a good father could sacrifice a son in payment for sin. Any father who did it, he was certain, "would be hanged." On the question of what fathers would or would not do, Lincoln reserved judgment.

To find reflections of nature's darkness, and his own, Lincoln turned instead to poetry. He missed many of the great poets of his time: Wordsworth, Coleridge, Keats, Shelley, Tennyson, Whitman never stirred his interest. His favorite poem, disconcertingly, was "Mortality," a lugubrious meditation on the vanity of human wishes by William Knox, a Scotsman who had died in 1825. Lincoln read it in New Salem, committed it to memory, and would recite it in later years. "I would give all I am worth, and go in debt," he once declared, "to be able to write so fine a piece as I think that is." More to his credit was his love of Robert Burns, whom he admired for his satire; "Holy Willie's Prayer," a send-up of a canting hypocrite, was a particular favorite of his.

A third discovery in New Salem was Lord Byron. It is hard now to understand what Byron was to the early nineteenth century. He was both

a poet and a personality, an actor and a hero. He was beautiful, glamor-
ous, rich, witty, and damned—an irresistible combination. Byron's politics
were not unlike Paine's—he was a liberty-loving aristocrat who died in 1824
fighting to free Greece from the Ottoman Empire. But, unlike Paine, or any
other Enlightenment figure, he had access to all the dark emotions—depression, despair, nihilism, madness. The ease of his access makes us now
suspect that he was a bit of a poseur. Lincoln, like most of his contemporaries, loved him; when he was on the road, he would look up favorite passages
in other people's volumes of Byron (other people always had them).

Towering over all was Shakespeare. Lincoln never read all the plays.
This was characteristic of his learning; he was less well read than many
a professor or even journalist, but what he read he read deeply. His
favorites were the plays in minor keys—the tragedies and the histories
(though Shakespeare designed the histories to end well—springtime for
Tudors—there is a lot of grimness along the way). Lincoln's favorite of
favorites was *Macbeth*, the play that is set in motion by witches.

In his late twenties and thirties, Lincoln wrote poems of his own, all
sad. One, "The Suicide's Soliloquy," was thought to have been removed
from the files of the *Sangamo Journal*, the local newspaper that ran it,
as if to spare Lincoln from being associated with such a grim topic. A
scholar rediscovered it, however, in 2004. One stanza will suffice:

> *Yes! I've resolved the deed to do,*
> *And this the place to do it:*
> *This heart I'll rush a dagger through,*
> *Though I in hell should rue it!*

Lincoln failed utterly to match his words to the sentiments he wished
to evoke. The rhyme of "do it" and "rue it" is like rolling barrels down a
staircase.

Probably his best touch as a poet came in "The Bear Hunt," a long
description of a wild bear being run down and killed by mounted hunt-
ers and baying dogs. As the chase reaches a clamorous pitch, Lincoln,

whose sympathies are with the bear, drops in this mordant little line: "The world's alive with fun." Only a humorist could be that black.

Lincoln loved poetry and turned to it all his life: as a mirror for his moods, as a salve for them, as a capsule in which to deposit them. But he stopped writing it, and seldom quoted it in his speeches. He did better: he assimilated the moods and music, and learned to call on them, when needed, in his prose.

In January 1838 Lincoln gave a speech in which he brought together many of the things he had been learning about politics and self-expression. He also spoke of the founders—their legacy and their passing: what they had accomplished and what would become of it now that they were dead.

His venue was the Young Men's Lyceum of Springfield. Lyceums were discussion groups that met in American towns to hear edifying talks, either by locals or by traveling speakers. The highfalutin name (the original Lyceum was Aristotle's school in ancient Athens) showed the young country's ambition for self-improvement. Lincoln's audience at the Young Men's Lyceum was composed of striplings like Herndon and Matheny who were already his fans. Lincoln, on the eve of his twenty-ninth birthday, could still just claim to be one of them.

His topic was "The Perpetuation of Our Political Institutions"—a subject of obvious interest to a politician (he was in his second term in the Illinois House of Representatives). Rhetorically he was on his best behavior—perhaps too much so. His first sentence, after stating the topic, is a long rumble: "In the great journal of things happening under the sun the American people find our account running under date of the nineteenth century of the Christian era." This was as resonant as a drum, and as empty. But as the young statesman warmed to his subject, he had some interesting things to say.

Lincoln defined America's political institutions as a system "conducing . . . to the ends of civil and religious liberty," and he thanked the founders—"hardy, brave and patriotic"—for establishing it (he would come back to the founders twice more). Their handiwork, he went on, was safe from invasion. The War of 1812 had proved that point: the British, who had beaten Napoleon, had been unable to beat the United States.

America's institutions, however, faced a threat from within: mob violence. "Accounts of outrages committed by mobs," said Lincoln, "form the every day news of the times": "They have pervaded the country" and "have grown too familiar to attract anything more than an idle remark." He dwelled on two examples—a lynching of five gamblers in Vicksburg in 1835, and the lynching of Francis McIntosh, a colored man, in St. Louis in 1836. The victims were not lambs—both the gamblers and McIntosh were killers—but their deaths were brutal and entirely illegal: the gamblers had been strung up without trial, and McIntosh had been chained to a tree and slowly burned to death.

Here Lincoln showed his Whig partisanship. Andrew Jackson had left the White House at the end of his second term in 1837, to be succeeded by fellow Democrat Martin Van Buren. (The Whig Party had tried to beat Van Buren in the election of 1836 by running three presidential candidates, in hopes of sending a deadlocked election to the House of Representatives; their failure has dissuaded any party from trying that gambit again.) Van Buren was sleek, stout, courteous, and elegant—in short, no Andrew Jackson. But Jackson's hellion personality was still a political lightning rod. Whigs in Lincoln's audience would believe, without him having to argue the point, that an uncontrollable president had somehow given an impetus to lawless mobs. Both Mississippi and Missouri, where the lynchings had occurred, were Democratic states.

There was a third Democratic state that had also recently witnessed mob violence, and that was Illinois. Elijah Lovejoy, a Presbyterian minister from Maine, had settled in St. Louis, where he published an abolitionist newspaper. A mob had destroyed his presses after he had condemned the lynching of McIntosh, whereupon Lovejoy had restarted his newspaper across the Mississippi River in Alton, Illinois. In

November 1837 a mob there shot him to death and threw his presses into the water. Lincoln alluded to this crime in a list of the things mobs do: "burn churches, ravage and rob provision stores, *throw printing presses into rivers, shoot editors* . . . " (italics added). Lincoln did not mention Lovejoy by name, but only two months after the fact and sixty miles away (the distance between Alton and Springfield), everyone in the audience would have recognized him.

Lincoln milked these crimes for all their gruesomeness, but he argued that the worst thing about mob violence was its aftereffects. If life and property depended on "the caprice of a mob," decent men would become "alienated" from their government. Once that happened, ambitious men would be tempted to overturn it and start afresh. This was the great threat Lincoln saw to American institutions—not Andrew Jackson and his riotous imitators, but rebels who might arise in their place.

The spectacle of lawlessness would give such rebels their opportunity, but their incentive would be the chance of making a mark in history. Lincoln returned to the founders as a parallel. They had made their mark in history by establishing free government: "If they succeeded, they were to be immortalized." They had succeeded, and they had their reward: "This field of glory is harvested, and the crop is already appropriated."

"But," Lincoln went on, "new reapers will arise, and they too will seek a field." Would these new reapers find glory in maintaining the institutions that other men had created—even men as glorious as the founding fathers? Lincoln scoffed: "*Such [ambitions] belong not to the family of the lion, or the tribe of the eagle*. . . . Towering genius disdains a beaten path. It seeks regions hitherto unexplored."

These are almost the best lines of Lincoln's speech. Fields, reapers, and eagles are images as plain as anything in Paine (lions are a bit exotic), though Lincoln means them seriously, not sarcastically. They reach for poetry—and Lincoln had a poetical model for the towering genius he depicted. *Childe Harold's Pilgrimage* was one of Byron's most famous poems, a long rumination on life and modern Europe, and one of its most famous passages was a portrait of Napoleon.

But quiet to quick bosoms is a hell,
And there hath been thy bane; there is a fire
And motion of the soul which will not dwell
In its own narrow being, but aspire
Beyond the fitting medium of desire;
And, but once kindled, quenchless evermore,
Preys upon high adventure . . .

Napoleon's career was recent history—he had died in 1821—and everyone admired him for his abilities and against-all-odds boldness. But he was the archetype of the restless political adventurer; and any republican—like Byron, like Lincoln—deplored him for destroying the French republic and replacing it with his own personal empire.

How to forestall an American Napoleon? Lincoln turned once more to the founders.

The political institutions of the founders had been established and sustained, Lincoln argued, by passion—theirs, and ours. The founders had been passionately committed to the Revolution. Lincoln described how the struggle had galvanized them, focusing hatred on a common enemy and sinking ordinary rivalries in a common cause. So long as the founders lived, younger Americans felt a passionate commitment to them as heroes in their midst. "A *living history*" of the Revolution, Lincoln said, "was to be found in every family . . . in the limbs mangled, in the scars of wounds received."

But now the founders were dead—dead and gone. The ties of passion that had kept America connected to the Revolution were cut. The founders had been "a fortress of strength; but what the invading foeman could never do, the silent artillery of time has done—the leveling of its walls. . . . They were a forest of giant oaks; but the all resistless hurricane has swept over them, and left only here and there a lonely trunk." This passage, especially the phrase about time's artillery, is the finest in the Lyceum Address, the first anticipatory flash of the light to come.

Now that the founders had died, neither they nor our fading loyalty to them could stop the next Napoleon. What could Americans turn to instead? Lincoln's answer was reason: "Passion has helped us but can do so no more. Reason, cold, calculating, unimpassioned reason, must furnish all . . . our future support."

Lincoln's appeal to reason echoed Paine's great title, but Lincoln's Age of Reason, unlike Paine's, would be focused on politics, not religion. Reason would instruct Americans to honor the law: "Let reverence for the laws be breathed by every American mother to the lisping babe that prattles on her lap." Then American institutions would be safe from mobs, from alienation and from towering geniuses alike. Lincoln even hoped that law-abidingness would become a "political religion." But the new faith would be founded upon, and guided by, reason.

The Lyceum Address was printed in the *Sangamo Journal*, a Springfield newspaper, with a note of thanks from the Lyceum to "A. Lincoln, Esq."

There are problems with the Lyceum Address. There is a lot of rhetorical stuffing in it, which the eye now slides over ("lisping babe," indeed). Lincoln's picture of revolutionary-era America united in a glorious cause was historically false. There had been traitors, such as Benedict Arnold, and there had been thousands of loyalists engaged in violent resistance to the Revolution, both in New York and in the South. Parson Weems had followed his *Life of Washington* with a *Life of General Francis Marion*, the Swamp Fox of South Carolina, which covered the local civil war there in detail.

Lincoln's appeal to "cold, calculating, unimpassioned reason" was untrue to his own rhetorical efforts. If he loved reason's coldness so much, why had he used all the arts he possessed to make his case? Reasoners don't talk about resistless hurricanes or time's artillery.

A loose thread running through the address, neither cut nor tied off, was the issue of abolition. Lovejoy had been lynched for advocating it, and he and other abolitionists had deplored the lynching of McIntosh. Even the Mississippi lynchings had an abolitionist subtext: Vicksburg had turned on its gamblers in 1835 as part of a statewide alarm over a slave revolt that was supposedly being plotted by an unholy alliance of abolitionists and bandits. The fear was groundless, but the hangings that ensued were very real.

Lincoln had no truck with abolition. In the March 1837 Protest on Slavery, he and Dan Stone had maintained that abolitionist propaganda actually made slavery worse, presumably by causing panic among masters. Lincoln hated lynchings, but he also hated stirring up public wrath. Abolitionism struck him as a radical project, the kind of thing that might follow a descent into lawlessness. America's "towering genius," he warned in the Lyceum Address, might be equally capable of "emancipating slaves, or enslaving freemen." Lincoln's fear of a Napoleon-to-be, finally, was groundless. No such figure arose. The challenges Lincoln would face over the rest of his career took very different forms.

Yet there were Americans in the family of the lion and the tribe of the eagle, men with traces of towering genius, and though they would never found an empire, they would cross Lincoln's path, sometimes quite intimately.

The address was a marker of what he had learned by the end of his twenties: a try-out and a rehearsal of arguments. He had not yet figured out how to use humor in a serious setting, but he made his first essays in poetry—not jingles about suicide or bear hunts, but the true poetry of liberty, death, and humanity.

Lincoln called on the founders. He called clumsily. He lifted Reason (shorn of anti-Christian mockery) from Paine. He invoked the founding generation as wraiths, venerable but vanished. At the tail end of the address, Lincoln even summoned George Washington: "That we remained free . . . shall be that which to learn the last trump shall awaken our WASHING-TON" (Lincoln's caps). Washington had fought for freedom—once upon a time. He could not help us now, because he was dead, but when he should be resurrected, he would learn that we had helped ourselves.

That was rather curt. But Lincoln would be coming back to the founders again.

Five

1840–1852: MATURITY

TOWERING GENIUS, AS LINCOLN SAID, DISDAINS THE BEATEN
path. In his thirties, Lincoln followed it. The beaten path led him
to the mature walks of life, professional and personal.

As his legal practice grew, he traveled the roads, dusty or muddy by
turns, of central Illinois, arguing cases in county courthouses. In politics
he clambered up the ladder of ambition until he was sent to Washington
as a congressman. He made money, labored for his party, and attacked
a president (of the other party) and a war (begun by the other party).

Along the way he sank into despair, married, and started a family.

He had some further encounters with George Washington, but they
were muffled by official piety or partisanship. The beaten path can be a
busy and distracting place.

———

Despite Lincoln's fears of real mobs and possible Napoleons, Illinois politics followed ordinary democratic paths, both intricate and

boisterous. A few of the incidents in which Lincoln figured stood out for their local color.

In December 1840 Illinois Democrats tried to adjourn the legislature, which would cause a law offering relief to the Illinois state bank to lapse. Local Democrats opposed the state bank for the same reasons Andrew Jackson had fought the Second Bank of the United States— they claimed it favored businessmen and the rich, not the common man. Lincoln and his fellow Whigs argued that the state bank offered credit to all and wanted to protect it by keeping the legislature in session. To block a motion to adjourn, most Whigs absented themselves, depriving the legislature of a quorum; only Lincoln and a few others stayed behind to keep an eye on things. But the Whig watchdogs miscounted: Lincoln and friends plus the Democrats were just enough to make a quorum after all. When the Whigs saw their error, they tried to leave the statehouse, but the Democrats barred the door. So Lincoln and his friends jumped out of a second-story window. Democratic newspapers joked about raising the building another story.

Two years later Lincoln was involved in a more serious spat, though still a grotesque one. By 1842 the Illinois state bank was so weakened that the state refused to accept its currency in payment of debts, a policy announced by the state auditor, James Shields, who was a Democrat. Lincoln believed that the Democrats, who had attacked the bank for years, were reaping the fruit of their own demagogy, and he decided to make fun of Shields in a pseudonymous letter to the *Sangamo Journal*.

Lincoln's letter appeared in August. His persona was Aunt Becca, a chatty old countrywoman; her message was that Shields was imperious and high-handed. There was one funny line in the piece, describing Shields (who must have been a bit of a dandy) at a party: "Dear girls," he says to the assembled ladies, "it is not my fault that I am *so* handsome and *so* interesting."

Shields was not amused, and he challenged Lincoln to a duel. The deaths in duels of Alexander Hamilton in 1804 and of naval hero Stephen

Decatur in 1820 had thrown the practice into disrepute—somewhat. But Shields and Lincoln took the matter seriously. As the challenged party, Lincoln got to pick the weapons; he chose cavalry broadswords, to take advantage of his long arms (Shields was of average size). In September the parties and their seconds met on an island in the Mississippi, opposite Alton, where the affair was finally resolved short of combat, Lincoln declaring that Aunt Becca's letter had been written "wholly for political effect," and not to impugn Shields's character.

Lincoln learned from these encounters to make better vote counts, and not to push opponents too hard.

———

Such maneuvers and mind-games were the inside story of politics, absorbing to politicians and journalists, if to no one else. But there was also the outside story of politics: the public appeals that politicians and parties made to establish their claim to rule.

Lincoln's party made one of the most effective appeals in American political history in the presidential election of 1840. After Jackson destroyed the Second Bank of the United States, the economy had collapsed on the head of his successor, Martin Van Buren. The Whigs were determined to ride through the ruins to victory—their first ever, if they succeeded. Their candidate in 1840 was William Henry Harrison, a hero of the War of 1812 who had also held a few political offices, though none of them recently. He seemed dignified and reasonably famous without being controversial.

Early in the campaign, a Democratic newspaper attacked Harrison as a nobody: if he were given a pension, he would "sit the remainder of his days in his log cabin." The Whigs immediately realized that this jibe, aimed at Harrison's obscurity, came off as disdain for his humble station in life—which also happened to be the station of the vast majority of voters. The Whigs embraced the insult, parading log cabins at Harrison rallies and marketing canes, handkerchiefs, soapboxes, joke books, and whiskey bottles decorated with log cabins.

The Log Cabin Campaign was literally false, since Harrison was no hick but the son of a Virginia grandee who had signed the Declaration of Independence. But the Whigs told a political truth: they had spent a decade in the wilderness, while Harrison's opponent, Van Buren, was the insider's insider presiding over a haggard administration. For all their hokum the Whigs had a point—in a two-party system, the challengers deserve a chance when the incumbents have been in office too long.

It was not the point Lincoln wished to make, however. He was an active Harrison supporter. He was a Whig presidential elector, in case Harrison carried Illinois; he ran a campaign newspaper called *The Old Soldier*; and he stumped the center of the state, debating Democrats. In one encounter with Stephen Douglas, another rising politician, Lincoln played the race card, reading from an old campaign biography of Van Buren to show that he had supported black suffrage in New York State (free blacks could not vote in Illinois). Lincoln did this to embarrass Douglas and he succeeded: "Damn such a book," Douglas cried, snatching it from his hands and flinging it into the crowd. Lincoln opposed lynching and called slavery unjust, but he was not above slyly trafficking in prejudice.

For the most part, however, he stuck to the issue that was then preoccupying him, and that would soon cause him to jump out the window of the state legislature: the Democratic Party's war on banks. Lincoln "drew a vivid picture of our prosperous and happy condition" under the Second Bank of the United States, according to one newspaper account of his stump speech. Lincoln, as the economic historian Gabor Boritt put it, was by nature a single-issue candidate. His issue after the collapse of the System was banking, and he focused on it, rather than log cabins.

Yet he would have had to be insensible not to notice the populist hoopla of the Whig onslaught, and careless not to file it for future reference. A serious single-issue candidate might not engage in such antics himself, but he could let his supporters do it for him.

Harrison won, with 234 electoral votes to Van Buren's 60, and 53 percent of the popular vote to Van Buren's 47 percent. He did not win Democratic Illinois, however, which Van Buren carried narrowly. Lincoln would not be casting an electoral vote. He also experienced a personal setback, for although he was elected to a fourth term in the state legislature, he won by the smallest margin of any of his races so far. The collapse of the System had crimped his popularity.

Nationally, the Whig triumph was cut short when the sixty-eight-year-old Harrison caught pneumonia and died in April 1841, a month after his inauguration. For the first time in American history, a vice president was obliged to fill a vacancy in the White House. But Harrison's vice president, John Tyler, was not a Whig at all, but a renegade Democrat who had been put on the ticket to increase its appeal. Once he became president he fought the Whigs who had unintentionally elevated him, vetoing a bill to restore the Second Bank of the United States. "By the course of Mr. Tyler," wrote Lincoln sourly, "the policy of our opponents has continued in operation."

The election of 1840 was not a total loss for Lincoln, however, for it introduced him to his future wife—though their courtship would be harder and longer than a presidential campaign.

―――

Mary Todd, almost ten years younger than Lincoln, grew up in a wealthy family in Lexington, Kentucky, bluegrass country—a different world from the one the Lincolns had left. She was a cousin of John Stuart, Lincoln's law partner, and two of her sisters had married into the Springfield elite. Mary came to pay her relatives an extended visit late in 1839.

Mary Todd was short, plump, and attractive; smart, lively, and pert. There is a story that Lincoln told her, at a ball that December, that he wanted to dance with her "in the worst way," and that she said later that "he certainly did." Some scholars doubt the truth of the tale, but its interest lies in what it says about Mary: a woman who was dull or placid would not have been assigned such a punchline.

Politics drew them together. Mary and her family, as well as her Illinois connections, were all Whigs. She was passionate about politics, especially in the banner year of 1840. Whig women threw themselves into the Harrison campaign, one Democrat even complaining that they wore ribbons across their chests "with two names printed on them" (Harrison and Tyler—one for each breast). For Lincoln and Mary the thrill of their newfound acquaintance was enhanced by the thrill of presidential politics.

Then, suddenly, it was over; the campaign romance did not survive the campaign. It is hard to figure out why exactly. Lincoln had more in common with his political lover than he had with Mary Owens. Perhaps the prospect of success alarmed him. Both Mary Todd and Lincoln began flirting with other people. In December 1840 Lincoln told his friend and roommate Joshua Speed that he had decided he would see Mary no more and that he would write her a letter saying so. Speed told him that he must tell her face to face. Mary cried, Lincoln kissed her. The campaign romance ended with a break-up kiss.

Lincoln was plunged into gloom. "I am now the most miserable man living," he wrote Stuart. "If what I feel were equally distributed to the whole human family, there would not be one cheerful face on the earth." Speed hid their knives and razors. Other acquaintances in the little world of Illinois politics gossiped about his distress. Lincoln reportedly had had "two cat fits and a duck fit," one woman wrote her brother, a Whig legislator. "Is it true? Do let us hear soon."

Lincoln stayed sad, if not suicidal, for much of 1841. Speed sold his share of his Springfield store and moved back to his family's estate outside Louisville, where Lincoln visited him in the late summer. Speed's mother gave Lincoln a Bible, perhaps to steady him. On the steamboat going home, he saw a sight that impressed and chastened him, and he described it in a letter to one of Speed's sisters: "A gentleman had purchased twelve Negroes . . . and was taking them to a farm in the South.

They were chained six and six together. A small iron clevis [a U-shaped shackle] was around the left wrist of each, and this fastened to the main chain . . . at a convenient distance from the others, so that the Negroes were strung together precisely like so many fish upon a trot-line." What struck Lincoln most was their good spirits. "In this condition they were being separated forever from the scenes of their childhood," and from their families and friends. "Yet amid all these distressing circumstances, as we would think them, they were the most cheerful and apparently happy creatures on board." One played a fiddle; "others danced, sung, cracked jokes, and played various games with cards."

There was a racist way to view the scene: Negroes are simple creatures, they will get over anything. Lincoln viewed it through the eyes of melancholy: even slaves can feel happy, unlike me. He spelled it out to Speed's sister: "[God] renders the worst of human conditions tolerable, while He permits the best to be nothing better than tolerable." Depression can seem absurdly self-aggrandizing to those who do not experience it themselves; that does not make it any less painful to those who do.

Lincoln began to emerge from his funk by helping Speed out of a funk of his own. In the summer of 1841 Speed fell in love with a young woman, Fanny Henning, and then fell into gloomy fears. He worried that he did not love her; he imagined that she would die young. Lincoln wrote him hortatory letters in January and February 1842 as his wedding day approached. Speed's problem, Lincoln decided, was "nervous debility." Speaking as a fellow-sufferer, he assured Speed that "our forebodings . . . are all the worst sort of nonsense." It was in these letters that Lincoln recalled his father's saying: "If you make a bad bargain, hug it the tighter." A medical diagnosis that explained nothing, an airy dismissal, and an opaque proverb were not very lucid encouragements, but they may have helped get Speed over his reluctance; in February 1842 the wedding to Fanny came off as planned.

Once his friend was married, Lincoln turned his thoughts back to Mary Todd, though still with an odd passivity. Lincoln wrote Speed on the Fourth of July to say that, even as "God made me one of the instruments" of your happiness, He would somehow provide for Lincoln, too. "Stand still and see the salvation of the Lord," he added, quoting a command God gives Israel in the Bible, promising to fight her battles Himself.

Lincoln's almost-fight with James Shields in September 1842 seems to have concentrated his mind. Politics helped his courtship in the home stretch, as it had at the start: Whig friends arranged for him and Mary Todd to meet again. Mary was more persevering, and more forgiving, than Mary Owens. Lincoln wrote Speed a last nervous letter, asking if he was truly glad to be married. Speed must have said yes; Lincoln and Mary Todd were married in November.

The happy ending did not make for a happy marriage. Neither of the Lincolns was easy to live with. One friend of the couple described Mary as "always either in the garret or the cellar"—exalted or downcast. Abraham was generally the latter. Mary's mood swings were accompanied by a temper. In moments of distress she would beseech her husband, berate him, even throw things at him. In response he would read the newspaper, play with his children, or otherwise detach himself.

Mary Lincoln's eccentricities would cause Abraham political headaches during his presidency. Against this must be set her political interests, which kept her engaged in his career, and her political instincts, which could be sharp. (She accused him of being too trusting, which he was, though that probably benefited him in the long run.)

Lincoln's marriage would be of no interest to history, except for what it lacked. Public achievements are not always compensations for personal deprivation; there have been great men whose private lives were filled with blessings—wonderful parents, happy marriages, splendid children. Lincoln, however, was a wanderer in his own life, looking for something he never quite had. He chose issues in public life for sufficient political and moral reasons, but he came to them with passion to spare.

In the depths of his depression in 1841 he told Speed that "he had done nothing to make any human being remember that he had lived."

He did not expect family life to generate saving memories of him, and he had not yet earned them from politics.

———

Lincoln's law partner John Stuart had been elected to Congress in 1838 and reelected in 1840. In 1841 the two men recognized that the time Stuart spent in Washington made the partnership impracticable, so they dissolved it, and Lincoln joined forces with another Whig lawyer-politician, Stephen Logan. They worked together until 1844, when Lincoln took on his third, last, and longest-serving partner, Speed's former clerk William Herndon.

Much of Lincoln's legal work was done in Springfield, where the state supreme court and federal courts sat; but twice a year—in the spring and the fall—he traveled the Eighth Judicial Circuit of Illinois, arguing cases in county courthouses. The Eighth Circuit was as big as Connecticut, and each road trip took ten weeks. Accommodation could be almost as primitive as the family cabin back in Indiana, the cases were routine, and the fees were tiny. But Lincoln liked the camaraderie of his fellow lawyers, and his travels made him known throughout central Illinois (his judicial circuit overlapped most of his congressional district).

Lincoln the lawyer cut a homely figure. In his Springfield office he stuffed letters, bills, and notes to himself in an old silk hat, or in a bundle of papers on his desk with a reminder slipped under the string: "When you can't find it anywhere else, look in this." On the road he wore a coat that was loose and pants that were short, and carried an umbrella that had no knob and a carpetbag packed with documents and underwear. He was genuinely indifferent to what he wore and ate and where he slept, but his slovenliness was also an extension of his rube/boob persona, which served several functions. It put ordinary clients and jurors at ease, and it took opposing counsel off their guard. "Any man who took Lincoln for a simple minded man," said one fellow lawyer, "would very soon wake up with his back in a ditch."

Lincoln's strength as a lawyer was his ability to focus on the case at hand. Logan, his second law partner, rated his general knowledge of the law as "never very formidable"—the legacy of his do-it-yourself education—but he bore down on anything he handled, mastering both the details of the case itself and the principles involved. "He not only went to the root of the question," wrote Herndon, "but dug up the root."

When Lincoln took on Herndon as a law partner, he also acquired a biographer. Herndon put off writing until he was an old man who needed the help of an amanuensis, but preparing and planning the biography was the project of his life. Herndon realized early on that Lincoln was unusual; he observed him, and endeavored to draw him out. Much of what we know about Lincoln's prepresidential appearance and habits comes from Herndon or from the many interviews with family and friends that Herndon conducted after Lincoln's death. Herndon was alert to Lincoln's melancholy, which "dripped from him as he walked." He understood how Lincoln used humor to keep himself afloat—"to whistle off sadness," as one of Herndon's informants put it.

Herndon described a strain of fatalism that ran through Lincoln's mind. Lincoln used a little catchphrase to express it that both Herndon and Mary Lincoln recalled: "What is to be will be, and no prayers of ours can reverse the decree." His fatalism may have begun as a legacy of his parents' religion; the particular sect of Baptists to which they belonged believed in predestination. Lincoln left the church, but kept the belief. Fatalism became a way of explaining his gloom to himself: The reason I feel so bad is because it could not have been any other way. I am damned because I was doomed. "There are no accidents in my philosophy," Lincoln told Herndon one day. Every action was a link in an "endless chain" of cause and effect. "The motive was born before the man." The motive, and the moods.

In the early 1850s, Lincoln pursued a new intellectual interest on the circuit, working his way through the first six books of Euclid's *Elements of Geometry*. He was proud enough of this accomplishment to mention it in a campaign autobiography when he ran for president.

Euclid pleases minds enamored of logic. Thomas Hobbes admired him; so did Thomas Paine, who declared in *The Age of Reason* that Euclid, unlike the authors of the Bible, proved everything he said (Paine called the *Elements* a book of "self-evident demonstration"). The chains of proof, each building on the one that went before, unwind like cause and effect in Lincoln's view of the world. But Euclid offered something that fatalism did not: clarity and definition. He tells us what things are. Fatalism locks us in place; Euclid is a means, austere but certain, of understanding.

Lincoln the lawyer was no mere reasoning machine. He could summon the passions when he had to. Herndon recorded the case of Rebecca Thomas, the widow of a Revolutionary War veteran, who had been bilked by an agent she had hired to collect her husband's pension. She "came hobbling into the office" one day in 1846, Herndon wrote, "and told her story. It stirred Lincoln up." The day before the trial he asked Herndon to get him a history of the Revolution, for refreshing his memory; the next day, in court, he went to work. He only called one witness—Mrs. Thomas herself—then summed up for the jury. He "drew a vivid picture of the hardships of Valley Forge, describing with minuteness the men, barefooted and with bleeding feet, creeping over the ice." Shades of Weems and the crossing of the Delaware. Lincoln concluded: "Time rolls by, the heroes of '76 have passed away and are encamped on the other shore. The soldier has gone to rest, and now, crippled, blind and broken, his widow comes to you and to me, gentlemen of the jury, to right her wrongs. She was not always thus. She was once a beautiful young woman. Her step was elastic, her face fair. . . . But now she is poor and defenseless. . . . She appeals to us, who enjoy the privileges achieved for us by the patriots of the Revolution, for our sympathetic and manly protection. All I ask is, shall we befriend her?" The jury was in tears; Lincoln won the case, and charged no fee.

This speech was not for a general audience and was not printed until Herndon published this reconstruction of it decades later. But it corrects what Lincoln said about the founders in the Lyceum Address.

The heroes of '76 are dead, but they can be summoned; we, their beneficiaries, have an obligation to summon them, especially when there are
wrongs to be righted. Even in death they help us (we enjoy the privileges
they achieved); so we must help others (with sympathetic and manly
protection); the heroic dead can inspire us to do it. Reason is powerful,
but so is memory. Lincoln would make this appeal again, to a larger
audience, for a greater cause.

———

While Lincoln practiced law, he simultaneously pursued his political
career. Stuart decided not to run for Congress again in 1842, which
opened up the one safe Whig seat in Illinois. Three Whig lawyers, all in
their early thirties, wanted it: Lincoln, John Hardin, and Edward Baker.

One way Lincoln positioned himself to be a candidate was by campaigning for temperance. Temperance was a religiously tinged movement of moral reform, one of several that flourished in the 1830s and
1840s (Sabbath observance was another). Whigs tended to be more
hospitable to such impulses than Democrats; Lyman Beecher, a Connecticut minister, wrote that the Democratic Party in his state had been
founded by "rum-selling tippling folk, infidels and ruff-scuff generally."
Lincoln did not drink, which suited him to this new role; on the other
hand, temperance crusaders often employed a hectoring tone that he
did not like.

On Washington's Birthday in 1842 Lincoln gave a speech in Springfield's Presbyterian Church to a meeting of a temperance society named
for the first president. Lincoln urged the temperance advocates to drop
the fire and brimstone: "It is an old and true maxim that a 'drop of honey
catches more flies than a gallon of gall.'" Unfortunately the speech as a
whole was the most fustian performance he would ever give; it ended
with a paean to Washington as the Father of Temperance: "Washington
is the mightiest name of earth—long since mightiest in the cause of
civil liberty; still mightiest in moral reformation." This was the legacy of
Weems's stories about the apple orchard and the cherry tree, erecting

Washington into an icon of virtue—only now Lincoln, and those who had named the temperance society for Washington, were addressing adults. It seems that Lincoln overdid it: Herndon, who stood at the church door listening to the crowd as it left, claimed they thought Lincoln was making fun of them. Thanks to carelessness, or unhappiness with his task, Lincoln had not made good use of Washington.

The three Whig politicians ended up trading the congressional seat among themselves, Hardin running in 1842, Baker in 1844, and Lincoln in 1846. It looked like a formal division of the spoils, but it was accompanied by much off-stage elbowing and body-blocking. One maneuver was for each man's supporters to suggest that one of the other Whigs be their party's candidate for governor instead. No one took the bait (in Democratic Illinois, Whig gubernatorial candidates were almost certain to lose).

As Baker's term wound down in 1846, Hardin gave signs of wanting another term for himself. A congressional seat, he wrote Lincoln, was not "a horse which each candidate may mount and ride [for] a two mile heat." Lincoln caught the metaphor and threw it back at him, asking Hardin if he thought the seat was "a horse which, the first jockey that can mount him, may whip and spur round and round, till jockey, or horse, or both, fall dead." Hardin backed off, and Lincoln won the Whig nomination in 1846 without a fight.

His Democratic opponent, Peter Cartwright, charged him with irreligion, raking up memories of his Paine-ite talk in New Salem and his early days in Springfield, which prompted Lincoln to issue a handbill declaring that he had never openly scoffed at Christianity. He admitted to being a fatalist, who believed "that the human mind is impelled to action or held in rest by some power over which the mind itself has no control." But he noted that "several of the Christian denominations" shared that opinion (his parents' denomination, for instance). The Democratic charge did not stick, and Lincoln won handily.

Lincoln's local campaigns played out against a backdrop of turbulent presidential politics, exacerbated by questions of expansion and war.

President Tyler, who had the unusual distinction of having betrayed both major parties, was the candidate of neither in 1844. The Whigs nominated Henry Clay of Kentucky, former congressman, Speaker of the House, secretary of state, and senator—a fixture in national politics since before the War of 1812 (he had already run for president—unsuccessfully—in 1824 and 1832). The Democrats chose James Polk, who had his own achievements—he, too, had been Speaker of the House, as well as governor of Tennessee. Yet Polk, who was almost twenty years younger than Clay—forty-eight years old to Clay's sixty-seven—was a fresher face.

Polk also had a clear issue—national expansion. The United States had been essentially the same size since the Louisiana Purchase in 1803. Polk now argued for annexing the Pacific Northwest and Texas, an independent country run by American emigrants who had revolted from Mexico in 1836.

Clay, like most Whigs, feared that annexing Texas would provoke a war with Mexico; the boundary between the two countries was disputed, and Mexico had never recognized the independence of its former province. But he also wanted votes in the South, where Texas—a republic of slave owners—would be welcomed as a new slave state. So Clay hedged, and a tiny abolitionist third party, the Liberty Party, peeled off enough anti-Texas Whigs in New York to cost Clay the state and its 36 electoral votes. Polk took 49.5 percent of the popular vote and 170 electoral votes, Clay won 48 percent and 105 electoral votes. If Clay had carried New York he would have won, with 141 electoral votes to 136. As usual, the Democrats carried Illinois.

Lincoln had stumped for Clay throughout his district and even across the state line in southwestern Indiana, his former home. He analyzed the Whig loss in a letter to a Liberty Party supporter in northern Illinois. Lincoln assumed that Clay, for all his waffling, would not have annexed Texas, and asked why the Liberty Party had turned on him. "As

I always understood it, the Liberty-men deprecated the annexation of Texas extremely; and, this being so, why they should refuse to so cast their votes as to prevent it . . . seemed wonderful." Lincoln did not believe in compromise for its own sake, or in surrendering essential goals; he was telling the Liberty man that he should have swallowed Clay in order to achieve his goal.

Polk accepted Texas as a new state in 1845 and sent troops to its disputed border (their commander was Zachary Taylor, a veteran of the Black Hawk War). In the spring of 1846 there was a clash, and the war Clay had feared came to pass.

America won an astonishing string of victories, but the fighting was brutal. John Hardin was killed on Washington's Birthday in 1847 at the Battle of Buena Vista (so was one of Clay's sons). James Shields, who had challenged Lincoln to a duel, was wounded at the Battle of Cerro Gordo in April; Edward Baker took charge of Shields's unit in his place. Lincoln was a lifelong civilian after his Black Hawk War days, but he could not insulate himself from battle and its handiwork. The fighting finally ended in September 1847, when American troops under Winfield Scott captured Mexico City.

In the nineteenth century there was a long lag between elections and convening new sessions of Congress. Although Lincoln had won his seat in November 1846, he did not occupy it until December 1847.

He left Springfield for Washington at the end of October with his family—Mary and their two sons, Robert, born in 1843, and Edward, born in 1846 (despite his rivalry with Edward Baker, Lincoln named a son after him). The Lincolns would have two more children—William (Willie) in 1850 and Thomas (Tad) in 1853. Lincoln was an indulgent parent—there would be no laboring in the fields for these boys, and virtually no discipline of any kind. Herndon thought the Lincoln children were brats—but then he also disliked their mother (he was jealous of anyone who might be closer to his idol than he was).

By the beginning of Lincoln's congressional term, the war was over; only the terms of the peace treaty remained to be worked out. But the Whigs, who had rallied to the flag once the fighting began, still sniped at Polk any way they could. Lincoln threw himself into this political warfare as soon as he arrived in Washington.

He tried to refight the opening shots of the war. Polk claimed the fighting had started on the American side of the Texas border: American troops had repelled an attack on them, in American territory. But the Whigs insisted that the fighting started only after American troops had crossed into Mexico. In December Lincoln introduced a set of resolutions in the House demanding that the president reveal "the spot of soil" on which the first hostilities had occurred. In January 1848 he gave a speech repeating his demands, and warning Polk to respond truthfully. Lincoln invoked the mightiest name: "Let [Polk] remember he sits where Washington sat, and so remembering, let him answer as Washington would answer."

Lincoln's questions backfired. Democratic newspapers in Illinois seized on the humorous possibilities of the word "spot," calling him "spotty Lincoln" and reporting that he had come down with "spotted fever." Lincoln's invocation of George Washington also fell flat. It was not as turgid as the conclusion of his Temperance Address, but it was equally hollow. He might have cited Washington's opinions with effect—the first president was a military hero who nevertheless urged his countrymen to "cultivate peace and harmony" with all nations. Lincoln did none of that; he simply gestured at Washington as at a moral yardstick.

A better anti-Polk speech was given in February by one of Lincoln's fellow Whigs, Alexander Stephens of Georgia. Three years younger than Lincoln, he was in his third term in the House. Lincoln described him as a "little slim, pale-faced, consumptive man"—he never weighed over one hundred pounds—but he was intelligent, eloquent, and caustic. He savaged the terms Polk was trying to impose on Mexico at war's end, and concluded with a denunciation of the president's appetite for Mexican territory. "I have heard of nations whose honor could be satisfied with gold . . . but never did I expect to live to see the day when the Executive of this country should announce that our honor . . . must feed on earth—gross, vile dirt!" In a letter to Herndon, Lincoln called this "the very best speech of an hour's length I ever heard." Lincoln did not say what he admired about it, but Stephens's reduction of a grand but false idea (war with Mexico) to something concrete and small (dirt) was a technique Lincoln had read in Paine and would later use himself.

Polk paid no attention to Lincoln's questions or Stephens's speech. The Treaty of Guadalupe Hidalgo, signed in Mexico the very day Stephens spoke, gave the United States quite a bit of dirt: a comfortable border for Texas, plus the Mexican provinces of Nueva Mexico and Alta California (the future states of New Mexico, Arizona, California, Nevada, and Utah as well as slices of Wyoming and Colorado)—750,000 square miles.

———

That summer official Washington attended a more solemn invocation of Washington's name when the cornerstone of his monument was laid.

America had begun scrambling to honor Washington in his own life-time. The State of Virginia commissioned a statue of him from the great French sculptor Jean-Antoine Houdon that still stands, in more than regal dignity, in the statehouse in Richmond. After Washington's death and burial at Mount Vernon there was talk of exhuming and reburying him under the dome of the US Capitol; the Washington family vetoed that plan. After many false starts the construction of the present monument began on July 4, 1848.

There were no founders left to attend the ceremony, but there were two founders' widows on the podium, as frail as Lincoln's client Rebecca Thomas back in Illinois: Dolley Madison (eighty years old) and Eliza Hamilton (almost ninety-one). Also in attendance was George Washington Parke Custis, the founding father's last surviving step-grandchild (spry, only relatively, at sixty-seven). America clutched at these survivors as living ghosts.

The honor of giving the oration was offered to another living ghost, former president John Quincy Adams. After leaving the White House, Adams had served in the House of Representatives as a Whig from Massachusetts. More relevant to his task as orator, he was the son of a founder, John Adams, and acquainted with many of the other founders personally; he had been given his first government job—minister to Holland—by George Washington himself. Adams declined the offer to speak, however, pleading ill health, and then died in February. The oration was instead delivered by the Speaker of the House, Robert Winthrop, another Massachusetts Whig.

Winthrop's most original touch was to link Washington to current events in Europe. A wave of revolution had washed over the continent in 1848, beginning with riots in Paris. After more than forty years under an emperor and three kings, France had become a republic once more. The New World, said Winthrop, could be an example to the Old, a thought he expressed in a lively if clumsy metaphor: "The great upward and downward trains on the track of human freedom have at last come into collision! . . . The great America-built locomotive, 'Liberty,' still holds on its course, unimpeded and unimpaired."

Winthrop offered Washington's self-control and devotion to republican government as models to European revolutionaries, and quoted Europeans who agreed with him: "The want of the age," said the poet Alphonse de Lamartine, provisional leader of the new French government, "is a European Washington." A great model, but a hard one to emulate. Lamartine was falling from power even as Winthrop spoke. The Second Republic would sputter along for three more years, when another Napoleon, nephew of the first, overthrew it.

But Winthrop knew that his most important theme must be what Washington could offer in 1848 to America. Winthrop's answer was reverence for the Union: "complete, cordial and indissoluble." Maintaining the Union had indeed been a preoccupation of Washington's.

His presidency had seen an armed tax revolt in Pennsylvania and the rancorous birth of the first two-party system. (The husbands of the old ladies on the podium had been among the most prominent partisans: James Madison, cofounder of the Republicans, and Alexander Hamilton, champion of the Federalists.) Although Washington was himself a Federalist, he feared, with some reason, that political passions might cause the country over which he presided to fly apart. In his Farewell Address at the end of his second term, he urged Americans to "cherish a cordial, habitual, immovable attachment" to the Union.

The fate of the Union would become problematic once again thanks to the windfall of the Treaty of Guadalupe Hidalgo. Peace would be even more contentious than the Mexican War. What would become of those 750,000 newly acquired square miles? How would they be administered? What states would be carved from them? Mexico had abolished slavery in 1824. Would the territory America had taken from her be slave or free?

Winthrop had nothing to say about that. "I may not, I will not, disturb the harmony of the scene before me by the slightest allusion of a party character." Winthrop's reticence was ironic. After praising the Union in his Farewell Address, Washington had gone on to give a rather partisan speech, singling out policies—sound finances at home, peace abroad—that were the special concern of Federalists. The founding father wanted unity—but he wanted it on his terms. He was bolder, and more particular, than his children.

Winthrop's speech was delivered at a grander occasion than Lincoln using Washington to needle the president, or holding him up as a model of moral reformation. Yet all three occasions partook of the same spirit. Their version of Washington was a man of marble, spotless but blank. Lincoln had done better when he invoked the Revolution to help Rebecca Thomas get her husband's pension. His appeals to Washington in the 1840s were opportunistic or empty. Unfortunately, orators more prominent than he was made the same noises.

Lincoln wrote no letter to Herndon, or to anyone else, about Winthrop's speech.

———

Lincoln's congressional term ended with an idea that was interesting but stillborn. He proposed a plan to abolish slavery in the District of Columbia.

Although the District was small—Washington was barely in the top twenty of American cities, just ahead of Newark, New Jersey, but behind Providence, Rhode Island—it was symbolically important as the home of the federal government. The presence of slaves and slave traders there—"a sort of negro livery stable," as Lincoln called it, stood only seven blocks from the Capitol—seemed grotesque to antislavery men.

In a brief speech on the House floor in January 1849 Lincoln offered a plan of gradual and compensated emancipation. Any children of slaves born in the District after 1849 should be free; slaves who were living there as of 1849 could be freed by the federal government paying full value to their owners.

Lincoln limited his plan in several ways. The freeborn children of the future would have to serve apprenticeships to their masters until they reached adulthood; any slave owner who did not want to free a slave in return for payment would not have to do it. Finally, Lincoln's plan had to be submitted to the District's voters; it would go into effect only if they approved. In this, Lincoln was consistent with his 1837 Protest on Slavery in the Illinois legislature. Then, he and Dan Stone had noted that Congress had the power to abolish slavery in the District, though it should only do so "at the request of the people of said District."

Lincoln believed emancipation had to come via voter approval. This was an obligation of republican government; a "duty," as he put it, "due . . . to liberty itself (paradox though it may seem)." Free men had to choose to free their slaves.

It is always easier to free slaves from the top down. The greatest manumission in the world so far, the abolition of slavery in the British Empire in 1834, had been such an act. Seven hundred thousand slaves in the West Indies were freed not by the assemblies of the colonies in which they were held, but by Parliament in London. In 1848 there were smaller manumissions in the empires of France and Denmark that happened in the same way: as acts of imperial noblesse oblige, not self-government. In the Lyceum Address, Lincoln had even warned that emancipation from on high might be one of the projects of the tyrannical "towering genius." He wanted no part of that.

Lincoln told the House his plan had the support of "leading citizens" in the District (the mayor of Washington, DC, was a fellow Whig). Once Lincoln offered his plan publicly, however, the citizens got cold feet (no leadership from them). He let his suddenly friendless proposal drop, never even introducing it as a bill.

Lincoln had been cautious and careful: he had built on his own earlier efforts, and he had accomplished nothing. Two months later, on March 4, 1849, Congress adjourned. The Whig nomination in his district had rotated in 1848 to yet another politician, Stephen Logan, his second law partner, who lost to a Democratic Mexican War veteran. Lincoln's career as a congressman was over.

Six

HENRY CLAY AND THE FOURTH OF JULY

THE MAIN FIGURE IN LINCOLN'S POLITICAL WORLD DURING the 1840s was the aging Whig lion Henry Clay. Clay charmed Americans with his eloquence, and loomed over successive presidential elections on account of his mountainous ambition. Lincoln was not so impressed with him as an orator or a presidential candidate. He had more sympathy with Clay's mastery of the arts of compromise and with his economic program.

Most important, at the end of this period of Lincoln's life Clay shaped his understanding of the founding and showed him its relevance to the politics of slavery. Though not a founder himself, Clay taught Lincoln what the Fourth of July meant, and what it might mean to a country that was tearing itself apart. He led Lincoln to what would become one of the touchstones of his career, the Declaration of Independence.

Clay, born in 1777 in Virginia, moved to Kentucky in 1797—the same path as Thomas Lincoln and Nancy Hanks, though Clay was marked for greater things. As a teenager, he had read law with the Virginian jurist George Wythe, signer of the Declaration and teacher of Thomas Jefferson. In Kentucky Clay opened a practice, married a rich man's daughter, and made a brilliant start in politics. He joined the first Republican Party—there were few Federalists in Kentucky—and was elected to the state legislature, which twice sent him to the US Senate to serve the stubs of terms left vacant by resignation. In 1810 he was elected to the House of Representatives, which chose him to be Speaker on his first day in office (the first, and still the only member of Congress to have risen so fast). He was only thirty-four years old.

Over the next forty years Kentucky sent him to the House or the Senate more or less whenever he wished (he took time off in the 1820s to be US secretary of state). He was a man of many political talents—a wily parliamentarian and a patient deal-maker—but his hold on the public rested on his skill as a performer. One listener described him in full cry: "He spoke to his audience very much as an ardent lover speaks to his sweetheart. . . . His voice was full, rich, clear, sweet, musical, and as inspiring as a trumpet. . . . His tall form would seem to grow taller and taller with every new statement, until it reached a supernatural height." He was "the *livest* man of whom it is possible to conceive."

Clay was one of the first politicians to note the aging of the founders (not yet their passing, for Jefferson and Madison were still active when he first came to Washington). As early as 1810 he spoke of them thus: "The withered arm and wrinkled brow of the illustrious founders of our freedom are melancholy indications that they will shortly be removed from us. . . . We shall want the presence and living example of a new race of heroes to supply their places."

Clay intended to be one of those heroes. He showed his mettle by defusing two crises as great as anything Washington had faced as president.

In 1819—when Lincoln was still a child in Indiana—Missouri applied for statehood. It would be the second state carved out of the Louisiana Territory, after Louisiana itself, and the first that was entirely west of the Mississippi. Would the new state in the new American West admit slaves? The House, where the more populous free states commanded a majority, wanted Missouri to be free, but the Senate, where slave states and free states were in balance, would not agree. House and Senate, North and South, became fixed in an acrid deadlock. Clay, who was Speaker as the crisis began, engineered a compromise whereby Missouri would be admitted as a slave state, balanced by Maine (hitherto a part of Massachusetts) as a free state, while in the rest of the Louisiana Territory slavery would be forbidden north of a line running west at latitude 36°30' N—known thereafter as the Missouri line. He had saved the Union, though southern diehards never quite trusted him again.

In 1832 came a second almost-explosion. South Carolina was rich in slaves and cotton but dependent for its necessities on imports. After Congress passed a high tariff to protect northern manufacturers, the state announced that it would nullify the law within its borders. President Jackson threatened, South Carolina blustered. Clay, now a senator, arranged a gradual lessening of the tariff, and the rebellious state withdrew its ordinance of nullification.

The Missouri clash split the country on sectional lines; South Carolina's nullification ordinance challenged the very structure of the Constitution, where setting tariffs is made the responsibility of the federal government (Article I, Sections 8 and 10). The last of the founders anxiously watched these threats to their handiwork. Jefferson called the Missouri crisis "the knell of the union." Madison accused the South Carolina nullifiers of fomenting "disgust with the union." Clay had helped beat back both threats; his handiwork earned him the title of the Great Compromiser.

But he coveted an even greater title. Clay reputedly said he would rather be right than president. His desire to be right must have been very great then, for he desperately wanted to be president. He first ran in 1824, in the four-way race to succeed the last founder president, James Monroe. He came in fourth, with 37 electoral votes. One of the other candidates—all of them, like Clay, Republicans—was Andrew Jackson; their rivalry would polarize the next two-party system. In 1832 Clay ran head to head against Jackson, this time calling himself a National Republican; Jackson buried him, with 219 electoral votes to 49. Clay lost again in 1844, running as a Whig—which made him the first three-time loser in the history of presidential elections. But Clay had wanted two more shots, seeking (and failing) to win the Whig nomination in 1840 and 1848.

What did Lincoln think of this gaudy, capable, egotistical man?

Lincoln never heard Clay speak in Congress, for Clay left the Senate in 1842 to prepare for his next presidential campaign and did not return until 1849, after Lincoln left the House. Lincoln did hear him in November 1847 in Lexington, Kentucky, when the Lincoln family stopped in Mary's hometown on their way to Washington. Clay denounced the Mexican War as a war of aggression—the very argument Lincoln would make in his "spot" resolutions the following month.

Lincoln never said much about Clay's oratory; the one time he praised it, after Clay's death, he did so by quoting a newspaper obituary—praise at arm's length. Their styles would never be alike. Lincoln learned to summon the passions, but he never addressed audiences as sweethearts (he hardly addressed his sweethearts as sweethearts). As Lincoln came into his own as a speaker, he strove for the hard glow of literary permanence. Clay's speeches, as even his admirers admitted, were not meant to be read, but to be absorbed in the rush of the moment. Clay's compromises were more to Lincoln's taste, as his letter to the Illinois Liberty Party supporter showed. If you keep your main point, why not surrender subsidiary ones?

Clay was most disappointing to Lincoln as a presidential candidate. Lincoln the Whig stalwart wanted victories—and Clay was unable to supply them. In addition to the talents he actually possessed, Clay fancied himself a clever campaigner. He was ever thinking of the twist, the turn, the quickstep that would carry him over the finish line, but he only managed to stumble. In 1839, he gave a speech attacking abolitionists, because he honestly deplored their criticism of the Constitution, and because he wanted to shore up support in the South. But he went so far that he only offended northern Whig leaders, who swung the party's nomination to Harrison. As the Whig candidate in 1844, Clay made a similar mistake concerning the annexation of Texas, driving northern voters to the Liberty Party. Despite all his efforts to conciliate the South, supporters of slavery mocked him; one rhymester wrote of Clay and his 1844 running mate, Theodore Frelinghuysen: "De niggar vote am quite surprising, / We's all for Clay and Frelinghuysing."

As the 1848 election approached, Clay stirred again (he would be seventy-one years old). A cadre of younger Whigs, called Young Indians, was determined to stop him and nominate a war hero instead. That credential had worked for Harrison in 1840; as it happened, the two best generals of the Mexican War, Zachary Taylor and Winfield Scott, were both Whigs. The party could still blame Polk for waging the war, so long as it was led by one of the men who had won it.

Alexander Stephens, the congressman whose speech Lincoln had so admired, was a Young Indian. So was Lincoln. In June 1848 Lincoln went to the Whig convention in Philadelphia to support Taylor, who was nominated on the first ballot. "We shall have a most overwhelming, glorious triumph," Lincoln predicted in a letter to Herndon. The Democrats nominated Lewis Cass, a Michigan politician who had served in the War of 1812 (in a speech in the House, Lincoln laughingly compared Cass's slender war record with his own in the Black Hawk War). There was also a significant third party in this contest, called Free Soil—a coalition of Liberty Party abolitionists and those who would not end slavery outright, but opposed letting it expand into the territories that America had wrung from Mexico. Their nomination went to former president Martin Van Buren, trying to get back into the game.

Lincoln opposed slavery's expansion, too—if America did not "find new places for it to live in," he wrote, it would die "a natural death"—but he thought, as he had in 1844, that the Whigs were the best means of achieving that goal. He campaigned for Taylor in Maryland, Massachusetts, and back home in Illinois. Taylor won with 163 electoral votes to Cass's 127. The Free Soil Party won no electoral votes, though it got 10 percent of the popular vote. Once again the Democrats took Illinois.

Lincoln was not rewarded for backing the winner. He angled for a federal appointment as a land office administrator; the new administration gave it instead to a former Clay backer. He was offered a job in the Oregon Territory as a consolation prize, but decided to stay in Illinois and (for now) in private life.

———

Lincoln found Clay to be a mixed political leader. But he endorsed Clay's economic program wholeheartedly.

Clay's vision, which he called the American System, was an interlocking structure of internal improvements, a national bank, and protective tariffs (though he was willing to cut tariffs when a crisis loomed). As a young politician Lincoln had supported both internal improvements in Illinois and the Second Bank of the United States.

But the purpose of the American System was not just to make infrastructure or make money; it was to make men—to develop the talents of individual Americans and the national character. Clay wanted an economy that was diversified and progressive, which would give his countrymen the chance to move beyond hardscrabble farming. He is credited, wrongly, with inventing the phrase "self-made man." But he had highlighted it in a long Senate speech expounding his economic views during the 1832 campaign. "In Kentucky," he said, every factory "known to me is in the hands of enterprising, self-made men, who have acquired whatever wealth they possess by patient and diligent labor." *Enterprising, self-made, patient, diligent*—these words were moral and economic touchstones for Clay.

Who would reject such a vision? Plenty of people. There was already in American politics a long thread of polemic against the wealthy, especially businessmen or bankers—anyone who seemed to have too much money. Madison, cofounder with Jefferson of the first Republican Party, dismissed such folk as "the opulent." Andrew Jackson's Democrats carried on the attack in their struggle against the Second Bank of the United States. Jefferson, Madison, and Jackson were wealthy men, but since their wealth came from agriculture, not manufacturing, they and their supporters considered it virtuous.

Clay addressed that point in 1832. Manufacturing, he admitted, was accused of "favoring the growth of aristocracy. . . . But is there more tendency to aristocracy in a . . . factory supporting hundreds of freemen, or in a cotton plantation, with its not less numerous slaves, sustaining, perhaps, only two white families—that of the master and the overseer?" Lincoln might have added another point of comparison to Clay's—though there was no tendency to aristocracy in a farm like Thomas Lincoln's, it offered little reward (beyond subsistence) for patient and diligent labor.

Neither party was a monolith. The Democrats of Clay's and Lincoln's day, like the first Republican Party, embraced many self-made men—workers, artisans, businessmen—while the Whigs made a successful pitch for the rural poor with the Log Cabin Campaign of 1840. But each party had its favorite stock of tropes, which they strove (inconsistently) to live up to. Clay, Lincoln, and most Whigs believed in economic development leading to self-improvement.

There was a founding father from whom Lincoln could have learned this message. Alexander Hamilton was the self-made man among the founders, even more than Benjamin Franklin (both started poor, but Hamilton, an illegitimate immigrant, started even further back). As first treasury secretary, Hamilton had offered a program of national development, including the first Bank of the United States and a vision of a diverse American economy, with factories as well as farms. His goal was to foster a nation of Hamiltons—economics as soul-craft. "When all the different kinds of industry obtain in a community," he wrote, "each individual can find his proper element, and can call into activity the whole vigor of his nature."

Lincoln seems to have been hardly aware of Hamilton (he appears briefly in Weems's *Life of Washington* not as treasury secretary but as a heedless duelist, "pursuing the phantom honor up to the pistol's mouth"). Hamilton's early death in 1804, and the death of his Federalist Party a dozen years later, left a vacuum where his reputation should have been. Hamilton's Republican enemies—Jefferson, Madison, Monroe—not only outlived him, they occupied the White House for twenty-four years. The Federalists, meanwhile, were disgraced by their opposition to the War of 1812. In New York, Hamilton's state, and in New England, where Federalism survived the longest, he was still sometimes remembered. Elsewhere he was an honored cipher—a hero of the Revolution (Weems conceded that he was "gallant"), whose widow was entitled to a seat on the podium when the cornerstone of the Washington Monument was laid, but not a usable political example.

Henry Clay was usable, even though his economic program had suffered as many setbacks as his presidential ambitions. Tariffs had to be cut after the Nullification Crisis, and the Second Bank of the United States had never been resurrected. Yet Clay remained a living advocate of ideas that went beyond his hunger for office. Lincoln tired of him as a presidential candidate, but thought he was right.

———

When Clay returned to the Senate for the last time in December 1849, the issue before the country was not economics, but the fate of its new Southwest.

California was in the midst of a gold rush and clamoring for immediate statehood. Texas claimed a western border running all the way to Santa Fe. The question of slavery embittered every other question. Would the Missouri line, drawn to resolve a crisis thirty years earlier, be extended all the way to the Pacific, splitting California in half? Would Texas be allowed to carry slavery into New Mexico, where it did not exist? Should slavery be allowed into all of America's new territories? Into none of them? The answers to these questions would reach beyond the Southwest to touch the balance of power in Congress and the future of American politics.

America's divisions over slavery seemed to be woven into Clay's own life. For all his mockery of cotton planters, he was himself a slave owner—the largest in Kentucky (his plantation in Lexington grew hemp, which was made into rope in Louisville factories—so the American System was still upheld). Yet Clay had hoped that his state might take the route of gradual emancipation. Two state constitutional conventions, fifty years apart—in 1799 and 1849—actually considered the question, but failed to act.

Perhaps Clay's split personality made him the ideal man to settle the question of slavery nationally. In his last compromise—the Compromise of 1850—he tried to offer something to everyone. California would be admitted, whole, as a free state. Utah, home of the persecuted Mormons, and New Mexico, which included present-day Arizona, could be future slave territories if they chose. Texas would accept a restricted boundary in return for having the United States pay off its independence-era debts. In addition, Clay offered to end the slave trade in the District of Columbia—no more Negro livery stables on Capitol Hill—and to impose a tough federal fugitive slave law.

Clay invoked George Washington, displaying on the Senate floor a fragment of his coffin. (Clay was close to the grave himself, age seventy-two going on seventy-three, and coughing from tuberculosis.) A man who was interested in preserving Mount Vernon, Washington's old estate, had given Clay "the precious relic" while he was working on his speech in support of the compromise. Was it, Clay asked, "a sad presage" of the impending death of the country? He answered his own question: "No, sir, no. It was a warning voice" asking Congress "to beware, to pause, to reflect."

After six months of reflection, the Senate rejected Clay's compromise. Free Soil northerners did not want slavery to expand anywhere. Southern diehards could not accept California as a free state, or Texas's loss of its far western border. These, united with mere obstructionists who had personal quarrels with the old orator, managed to block his last great effort. Clay retired to Newport, Rhode Island, to take care of his ravaged lungs.

But his last effort was salvaged by an acquaintance of Lincoln's—Senator Stephen Douglas of Illinois. Douglas had risen from clashing with Lincoln in local disputes to winning all the prizes that were open to a talented Democrat in a Democratic state—secretary of state, state supreme court judge, congressman, and, since 1847, US senator. Once he had vaulted onto the national stage, he had assumed a starring role. In midsummer 1850 Douglas split Clay's compromise into its constituent parts, and by the middle of September he had rounded up enough votes for each proposal to pass all of them.

Lincoln watched from afar but made no comments on the great compromise—except possibly in one exchange with his first law partner, John Stuart. Sometime in 1850, as Stuart remembered it, he and Lincoln were on the road, tending to legal business in Tazewell County, south of Peoria. "As we were coming down [a] hill . . . I said, 'Lincoln, the time is coming when we shall have to be all either Abolitionists or Democrats.'" Stuart assumed that, in a reshuffling of parties, the Democrats would be the party of slavery. Lincoln, he went on, "thought a moment and then answered, ruefully and emphatically, 'When that time comes my mind is made up, for I believe the slavery question can never be successfully compromised.'"

Stuart was hazy about the date; possibly he was imputing more foresight to himself and to Lincoln than they had shown. By the end of 1850, thanks to Henry Clay (and Stephen Douglas), the future of slavery in the United States seemed settled—provided everyone kept to the settlement.

———

Clay died, age seventy-five, at the end of June 1852. The founders were dead, and now so was the new race of heroes to which Clay had

nominated himself. Lincoln delivered a eulogy in Springfield a week
later. The eulogy showed some reserve, some holding back, especially
on the subject of Clay's oratory. But Lincoln found something important
in the dead man's life and words—a path, back through Clay himself, to
the founders and the first principles of America.

Lincoln began with a coincidence. Clay was born in the first year after
the United States' birth (April 1777). "The infant nation, and the infant
child began the race of life together. For three quarters of a century they
have travelled hand in hand." Lincoln equated Clay with America—but
what about him was particularly American?

He described Clay's eloquence with a quotation from an obituary—
two pages of what was, in effect, oratory about an orator. Useful for
pressing flowers, maybe. Then Lincoln decided, as Herndon might have
put it, to dig up the root. "Mr. Clay's predominant sentiment, from first
to last, was a deep devotion to the cause of human liberty. . . . He loved
his country partly because it was his own country, but mostly because
it was a free country." Clay was known as the Great Compromiser, and
Lincoln was about to survey his achievements in that line. But he asserted that Clay's compromises all had a goal, which was freedom.

Lincoln discussed the Missouri Compromise, the Nullification Crisis, and the Compromise of 1850. Then he returned to liberty—and
turned to present-day politics. Clay "ever was, on principle and in feeling, opposed to slavery." What then had he done about it? Nothing
much, or so at first it seemed in Lincoln's presentation. Clay's "feeling
and his judgment," said Lincoln, "ever led him to oppose both extremes
of opinion on the subject." This looks like one of the weariest rhetorical
dodges in the world: Clay's opponents were all extremists; the truth lay
between them.

Yet Lincoln was quite precise as to what the extremists had been
saying. Clay's opponents attacked America's two founding documents.
Abolitionists wanted to "tear to tatters" the Constitution because of
the protections it offered slavery. (In 1842 William Lloyd Garrison had
arraigned the Constitution as "a covenant with death, and with Hell.")

But partisans of slavery, Lincoln added, were "beginning to assail and to ridicule . . . the declaration that 'all men are created free and equal.'"

Here, at the climax of his eulogy, Lincoln quoted Clay himself, reaching back to a speech Clay had delivered to the American Colonization Society in 1827. Colonization was a plan to send free Negroes back to Africa—the same that James Madison had discussed with Harriet Martineau. A protectorate had been set up on Africa's Atlantic coast, which would take the name Liberia. Henry Clay was a supporter of the scheme. So was Lincoln, and he would continue to be so until the middle of the Civil War. But the passage of Clay's long-ago speech that he quoted in 1852 was not about Liberia, but about America.

The American Colonization Society had critics: abolitionists (including Martineau) thought it was a futile project whose only effect would be to rid America of free blacks. But some slave owners thought it put dangerous dreams of freedom in black minds. It was the latter that Clay had addressed:

> What would they, who reproach us [for stirring up blacks], have done? If they would repress all tendencies towards liberty . . . they must do more than put down the benevolent efforts of this society. They must go back to the era of our liberty and independence, and muzzle the cannon which thunders its annual joyous return. . . . They must blow out the moral lights around us, and extinguish that greatest torch of all which America presents to a benighted world— pointing the way to their rights, their liberties, and their happiness. And when they have achieved all those purposes their work will be yet incomplete. They must penetrate the human soul, and eradicate the light of reason, and the love of liberty. Then, and not till then . . . can you perpetuate slavery.

All his life Clay talked for effect, but here he was as clear and sequential as Euclid. This paragraph moved, in three steps, from the news to history to the soul. Slavery was the problem before Clay and his audience.

But slavery was opposed to the spirit of the founders (the thundering cannon celebrated the Fourth of July). And the founders, whom Americans celebrated, had expressed a truth about human nature—that all men yearn for liberty, and as men, deserve it. There is poetry here, and reason, and orderly arrangement. No wonder Lincoln loved this passage, and would come back to it repeatedly (he would quote it at least three times when he ran for Senate in 1858, and again as he prepared to run for president).

Lincoln had been driven to think about Clay's passage by events— by Clay's death, obviously, but also by a sense that Clay's great compromises, his life's work, were a patchwork, liable at any moment, as John Stuart said on the hill outside Peoria, to be torn apart. If that happened, what should be done next? If that happened, what would the founders do?

Henry Clay was not the only American to bring the founders to bear on the question of slavery. Abolitionists and Free Soil men made the Declaration of Independence a holy document. The *Western Citizen*, an abolitionist newspaper published in Chicago, printed the Preamble of the Declaration on the front page of every issue. Lincoln was familiar with writing of this kind; his partner Herndon, an abolitionist, subscribed to their publications and kept copies in the office. Lincoln, however, found a more congenial expression of the antagonism between the founders and slavery in a man more congenial to him—in a compromiser, in a lover of the Constitution, in a Whig—in Henry Clay.

But Lincoln was delivering a eulogy—a speech after a death. His ending was short and not sweet. "But Henry Clay is dead." A few sentences followed, then Lincoln added, "but he is gone." Gone as the coffin fragments and fustian of a decade of orators; gone as a rained-on grave.

Lincoln would come back to the dead again.

PART
TWO

Seven

1854: THE REPEAL OF THE MISSOURI COMPROMISE

H ENRY CLAY'S DEATH IN 1852 WAS FOLLOWED, IN 1854, BY the repeal of his first great achievement, the Missouri Compromise. The repeal, as Lincoln wrote, would "arouse . . . him as never before" and set the trajectory of his life for the next six years.

The repeal involved Lincoln in a long battle with his fellow Illinoisan Stephen Douglas—over their political futures, over the future of the United States, and over the intentions of the founding fathers. Both men believed that the opinions of the founders carried special weight, and each believed he understood them best.

But before that, Lincoln witnessed a parade of deaths.

———

In February 1850 Lincoln's second son, Edward, died after a two-month illness, not quite four years old. Lincoln wrote of it, with some asperity, to his stepbrother John Johnston, who had approached him asking for various favors. "As you make no mention of it," Lincoln replied, "I suppose you had not learned that we lost our little boy. . . . We miss him very much." Johnston's selfishness, at that particular moment, no doubt grated even more than usual.

The funeral was conducted by the Reverend James Smith, a Scotsman who had recently become pastor of a Presbyterian church in Springfield. Smith believed that Lincoln turned to Christianity in the 1850s and that Smith had showed him the way. "[I had] the high honor," he wrote Herndon, "to place before Mr. Lincoln arguments designed to prove the divine authority of the Scriptures accompanied by the arguments of infidel objectors in their own language. To the arguments on both sides Mr. Lincoln gave a most patient, impartial and searching investigation. . . . The result was the announcement by himself that the argument in favor of the divine authority and inspiration of the Scripture was unanswerable."

Herndon hated Smith, and wrote on the letter: "Foolish. . . . Knows nothing of Lincoln." Smith had as much regard for Smith as he did for Lincoln or for Scripture, and his account reeks of wish-fulfillment. But that does not mean that Lincoln did not return to the greatest questions in the wake of his son's death. There is no evidence that he came to any new conclusions in the 1850s, but he would have more occasions to do so later on.

In the summer of 1850 Zachary Taylor, the second Whig president, became the second president to die in office. He had lasted longer than William Henry Harrison, but after two years in the White House he succumbed, age sixty-five, to acute gastroenteritis after eating contaminated food on the Fourth of July. Lincoln delivered a eulogy in Chicago. It was not as interesting as his eulogy of Clay would be two years later, though it included a shrewd estimate of Taylor's character: "He could not be flurried, and he could not be scared." Taylor, a patriotic old soldier, had wanted California and New Mexico admitted as free states, even though he was a Louisiana plantation owner, and he threatened to hang any of his fellow southerners who objected. His successor in office, Millard Fillmore, a New York Whig, was as sleek as Taylor was rough, but without any of his force of character.

The Whig Party was dying along with its presidents. Its nomination in 1852 went not to Fillmore but to the other hero of the Mexican War, Winfield Scott. Scott was a better general than Taylor or Harrison—probably the greatest American general between George Washington and Ulysses Grant—but he was also pompous, acerbic, and enamored of the figure he cut in his splendid uniforms. This would be no Log Cabin Campaign. That summer Lincoln gave a speech for Scott in Springfield, answering a Democratic campaign speech that Stephen Douglas had given in Richmond. Lincoln's effort was long and rambling, strewn with jokes and partisan quibbles. Maybe he sensed which way the race was going. In the fall the Democrat Franklin Pierce crushed Scott with 254 electoral votes to 42. Yet again, the Democrats carried Illinois.

How does a major party die? The greatest Whig never won the White House, neither of the Whig Party's winners completed a term there, Whig Party faithful had enjoyed scant federal patronage, the economic program of the Whigs was never enacted. As an Illinois Whig, Lincoln was accustomed to failure, but his party nationwide was sinking from sight.

Lincoln had arrived at midlife, but he was already calling himself an old man. As early as his years in Congress, when he was still in his thirties, his letters home were full of references to his age: "my old, withered, dry eyes"; "I am now one of the old men"; "I was young once." This was a new way for Lincoln to poor-mouth himself; the rube/boob could now be the old rube/boob. But a sense of premature age can also arise from a fear (or a conviction) of futility. Lincoln was still ambitious; he was always ambitious. "His ambition," as Herndon wrote, "was a little engine that knew no rest." Yet what did he have to show for it?

His speech for Winfield Scott had been marred by his envy of the man he was rebutting, Stephen Douglas. "When I first saw his speech," Lincoln began, "I was reminded of old times—of the times when . . .

Douglas was not so much [a] greater man than all the rest of us, as he now is." The contrast between the two Illinoisans was stark. In 1852 Lincoln was a former congressman; Douglas was a lord of the Senate. Lincoln had given a eulogy for Henry Clay, a man whom he had never met, in Springfield; Douglas had been at Clay's right hand in Washington, helping the great man save the nation.

By the time Lincoln reached his early forties he had not done one important thing. He had led an interesting life, yet he would have had to be a great memoirist, or be imagined by a great novelist, for anyone to recognize it. He was a self-made man of no consequence.

In 1854 Stephen Douglas changed Lincoln's prospects and American politics.

Douglas, four years younger than Lincoln, had moved to Illinois from Vermont when he was twenty. He was first elected to the state legislature in 1836, two years after Lincoln, but his rise was faster. He went to the US House of Representatives in 1843; four years later, the Democratic legislature chose him to be a senator on the eve of his thirty-fourth birthday.

Douglas was short, deep-chested, smart, quick, aggressive. He was one of those small men who dominate a room by their energy and their presence. Photographs show an unflattering line across the bridge of his nose, as if he had butted heads with a locomotive, but no one thought less of him for it. Herndon testified that he had "that unique trait, magnetism." Lincoln joked about the Man of Audacity; Douglas was that man.

Piecing together the Compromise of 1850, while still in his thirties, was a considerable achievement. But Douglas had his sights on others.

Now that the country had a Pacific coast, it needed a quicker means of getting there than horse-drawn wagons or ships sailing around Cape Horn. The means of the future was obviously the railroad. A transcontinental line anchored in Illinois would be a boon to the state—an iron Erie Canal—and to the man who made it happen.

Douglas wanted to be president. His name had been placed in nomination at the Democratic convention of 1852, and he had actually led the field for two ballots. Franklin Pierce, the eventual winner, was a dark horse who had triumphed on the forty-ninth ballot. Douglas had been only thirty-nine at the time. If he were to win the nomination and the election in 1856, he would still be the youngest man to have reached the White House.

Douglas's chances of winning both the railroad and the presidency seemed to be enhanced by his position as chairman of the Senate's Committee on Territories. The Compromise of 1850 had divided the American Southwest into states and territories, but one great swath of land in the middle of the continent remained without formal government. Two more states had been fashioned out of the old Louisiana Territory after the admission of Missouri—Arkansas and Iowa—and the northeastern corner of it had been organized as the Minnesota Territory. But between the Missouri River and the Rockies there was nothing but plains, mountains, bison, and Indians, with a few forts. Most of this wilderness lay north of the Missouri line. A transcontinental railroad linked to Chicago would have to pass somewhere west of Missouri or Iowa. The region needed territorial government, followed by statehood.

Wrangling over new territories and states had almost torn the country apart in 1850, but Douglas had surmounted that crisis. He was sure he could handle any problems that might now arise.

He went to work in January 1854 and produced a bold bill. Douglas proposed two new territories—Kansas (the present state, plus a slice of Colorado) and Nebraska (everything else all the way to Canada). Whether these territories would admit slavery would be left to the decision of the inhabitants. Douglas said he was following the principles of the Compromise of 1850, under which the territories of New Mexico and Utah had been allowed to choose slavery or not as they wished. That option was simply being extended to Kansas and Nebraska.

By leaving slavery up to the people of the new territories, Douglas claimed to be taking it off the table of national politics. His bill was a recipe for peace and quiet; it would, as he put it, "avoid the perils of . . . agitation by withdrawing the question of slavery from the halls of Congress and the political arena, and committing it to the arbitrament [judgment] of those who were immediately interested in it." The name for Douglas's new principle was "popular sovereignty," a phrase that had been first used a few years earlier by presidential candidate Lewis Cass. Now Douglas made it his own.

By embracing popular sovereignty, Douglas claimed to be beyond politics, but he had nevertheless offered a political deal along the way. Allowing slavery north of the Missouri line (if the residents wished it) meant repealing the Missouri Compromise. Many southerners had resented the compromise as a rebuke to slavery and to themselves as slave owners. (Why limit the spread of slavery unless it was a bad thing?) Douglas hoped his bill would win him southern support at the next Democratic convention.

For the rest of the winter and all through the spring, Douglas labored to pass his bill. He approached President Pierce in January, calling at the White House on a Sunday, which Pierce considered Sabbath-breaking. But Pierce's secretary of war, Jefferson Davis, got the two men to sit down and talk; as a result, Pierce supported the bill. Douglas out-argued and arm-twisted his fellow senators, winning their approval by a comfortable margin. The House, with its northern majority, was harder, but he lobbied on the House floor (which senators are not supposed to do) for a narrow victory. The bill became law at the end of May 1854. "I passed the Kansas-Nebraska Act myself," Douglas told his father-in-law, by "the marshalling and directing of men. . . . I had the authority and power of a dictator throughout the whole controversy."

———

Dictating to congressmen was one thing; persuading their constituents, another. The Kansas-Nebraska Act (often called the Nebraska bill or act, for short) was greeted in the North with rage. Every sectional dispute for the past thirty-plus years had been resolved with some sort of deal: Missouri became a state, but so did Maine; South Carolina dropped nullification, but tariffs had been lowered; Texas had been annexed, but so had the Pacific Northwest; the Compromise of 1850 was a cat's cradle of trade-offs. Now Douglas had given slavery and the South an opening for nothing in return, and he had obliterated one of the key provisions of an earlier deal—the Missouri line—to do it. Northern politicians, both Whigs and Democrats, denounced him.

Lincoln waited until later in the year to say anything in public about Douglas's latest deed, but then he would not relent for the rest of the decade. The Lincoln-Douglas debates, which all the world now knows about, happened in 1858, but the six years from 1854 to 1860 were one long Lincoln-Douglas debate. Lincoln made it his business to shadow Douglas, speaking where he spoke and replying to what he said, as he tried, in succession, to join him in the Senate, to replace him in the Senate, and finally, to beat him to the White House. Their contest was a local matter, but it had national implications, for slavery was a national issue, Douglas was a national figure, and Illinois was becoming a more significant state (in the 1850s its population would double, boosting it from the ninth most populous state to the fourth). The contest began on unequal terms, as Lincoln was well aware, for Douglas in 1854 was a success and Lincoln was, if not quite a failure, certainly no success. But Lincoln hung on Douglas's shoulder like a jockey trailing another down the backstretch and around the clubhouse turn, waiting for the chance to pull ahead.

All the elements of Lincoln's mind and personality, which had lain about like engine parts in a workshop, finally came together into something coherent and ultimately powerful. He made use of humor, logic, and eloquence, each trait now purged of grossness, rigidity, or bombast.

Equally important—maybe most important—he had help, from the dead.

Lincoln addressed the repeal of the Missouri Compromise twice in October 1854, first in Springfield, then in Peoria. Both times he was paired with Douglas, in Springfield speaking a day later, in Peoria a few hours later. Both of Lincoln's speeches were essentially the same, but the second was printed, with his corrections, so it has come to be known as the Peoria speech.

It was a major effort, three hours long, one of the longest speeches he would ever give. When speaking on the stump, Lincoln would occasionally read out quotations or pause to glance at notes in his pocket, but mostly he spoke from memory (as did Douglas, and all other orators worth their salt). After years of campaigning and courtroom pleading no one needed prompters. Lincoln did not pace, or saw the air with his arms in the manner of Henry Clay. One hand might hold the opposite wrist, or a lapel. His voice was high and slightly whining—a useful timbre for addressing crowds in the open air—but as he warmed up it deepened a bit. Some listeners noted the remains of a Kentucky accent.

Although he went into many details in Peoria, Lincoln had one simple theme: he wanted to repeal the Kansas-Nebraska Act, restore the Missouri Compromise and the Missouri line, and block the extension of slavery. Following the pattern of the Henry Clay paragraph he loved, he argued that the Kansas-Nebraska Act was bad politics, false to history and false to human nature.

The bad politics of Douglas's handiwork was the easiest point to establish. Douglas had said that leaving slavery in Kansas and Nebraska to local option was a way to avoid strife, yet his law had plunged the nation into it, as Americans argued whether or not slavery should be admitted into the new territories. "Every inch of territory we owned," said Lincoln, "already had a definite settlement of the slavery question." But as soon as the Missouri Compromise was repealed, "here we are in the midst of a new slavery agitation."

Lincoln ransacked history for instances in which the United States, contrary to the principle of the Kansas-Nebraska Act, had restricted slavery, either by limiting the spread of it or by interfering with the slave trade. A Democratic newspaper noted that "he had been nosing for weeks in the state library" in Springfield, looking up facts. He paid special attention to the slavery prohibition of the Northwest Ordinance, which he saw as a model for future restrictions. This was a powerful argument locally, for the Northwest Ordinance had helped determine the future of Illinois. It was also a powerful argument personally, for the Lincoln family had left Kentucky partly to escape the competition of slave labor.

When Lincoln condemned the Kansas-Nebraska Act as an offense to human nature, he echoed Clay directly. "Slavery is founded in the selfishness of man's nature—opposition to it, in his love of justice. . . . Repeal the Missouri Compromise—repeal all compromises—repeal the Declaration of Independence—repeal all past history, you still cannot repeal human nature." For good measure Lincoln added an echo of Christ. "It still will be the abundance of man's heart, that slavery extension is wrong, and out of the abundance of his heart, his mouth will continue to speak." ("A good man out of the good treasures of his heart bringeth forth that which is good . . . for of the abundance of the heart his mouth speaketh" [Luke 6:45].) Whatever Lincoln thought about Rev. Smith and the divine authority of the Scriptures, he certainly read them.

In the Peoria speech Lincoln brought his rhetorical techniques to a new level. His audiences expected him to tell rube/boob jokes—Democratic journalists called them "Lincolnisms"—and there was one such in the Peoria speech, a couple minutes in, when Lincoln described part of Ohio as "beat[ing] all creation at making cheese." By gum! He made some other jokes over the next two hours and fifty-eight minutes, but they were very different.

Three notable ones came in a cluster. Lincoln began the series by criticizing an opinion common among proslavery hardliners. "Equal justice to the south, it is said, requires us to consent to the extending of slavery to new [territories]. That is to say, inasmuch as you do not object to my taking my hog to Nebraska, therefore I must not object to you taking your slave. Now, I admit this is perfectly logical, if there is no difference between hogs and Negroes." Lincoln's starchiness—"it is said," "that is to say," "inasmuch"—set his listeners up; the sudden appearance of "my hog" knocked them down; the conjunction of "hogs and Negroes" made the joke, and the point—they were side by side in the sentence, but miles apart in their nature.

A few minutes later, Lincoln referred to the transatlantic slave trade, which Congress had defined as piracy in 1820. "The practice was no more than bringing wild Negroes from Africa, to sell to such as would buy them. But you never thought of hanging men for catching and selling wild horses, wild buffaloes or wild bears." Here Lincoln contrasted Negroes with a whole menagerie—to make the point that they did not belong in a menagerie.

Lincoln moved on to consider free blacks. "There are in the United States and territories, including the District of Columbia, 433,643 free blacks." The solemn specificity of this—"including the District of Columbia"—was itself comic. "At $5.00 per head they are worth over two hundred millions of dollars." More specifics. "How comes this vast amount of property to be running about without owners? We do not see free horses or free cattle running at large." Most American blacks were slaves, but not all of them; most white northerners did not like free Negroes, but they did not revolt at their freedom—perhaps, Lincoln suggested, because they acknowledged that blacks were entitled to it as men.

Each of these jokes used Paine's favorite technique, the *reductio ad absurdum*, pushing an assumption until it broke down. Lincoln had finally learned to harness humor to serious purposes.

His jokes also all involved Negroes. There was a whiff of minstrelsy about this—using black folk to entertain white folk. But Lincoln was running a sly minstrel show, designed to show that his comic characters were men. He left his audience laughing—and thinking.

At other points, he dispensed with humor and served logic straight up. Stephen Douglas's doctrine of popular sovereignty expressed an old American principle (based on even older English principles):

self-government. Should there be slavery, or not? Let the people decide. Lincoln agreed that men should govern themselves. That was "right—absolutely and eternally right."

But, he argued, the application of self-government to the admission of slavery into Kansas and Nebraska "depends upon whether a Negro is *not* or *is* a man. If he is *not* a man, why in that case, he who *is* a man may, as a matter of self-government, do just as he pleases with him. But if the Negro *is* a man, is it not to that extent, a total destruction of self-government, to say that he too shall not govern *himself*?" Lincoln had screwed this point down pretty tight, but he gave it one more turn. "When the white man governs himself that is self-government; but when he governs himself, and also governs *another* man, that is *more* than self-government—that is despotism." If you have a good thing and add something more to it, you make it better, said Douglas. Depends what you add, said Lincoln: if you add slavery to liberty, you negate and destroy it. Euclid was never more terse, Paine never more pointed.

The founding fathers marched through Lincoln's speech—no longer dead and gone, but living presences. He invoked the "pure, fresh, free breath of the revolution" as he began his oration, and "the principle of the REVOLUTION" (Lincoln's capital letters) as he wound up. He insisted that his position on slavery was the founders' position. "The plain unmistakable spirit of [their] age towards slavery was hostility to the PRINCIPLE and toleration ONLY BY NECESSITY" (Lincoln's capitals). Douglas and the Kansas-Nebraska Act had betrayed the founders. Lincoln wanted to return to their example, and he did it by citing three founding documents. Two of them expressed the founders' hostility to slavery.

The first that Lincoln cited was the Northwest Ordinance. In discussing the prehistory of this law, he made a mistake. In the early 1780s, Virginia had ceded to Congress a claim, derived from its colonial charter, to the old Northwest (many of the original thirteen colonies had paper claims to vast chunks of North America). What had once belonged to the colony and state of Virginia would now belong to the United States.

In Peoria Lincoln said that Virginia, in ceding its claim, had stipulated that its former territory be free of slavery—a stipulation he attributed to Thomas Jefferson, then a member of Congress.

But neither Virginia nor Jefferson had made any such stipulation. What Jefferson had actually done, in 1784, was propose to Congress that the entire American West, from the Appalachians to the Mississippi, be free of slavery. His plan was rejected, but three years later (Jefferson was in Paris at the time, serving as minister to France) Congress revisited the subject and passed the Northwest Ordinance, banning slavery there. In later years, Lincoln corrected the error.

But Lincoln was right to connect Jefferson in spirit with the Northwest Ordinance. The man who had wanted all of the West to be free certainly wanted the old Northwest to be free. By 1854 the Northwest Territory had become five states—Ohio, Indiana, Illinois, Michigan, and Wisconsin—which were now, Lincoln said, "what Jefferson foresaw and intended—the happy home of teeming millions of free, white, prosperous people, and no slave amongst them." Lincoln was right to appeal to Jefferson—and shrewd: he appropriated the founder of Douglas's party (Democrats claimed Jefferson and the first Republican Party as their direct ancestors). He also wrapped the Northwest Ordinance, via Jefferson, in the aura of the Revolution.

The second example of the founders' hostility toward slavery that Lincoln cited was the Declaration of Independence. He called it "the sheet anchor of American republicanism," the expression of "our ancient faith. . . . If the Negro is a man, why then my ancient faith teaches me that 'all men are created equal;' and there can be no moral right in connection with one man's making a slave of another." A sheet anchor is the strongest anchor a ship has, the last resort in a storm.

If there was no moral right in slavery, why then wasn't Lincoln an abolitionist? Because the founders, he explained, had accepted the existence of slavery "BY NECESSITY" (his capital letters) in the third founding document he cited, the Constitution.

The Constitution gave slavery certain guarantees: Lincoln mentioned the protection of the slave trade for twenty years, the obligation to return fugitive slaves, and the three-fifths rule, whereby slaves were counted in the apportionment of the House of Representatives. These had been necessary concessions to get slave states to accept the Constitution, and Lincoln accepted them in that spirit. "[They are] in the constitution; and I do not . . . propose to destroy, or alter, or disregard the constitution. I stand to it, fairly, fully, and firmly."

The founders, said Lincoln, had accepted slavery out of necessity. But acknowledging necessity did not mean approving slavery. "Necessity drove [the founders] so far, and farther, they would not go." Therefore Lincoln would not go farther himself. "Let us turn slavery . . . back upon its existing legal rights, and its arguments of 'necessity.' Let us return it to the position our founders gave it, and there let it rest in peace."

In his eulogy for Henry Clay, Lincoln had rebuked extremists who rejected either the Declaration or the Constitution. In Peoria, and for the rest of his life, he presented himself as the man who upheld both.

Several times in the Peoria speech Lincoln emphasized the oldness of the founders. The Declaration was "my ancient faith" and "our ancient faith": "I love the sentiments of those old-time men," he added a moment later. He may have intended a biblical echo; in the Book of Daniel, God is called "the Ancient of Days" ("the Ancient of days did sit, whose garment was white as snow" [Daniel 7:9]). In his own mind, he was turning his premature decrepitude to advantage: his old, withered, dry eyes made him like those old-time men.

Lincoln gave the founders another feature often associated with age: disease. In one of his references to the Constitution, he noted that the words "slave" and "slavery" never appear in it. Fugitive slaves are referred to as "Person[s] held to service or labour"; the slave trade as the "importation" of "Persons." "Thus," said Lincoln, "the thing is hid away in the constitution, just as an afflicted man hides away a wen or a cancer, which he dares not cut out at once, lest he bleed to death."

Those old-time men left a congenital illness, as well as an ancient faith. At least they had been ashamed of it.

How would Lincoln cut out the cancer? He gave hints only, none of them, he admitted, very attractive. Colonization was a possibility ("my first impulse would be to free all the slaves, and send them to Liberia"), but he knew that could happen only over the long run. Letting former slaves live as freemen in America would create its own problems. Either they would remain a permanent class of "underlings" or they would become the social and political equals of whites. The first option might not be much better than slavery; white people would not accept the second. Lincoln included himself as a recalcitrant white person: "My own feelings will not admit of" complete equality.

Those were problems for the future. Lincoln's goal at Peoria was to undo Douglas's law and stop the spread of slavery. His climax was poetic, almost prophetic: "Our republican robe is soiled, and trailed in the dust. Let us repurify it. Let us turn and wash it white, in the spirit, if not the blood, of the Revolution." In the Bible the Ancient of Days wears a white garment, and so do the souls of the saved: "These are they which came out of great tribulation, and have washed their robes, and made them white in the blood of the Lamb" (Revelation 7:14). Lincoln wanted a political salvation; he hoped it would not be a bloody one.

At Peoria Lincoln laid out themes that he would return to for years: accept slavery where it was, out of necessity; stop it from going anywhere else, out of principle; send freed slaves somewhere else at some later time, but recognize meanwhile that they were men. Do all these things in the spirit of the founders. Lincoln claimed the Northwest Ordinance as an Illinoisan, he admired the Declaration as a reasoner from first principles, and he honored the Constitution as a lawyer. He loved the Revolution as a poet, no longer of death and decay ("the silent artillery of time"), but of a powerful animating spirit.

Eight

1855–1858: RUNNING FOR SENATE

I N LATER YEARS, LINCOLN WOULD SAY THAT HE HAD NOT "controlled events, but confess plainly that events have controlled me."

He knew how to poor-mouth himself in order to deflect unwanted attention, and this line was in part such a maneuver. *Don't look at me, look at events (meanwhile, I will control all the events I can).*

But Lincoln's line also reflected the realism of the politician. You put your principles in order (if you have any). Then events bombard you with opportunities and conundrums. Politics is like making a journey on horseback that you have never made before. You may have directions, but they can be wrong. There may be roads, but they can turn out to be impassible or dead ends. Events always control you; they are the things you must deal with. How you deal with them is up to you.

The years following the Peoria speech placed both Lincoln and Douglas in a thicket of events as they fought for office. Along the way, they fought over the founders—each claiming them as guides and allies.

————

The first event, which their October speeches were made to affect, was the 1854 election in Illinois. It was a rebuke to Douglas—anti-Nebraska men won five of the state's nine seats in the House of Representatives and a narrow majority in the Illinois legislature.

Until ratification of the Seventeenth Amendment to the Constitution in the next century, state legislatures selected those who would be sent to Washington as US senators. Lincoln hoped the legislature would send him to the Senate in 1855 alongside Douglas. The incumbent, who was standing for a second term, was a Douglas ally, James Shields, the man whom Lincoln had almost dueled.

The Illinois legislature had 100 members. When it met in February 1855, Lincoln won 45 votes on the first ballot to 41 for Shields. But 5 votes went to Lyman Trumbull, an anti-Nebraska Democrat from Alton, with the rest scattered. Trumbull was not well-served by photographs, which show pinched eyes peering through narrow spectacles. Trumbull's supporters, who were already defying Douglas, could not go one step further and vote for an old Whig like Lincoln. On the seventh ballot, pro-Nebraska Democrats sprang a new candidate—Governor Joel Matteson. He, too, backed the Kansas-Nebraska Act, but not so vehemently as Shields, and he might win some Democrats by appealing to party loyalty, or by simply buying their votes. (Some things never change in Illinois.) Lincoln's total, meanwhile, began to dwindle as his supporters lost heart. On the tenth ballot he asked his diehards to switch to Trumbull, making him senator.

It was hard, Lincoln wrote afterward, for more than forty men to give way to five, "and a less good humored man than I perhaps would not have consented to it." Mary Lincoln never forgave Mrs. Trumbull, who had been one of her best friends. But Lincoln wanted a united front to put an anti-Nebraska man in the Senate. Later, that united front might unite behind him.

———

The next event to confront Lincoln and Douglas was the 1856 presidential election.

Anti-Nebraska men in northern states formed a new political party, bringing together Whigs and Democrats, Free Soilers and abolitionists. They took the name of Jefferson's old party, the Republicans. In Illinois its leaders included Lincoln, Trumbull, and Owen Lovejoy, younger brother of the murdered abolitionist editor Elijah Lovejoy. Herndon was an enthusiastic member; John Stuart, a dyed-in-the-wool Whig, would not join it, and was aghast that Lincoln had.

In May the Illinois Republicans held a convention in Bloomington, southwest of Peoria; Lincoln addressed them, giving what Herndon called the best speech of his life. "It was logic; it was pathos; it was enthusiasm; it was justice, equity, truth and right[;] . . . it was hard, heavy, knotty, gnarly, backed with wrath." Herndon was so carried away that he stopped taking notes after fifteen minutes. Unfortunately no one else recorded the speech either. We will have to be satisfied with the Lincoln speeches we have.

Douglas was nominated for president once again at the Democratic national convention in Cincinnati; he stayed in contention for sixteen ballots, peaking at second place. But all his labors for the Nebraska bill had given him not a clear path to the nomination, but a reputation as a fomenter of controversy. On the seventeenth ballot he gave way to James Buchanan, a sixty-five-year-old party hack who had spent the last four years of his long career in London, representing the United States at the Court of St. James, and thus had no record to defend on Douglas's bill.

There was a third party in the race, the Americans (called by their enemies the Know-Nothings). The Americans were, in inspiration, a nativist party that had formed in reaction to the floods of Irish and

German immigrants who had been coming to the United States since the 1840s, driven by famine or political unrest. The Americans also became a shelter for conservative Whigs. For their candidate they tapped the last Whig president, Millard Fillmore.

The Republicans held their convention in Philadelphia in late June, the latest of the three major parties. Lincoln wanted the new party to appeal to the old Whigs in its ranks and suggested nominating quite an old Whig to do it—John McLean, a seventy-one-year-old US Supreme Court justice: "His nomination would save every Whig," Lincoln wrote Trumbull. The convention went in the other direction, picking John C. Frémont, a forty-three-year-old Free Soil Democrat who was famous for exploring the Rockies and liberating California during the Mexican War. Free Soil, Free Men, and Frémont made a catchy slogan.

Although Lincoln did not attend the national convention, he was not ignored. The Illinois delegation backed him for the vice-presidential nomination, and he finished second in a straw poll of delegates, with 110 votes out of 607. The second spot on the ticket, however, went not to him but to William Dayton, another former Whig who had actually been a senator from New Jersey.

Frémont carried New England, New York, Ohio, and the upper Midwest—Michigan, Wisconsin, and Iowa—for 114 electoral votes. Fillmore took Maryland and its 8 votes. Buchanan carried every other state for 174 electoral votes and victory. His margin came from four swing states—New Jersey, Pennsylvania, Indiana, and Illinois—where he eked out tiny majorities (a hair over 50 percent in Pennsylvania, his home state) or won with pluralities. Frémont and Fillmore together took almost 56 percent of the vote in Illinois, but Buchanan's 44 percent was first past the post. The new Republican Party would need to win Illinois and other states like it if it were to elect a president in 1860.

————

Buchanan was inaugurated on March 4, 1857. Two days later the Supreme Court handed down perhaps its worst decision ever, certainly one of its most consequential. It forced both Lincoln and Douglas to scramble for new political ground.

Dred Scott was a slave whose master, an army surgeon, had taken him in the 1830s to forts in Illinois and the future Minnesota Territory, well north of the Missouri line. Later he served his master's wife in Missouri. After the surgeon died, Scott, with the help of abolitionist lawyers, sued for his freedom, on the grounds that living in a free state and a free territory had liberated him. *Scott v. Sandford* had been argued before the Supreme Court in 1856.

The majority opinion was written by Roger Taney, who would shortly celebrate both his eightieth birthday and his twenty-first year as chief justice. Taney ruled that Scott had no right to sue. Only citizens could do that, and blacks could not be citizens under the Constitution, because at the time of its ratification they were considered "beings of an inferior order" who "had no rights which the white man was bound to respect." Since the founders would not have respected Dred Scott, neither did the Constitution or the chief justice.

Taney went on to state that the Missouri Compromise, under which Scott claimed freedom, thanks to his having lived in the future Minnesota Territory, violated the Fifth Amendment. Since "no person" could be "deprived of property without due process of law," Congress could not pass a law that deprived slave owners of their property. Therefore owners could take their slaves into any territory whatsoever. Douglas and the Kansas-Nebraska Act had repealed the Missouri Compromise; now Taney and the Supreme Court declared it unconstitutional. Since the purpose of the Republican Party was to restore the Missouri Compromise, the *Dred Scott* decision was, as political scientist Harry Jaffa puts it, "a summons to the Republicans to disband."

As a boy and as an adult Lincoln had encountered views of George Washington, propagated by chapters of Parson Weems and orators like Robert Winthrop, depicting him as a blank symbol of virtue or national unity. Now Roger Taney was advancing the view that the founding fathers collectively had been patrons of slavery and racial hierarchy—that their Constitution treated slavery as a property right, and that they had regarded Negroes as beings with no rights.

In June 1857 Douglas addressed the *Dred Scott* decision in a speech in Springfield. On the face of it, Taney had demolished popular sovereignty along with the Missouri Compromise: If slaveholders had a right to bring their property into any territory, what point was there in letting the inhabitants pass laws about slavery? Douglas had found a loophole, however. The right to bring slaves would be "barren and worthless . . . unless sustained, protected and enforced by appropriate police regulations." In other words, if the people of a territory imposed slight or no penalties on helping runaways or preaching abolition, they could make slave-owning so precarious that the right became a dead letter. "Hence," he concluded, "the great principle of popular sovereignty . . . is sustained." Douglas could accept *Dred Scott*, yet at the same time urge Americans to evade it. This topic would come up again.

For the rest, Douglas agreed with Taney that blacks were an "inferior race," and he added that Republicans desired "amalgamation" with them.

Douglas's racial rhetoric would ring down the years. Racism was not peculiar to him. Almost every white American felt it, from wealthy planters to hardscrabble farmers to immigrants just off the boat. "My own feelings will not admit of" racial equality, Lincoln admitted in his Peoria speech. But Douglas was making racism a creed and a partisan plank of northern Democrats. For him it was not a passive prejudice, a piece of mental furniture, but a fighting faith. "No man of his time," wrote the black abolitionist Frederick Douglass (no relation) "has done more than he to intensify hatred of the negro." Douglas accompanied his racism with the charge that his Republican enemies were race-mixers (the word "miscegenation" would be invented in 1864 by a Democratic journalist for use against Republicans).

Douglas had his own view of the founding fathers, somewhat different from Taney's. He would expound it at length soon enough.

Lincoln answered both Taney and Douglas in Springfield later in June 1857. The question of how much deference should be accorded the

Court gave him some trouble. His old party, the Whigs, had come into existence to resist Andrew Jackson's willfulness, exemplified by, among other things, his rejection of Supreme Court decisions he disliked. Now Lincoln quoted Jackson himself, blasting *McCulloch v. Maryland*, the 1819 decision that had upheld the constitutionality of the Second Bank of the United States.

Lincoln was trying to wrong-foot Douglas, who was a Democrat, an old Jacksonian, and a long-ago enemy of Lincoln's in the Illinois bank wars: *here is what your old hero thought*. But in doing so, he risked wrong-footing himself: *I now find myself agreeing with my old villain*.

But Lincoln directed most of his fire not at the Supreme Court as an institution, but at Taney's reasoning in *Dred Scott*, and he focused it specifically on Taney's opinions of the founders. Lincoln seemed to shrug off Taney's attacks on the Missouri Compromise and the Republican Party. What the founding fathers really meant was more important to him. If Lincoln could get that right, the rest would follow.

Taney, said Lincoln, "insists at great length that negroes were no part of the people who made, or for whom was made," the Constitution or the Declaration. To prove that at least some Negroes were citizens under the Constitution, Lincoln relied on one of the dissenting opinions in *Dred Scott*, written by Justice Benjamin Curtis. Curtis noted that in 1787–1788, when the Constitution was ratified, five states (New Hampshire, Massachusetts, New York, New Jersey, and North Carolina) had allowed free Negroes to vote. White men in those states, far from not respecting the rights of free black men, as Taney claimed, had respected their right to vote; free black men had voted, along with white men, on the Constitution itself.

To prove that Negroes were included in the Declaration, Lincoln relied on his own thoughts, inspired by Clay and expressed at Peoria. At the time of the founding, "our Declaration of Independence was held sacred by all, and thought to include all." Why then had the signers not freed America's slaves? Because, said Lincoln, "they had no power to confer such a boon." They were not making laws; they were laying down a marker: "They meant to set up a standard maxim for free society, which should be familiar to all, and revered by all." For what purpose? "Its authors meant it to be, [as] thank God, it is now proving itself, a stumbling block to those who in after times might seek to turn a free people back into the hateful paths of despotism." Those in after times like Roger Taney and Stephen Douglas.

Lincoln had some fun with Douglas's charge of race-mixing. It was "counterfeit logic," he said, to argue "that, because I do not want a black woman for a slave I must necessarily want her for a wife. I need not have her for either, I can just leave her alone." This was a good line, and he would repeat it many times. It sprang from his own experience: he had left Mary Owens alone by dithering, and he left his wife alone by ignoring her whenever she bothered him; now he could use his difficulties with women in a higher cause.

But after the laughter, he passed immediately to moral reasoning. "In some respects [a black woman] certainly is not my equal; but in her natural right to eat the bread she earns with her own hands without asking leave of any one else, she is my equal, and the equal of all others." Counterfeit logic gave way to logic so austere, it was almost poetry.

Lincoln ended with a pitch for colonization, comparing slaves to Jews in the Bible. "The children of Israel . . . went out of Egyptian bondage in a body." So might Africans return to Africa.

———

The next events to come Lincoln's and Douglas's way arose in Kansas.

The Kansas-Nebraska Act had not only not pacified American politics, it had turned the Kansas Territory into a battlefield—literally. Settlers moving in from next-door Missouri and in greater numbers from the North came to blows, and soon there were two competing territorial governments adrift in a sea of freelance violence. *Terrorism* and *guerrilla war* were already familiar concepts, the first a legacy of the French Revolution, the second of the Napoleonic Wars in Spain. Now they stalked the plains.

In the summer of 1857, Kansas's proslavery government called for the election of delegates for a convention to write a territorial constitution. Antislavery men boycotted the election, believing it to be rigged, with the result that a proslavery convention met in Lecompton, twenty miles east of Topeka, and wrote a proslavery document. On December 8, 1857, President Buchanan endorsed the proposed constitution in his Annual Message to Congress (the equivalent of a State of the Union address). The next day Douglas responded in the Senate.

"It is none of my business," said Douglas, "which way the slavery clause [of the Lecompton Constitution] is decided. I care not whether it is voted down or voted up. . . . But if [the Lecompton] constitution is to be forced down our throats . . . under a mode of submission that is a mockery and an insult, I will resist it to the last. . . . I will stand on the great principle of popular sovereignty [and] I will follow that principle wherever its logical consequences may take me."

Douglas was prompted by intraparty politics, for he was feuding with Buchanan at the time. Although the president would prove to be a hopeless executive in a crisis, he was determined, like many weaklings, to rule in little things, and he had shut Douglas out of patronage. Yet Douglas also wanted to defend his great principle. The proposed constitution of Kansas followed the forms of popular sovereignty. The delegates to the Lecompton convention had been elected, and the Lecompton Constitution would be submitted to the voters. But if the convention had been rigged, and if the president meddled in the vote on its handiwork, then the process was a sham. Douglas had to reject it, if only to justify the past three years of his public life.

But defending popular sovereignty by attacking the Lecompton Constitution might also open up his future—and here Douglas truly showed himself to be the Man of Audacity. He had appealed to the South with the Kansas-Nebraska Act, with disastrous consequences. If he now gave something to the Republicans of the North, perhaps his fortunes might rebound.

Republicans in the Northeast (which was the stronghold of the party) were intrigued. The support, even opportunistic, of such a prominent

Democrat looked like a coup. Perhaps an alliance with Douglas was the way for a united northern party to take Illinois and the White House. Horace Greeley, the Republican editor of the *New York Tribune*, the newspaper with the largest circulation in the country, urged Republicans to "promptly and heartily tender their support to Mr. Douglas"— and Greeley was only printing what party leaders were thinking.

But if Republicans allied with Douglas, what would become of Lincoln? At the end of the year Lincoln wrote a tart letter to Trumbull in Washington asking what had possessed the easterners. "Have they concluded that the Republican cause generally can best be promoted by sacrificing us here in Illinois? If so we would like to know it soon; it will save us a great deal of labor to surrender at once."

Naturally, Lincoln was concerned for his political future. But he was also concerned with first principles, with digging to the roots of things. Douglas was for a fair vote in Kansas, which would almost certainly guarantee a free territory and state. (Kansas voters would reject the Lecompton Constitution, despite Buchanan's endorsement, by huge margins in two different votes in 1858.) But who could believe that Kansas would be the last struggle over slavery? And Douglas had said that he did not care whether slavery was voted down or up.

———

Both Lincoln and Douglas were under pressure because Douglas's current term as senator would end in March 1859. The future occupant of his seat would be chosen by the Illinois legislature that was to be elected in November 1858.

Douglas wanted a third term, and Lincoln wanted to replace him. Both men wanted a clean shot when the new legislature met, not a four-way struggle like the Shields-Lincoln-Trumbull-Matteson contest of 1855. Douglas asserted his dominance of the state's Democratic Party at a convention in Springfield in April 1858, which voted to support his reelection. (Buchanan had been trying to woo Illinois Democrats away from Douglas with federal patronage.) But Lincoln needed his own show of strength to impress out-of-state kibitzers like Greeley.

Illinois Republicans were happy to give it to him. Ex-Democrats in the party were still grateful for his selflessness in yielding to Trumbull in 1855. Ex-Whigs embraced him as one of their own. He was a fixture in state politics, and he had been acting as a scourge of Douglas since the Peoria speech. Illinoisans also resented the advice of easterners. The state's Republicans held their own convention in Springfield on June 16, which declared that Lincoln was their "first and only choice" for senator.

Lincoln addressed them that evening. He said nothing about the founders in this speech. The image that would give the speech its name came from the Bible (see Matthew 12:25 and Mark 3:25): "A house divided against itself cannot stand." Lincoln explained: "I believe the government cannot endure, permanently half slave and half free. . . . Either the opponents of slavery will arrest the further spread of it, and place it where the public mind shall rest in the belief that it is in course of ultimate extinction; or its advocates will push it forward, till it shall become alike lawful in all the states, old as well as new—North as well as South."

Douglas and the Democrats would assail Lincoln for the binary sweep of this prediction, and it made even some of his staunchest Republican allies blanch when he gave them a preview of the speech; one called it a "damned fool utterance." Lincoln was setting an end term to his policy of stopping the spread of slavery; the logical result, he admitted, would be to make slavery extinct. (How might this work? If slaves could not be sold to new owners in new places, the prices of slaves would stabilize, then drop. In time it would become realistic for the government to offer buy-outs and send the freed slaves abroad.) He still put slavery's consummation off to a distant, undefined day: the "course of ultimate extinction" could last for decades. In a note to himself about the time of the "House Divided" speech, Lincoln wrote that slavery might not end "within the term of my natural life"; in public, he would extend that to "a hundred years." Even such a long-range plan as this made a jolt in Illinois in 1858.

But Lincoln was also trying, with his prediction, to explain the dynamics of the 1850s. The advocates of slavery had indeed pushed slavery forward—into New Mexico and Utah (with trade-offs), above the Missouri line (with no trade-offs), deeper into the Constitution (via the *Dred Scott* decision), into the Lecompton Constitution (though that struggle was still ongoing).

They might push further still. In the "House Divided" speech Lincoln mentioned two possible ways in which slavery might expand. There might be a second *Dred Scott*–like decision, extending the right to take human property into free states. We may "awake to the reality," Lincoln warned, "that the Supreme Court has made Illinois a slave state."

Or there might be an effort to revive the slave trade. It had been considered piracy for thirty-eight years—indeed, a capital crime—but no one had ever been executed for slave-trading, and it had never been completely extirpated. If slaves could be carried into formerly free territories, why not allow them to be carried from Africa—especially since that was the cheapest place to buy them?

In a draft of the "House Divided" speech, Lincoln added a third arena for slavery's expansion: new slave territories in Central America or the Caribbean might be acquired by the United States. And indeed Americans from the South had been sponsoring freelance uprisings and invasions in that part of the world throughout the 1850s.

Who were the advocates of slavery pushing it forward? Lincoln answered with a metaphor. He had opened his speech with a biblical house, but halfway through he described a second house that was under construction, along with the workmen who were building it. "When we see a lot of framed timbers" gathered "by different workmen—Stephen, Franklin, Roger and James, for instance"—Lincoln's listeners would supply the surnames: Douglas, Pierce, Taney, and Buchanan—"and when we see these timbers joined together, and see they exactly make the frame of a house . . . all the tenons and mortices exactly fitting"—then,

Lincoln concluded, it was right to suspect that "a common plan or draft [had been] drawn up before the first lick was struck." The second house was a trap, like something out of a story by Poe or Hawthorne, representing the policies that would imprison Republicans and liberty itself. The four workmen, with their matching timbers, were also the jailers.

This was a conspiracy theory involving two presidents, a would-be president, and the chief justice of the US Supreme Court. It showed the desperation of Republicans in 1858, and their fear that, even as their party and the free states grew, the advocates of slavery would keep a lock on the government.

Was it crazy, simply because it was a conspiracy theory? Buchanan had been seen talking intently with Chief Justice Taney at his own inauguration. Had they been talking about the *Dred Scott* decision, shortly to come? Decades after Buchanan's death, his published papers would show that as president-elect he had been corresponding with other justices as they discussed the case, pushing them to issue the most sweeping proslavery decision possible. James and Roger had conspired, if not Franklin or Stephen.

Sometimes a conspiracy theorist, shooting at noises in the dark, hits real conspirators.

Lincoln ended with a rousing appeal. "Two years ago," the Republican Party had been formed to resist "a common danger. . . . Of strange, discordant, and even hostile elements, we gathered from the four winds. . . . Did we brave all then, to falter now? . . . The result is not doubtful. We shall not fail—if we stand firm, we shall not fail."

———

The nominations of Lincoln and Douglas earlier in 1858 allowed the two men to campaign across the state in the hope of affecting the elections to the legislature on November 2. After Lincoln twice found himself— first in Chicago, then in Springfield—speaking shortly after Douglas, the candidates agreed to appear together in seven other locations. Their schedule of debates was Ottawa (August 21), Freeport (August 27),

Jonesboro (September 15), Charleston (September 18), Galesburg (October 7), Quincy (October 13), and Alton (October 15). Their itinerary spanned the state: Freeport was near the Wisconsin border, Jonesboro in the tip of the wedge between Missouri and Kentucky. Republicans had wanted even more joint appearances, as many as fifty or one hundred. The actual schedule was numbing enough, as the candidates filled the days between debates with other speeches. Traveling by train, the two men logged almost 10,000 miles.

Such exertions for a Senate race were unheard of in American politics. (Presidential candidates did not campaign, either; when Winfield Scott made a few trips to army bases before the election of 1852, he was condemned for it.) In another innovation, the Chicago papers of both parties printed the texts of the debates, with ample notes of crowd reactions ("hit him," "that's so," "immense applause," "laughter and cheers").

The traditional arts of politics were also practiced. Buchanan still wanted to make trouble for Douglas in any way he could (these two workmen were not cooperating in the way Lincoln had charged), and his minions in Illinois ran a slate of independent candidates, who called themselves National Democrats (critics called them Buchaneers). Since the enemy of my enemy is my ally, the Republicans kept tabs on this effort via Herndon, whose father and brother were staunch Buchanan supporters. Since my liaison to my ally is not me, this allowed Lincoln to deny that he himself had "in any way promoted" the Buchaneers.

The format of the joint debates required one man to speak for an hour, the other to reply for ninety minutes, then the first to rejoin for thirty. Douglas opened and concluded the first debate, then the candidates successively switched positions. Douglas thus opened and closed in four debates, Lincoln in three—an advantage to Douglas, but as the incumbent and the man with the most to lose, he set the terms. Lincoln consistently called him "Judge Douglas"—a legitimate title, since Douglas had served on the state supreme court back in the 1840s; it also spared Lincoln calling him "Senator." Douglas addressed his opponent as "Mr. Lincoln."

The state was riveted. "The prairies are on fire," wrote the *New York Evening Post*. The audiences sometimes exceeded the population of the towns in which the debates were held; the dust raised by incoming horses and buggies clouded the air. There was some heckling, and a lot of cheering, but to an impressive degree people paid attention to what was said.

What they heard included a lot of repetition and a lot of small-bore disputation. The two candidates wrangled over party platforms and past statements, and they gave minute accounts of political maneuvers, which they professed to find shocking (or, when they were the maneuverers, unexceptionable). Even so, a lot of noteworthy things got said.

Douglas led off the first debate by patronizing Lincoln: "I have known him for nearly twenty-five years. . . . He could beat any of the boys wrestling, or running a foot race, in pitching quoits or tossing a copper; [he] could ruin more liquor than all the boys of the town together [uproarious laughter]." Since Lincoln was temperate and Douglas was a heavy drinker, that was a low blow. Douglas used Lincoln's rube/boob persona against him, depicting him as a yokel who had never amounted to anything—and that part of the charge was still painfully close to the truth.

Throughout the debates, Douglas tarred Lincoln as pro-black. He claimed that Frederick Douglass—whom he called a "rich black negro"—and other black abolitionists were campaigning for him, charges that were greeted with cries of "white men, white men," "down with the negro," and "he's a disgrace to white people." Frederick Douglass in fact scorned Lincoln as too conservative. Douglas accused the Republicans of tailoring their negrophilia to fit different parts of the state, the North being most antislavery, the South least. In Freeport and Chicago, said Douglas, Republicans were "jet black"; in central Illinois, "a decent mulatto"; in the southern part of the state, "almost white [shouts of laughter]."

Lincoln for his part insisted that he had no intention of introducing "political and social equality" between whites and blacks: "There is a

physical difference between the two, which in my judgment will probably forever forbid their living together. . . . I, as well as Judge Douglas,
am in favor of the race to which I belong having the superior position."
Lincoln made other demonstrations of his whiteness, using the words
nigger and *niggers* several times, as if to say, *Don't worry, I'm one of the
(white) guys too.* Some of his uses, however, put the words in Douglas's
mouth: "My friend Judge Douglas [says I want to] set the niggers and
white people to marrying together [laughter]." *I talk about niggers; but
Douglas worries about them.*

Lincoln told several versions of his joke about not having to marry
a black woman if she was not his slave. He concluded one recital of
it with a riff at Douglas's expense, which incidentally shows how he
worked a crowd. "I have never had the least apprehension that I or my
friends would marry negroes if there was no law to keep them from it
[laughter], but as Judge Douglas and his friends seem to be in great
apprehension that they might, if there were no law to keep them from
it [roars of laughter], I give him the most solemn pledge that I will to
the very last stand by the law of this state, which forbids the marrying
of white people with negroes [continued laughter and applause]." Lincoln had mined his own sexual insecurity to tell the marriage joke in
the first place; here he located an even greater insecurity in the racism
of Douglas.

The debates are best known for two sets of questions the candidates posed to each other early on, Douglas to Lincoln in Ottawa and
Lincoln to Douglas in Freeport. Douglas's questions sought to entangle
Lincoln with abolitionism—Did he favor repealing the federal fugitive
slave law, for instance? Lincoln had drawn the line between abolitionists and himself so clearly that he had little trouble answering: he said
he thought the fugitive slave law was constitutional. One of Lincoln's
questions homed in on the *Dred Scott* decision: Could the people of a
territory "in any lawful way . . . exclude slavery from its limits"? Douglas
answered that they could do it by "local police regulations." This was
not news. Douglas had given that answer in his speech on *Dred Scott*

in June 1857 in Springfield, and as he said at Freeport, he had given it "a hundred times from every stump in Illinois." But it was worthwhile to make him say yet again to what lengths he had been driven in order to square popular sovereignty with the Taney Court. Lincoln happily compelled him.

The issue overhanging all of the debates, however, was what the politicians on the podium thought of politicians who had never set foot in Illinois and who had, by 1858, all died years ago. Lincoln, Douglas, and their thousands of laughing, cheering, listening spectators wanted to know how the two candidates squared themselves with the founding fathers—and what that meant about the nature and future of the country. Chief Justice Taney had laid out his view of the founders, slavery, and race in a Supreme Court decision, and Lincoln had laid out his own in speeches since Peoria in 1854. Now Douglas and Lincoln expounded their conflicting views face to face on dusty Illinois podiums.

Douglas introduced his account of the founding fathers in his first speech in Ottawa. He began with a creation story of the federal government. The framers, he said, wrote a Constitution that recognized regional diversity and self-government. "Washington, Jefferson, Franklin, Madison, Hamilton, Jay and the great men of that day, made this government divided into free states and slave states, and left each state perfectly free to do as it pleased on the subject of slavery. [Right, right.]" "They knew," Douglas went on, " . . . that in a country as wide and broad as this, with such a variety of climate, production and interest, the people necessarily required different laws and institutions in different localities. . . . One of the reserved rights of the states was the right to regulate the relations between master and servant. . . . Why can [the government] not exist on the same principles on which our fathers made it? [It can.]"

So Douglas squared himself and slavery with the Constitution. In the third debate at Jonesboro, Douglas turned to the Declaration of Independence, arguing that it cast no rebuke on slavery because it applied only to white people. "The signers of the Declaration [made] no reference to the negro whatever when they declared all men to be created equal. They desired to express by that phrase white men, men of European birth and European descent, and had no reference either to the negro, the savage Indians, the Fejee, the Malay, or any other inferior and degraded race." The proof was that no signer of the Declaration had emancipated his own slaves, "yet if they had intended to declare that the negro was the equal of the white man . . . they were bound, as honest men, that day and hour," to have done so. "[Cheers]."

Lincoln was a bit slower to present his account of the founders. In the flow of the debates, Lincoln got better over time, apparently losing some nervousness, while Douglas wore out, losing his voice. In the sixth debate, in Quincy, Lincoln attacked Douglas's creation story: "When Judge Douglas undertakes to say that . . . the fathers of the government made this nation part slave and part free, he assumes what is historically a falsehood. [Long continued applause.]" The fathers bowed to what Lincoln had called, in his Peoria speech, necessity: "Our fathers did not make this nation half slave and half free, or part slave and part free. [Applause, and That's so.] . . . They found the institution of slavery existing among us. They did not make it so, but they left it so because they knew of no way to get rid of it at that time. [Good, Good, That's true.]"

The founders, Lincoln argued, nevertheless left "many clear marks of [their] disapprobation" of slavery. In the last debate, at Alton, he enumerated them. In the Declaration of Independence, the founders declared that all men are created equal, as "a standard maxim for free society" (Lincoln quoted his own speech on *Dred Scott* from 1857). They banned slavery in the Northwest Ordinance, and in the Constitution they allowed the slave trade to be ended after twenty years. "Why stop its spread in one direction and cut off its source in another, if they did not look to its being placed in the course of ultimate extinction?" The Constitution, it was true, gave guarantees to slavery (the three-fifths rule, the fugitive slave clause); yet its authors avoided the words *negro* and *slavery*, using "covert language" so that years later (a century later?), when slavery had finally disappeared, "there should be nothing on the face of the great charter of liberty suggesting that such a thing as negro slavery had ever existed among us. [Enthusiastic applause.]"

In the fifth debate, in Galesburg, Lincoln had quoted one more mark of the founders' disapprobation. Although "Mr. Jefferson was the owner of slaves, . . . in speaking upon this very subject, he used the strong language that 'he trembled for his country when he remembered that God was just.'" The line came from *Notes on Virginia*, Jefferson's long essay on his home state, which became the only book he ever published. Lincoln did not quote the rest of Jefferson's sentence: God's "justice," he wrote, "cannot sleep forever: . . . a revolution of the wheel of fortune, an exchange of situation is among possible events." Jefferson feared that slavery would end in a slave revolt and a race war; Lincoln hoped there would be no war. Time would show that both were mistaken.

Douglas's view of the founders came with a glowing corollary: follow their policy, and the United States would have a glorious future. He sketched it most eloquently in the sixth debate, at Quincy. "Let each state mind its own business and let its neighbors alone, there will be no trouble on this question [of slavery]. If we will stand by that principle, then . . . this Republic can exist forever divided into free and slave states, as our fathers made it. . . . Stand by that great principle," and the entire continent would become "one ocean-bound republic . . . the asylum of the oppressed of the whole earth."

Lincoln, holding a different view of the founders and their legacy, had a more anxious vision of the future, which he expressed at Alton: "The wisest and best men of the world," as he called the founders, had placed slavery in the course of ultimate extinction. But Douglas was willing to let it last forever, and even let it spread, because he saw nothing wrong in it.

"That is the real issue. That is the issue that will continue in this country when these poor tongues of Judge Douglas and myself shall be silent. It is the eternal struggle between these two principles—right and wrong—throughout the world." The principle of slavery "says, 'You work and toil and earn bread, and I'll eat it.' [Loud applause.] No matter in what shape it comes, whether from the mouth of a king who seeks to bestride the people of his own nation and live by the fruit of their labor, or from one race of men as an apology for enslaving another race, it is the same tyrannical principle." Here Lincoln fused the 1850s with the 1770s. Douglas, and those who praised slavery forthrightly, took the place of George III.

———

November 2, election day, was rainy. Even so, more voters went to the polls than in 1856, a presidential year. Slightly more Republicans than Democrats voted. But the Republicans were concentrated in too few districts; the newly elected legislature would be sending Stephen Douglas back to the Senate, by a vote of 54 to 46.

After it was all over, Lincoln wrote an old Springfield friend who had moved to Oregon that "though I now sink from view . . . I have made some marks which will tell for the cause of civil liberty long after I am gone." But the next day he wrote a friendly editor in Chicago asking for copies of the texts of all the debates. He planned to put them in a scrapbook, for the memories. A scrapbook would also assist typesetters if the debates were republished. He did not intend to sink from view just yet.

Nine

1859–1860: RUNNING FOR PRESIDENT

L INCOLN HAD PUT HIS LEGAL BUSINESS ON HOLD WHILE HE
ran for the Senate, and he needed to take it up again to earn some
money. By the late 1850s his clients had come to include major corporations, not just the litigious locals of the circuit. He defended railroads
in several important cases, arguing that the Illinois Central should be
free from county-level taxes, and that a bridge across the Mississippi
serving the Chicago, Rock Island and Pacific did not obstruct navigation
(steamboat companies, the competing form of transportation, naturally
argued that bridges did just that). Despite his services, the railroads had
given him no special treatment when he crisscrossed the state campaigning in 1858; Stephen Douglas, the powerful incumbent, was loaned
a private car.

Lincoln's most picturesque case had looked back to his past: early in
1858 he had saved the son of his old wrestling rival Jack Armstrong in a

murder trial, by showing that the prosecution's main witness could not have seen the deed on a night that was (according to a dramatically produced almanac) moonless. But the case that would be most important to his future had been a summons to Cincinnati in 1855 to advise the defense for Cyrus McCormick, inventor of the reaper, in a patent infringement suit. On second thought, McCormick's lawyers did not like the looks of their Illinois adviser, one of them, Edwin Stanton, calling him a "damned long-armed ape"—not to the ape's face, though Stanton's attitude was all too clear. Lincoln, who was given nothing to do, felt insulted but pocketed the fee. He and Stanton would meet again.

Lincoln experimented with a new rhetorical genre after his Senate loss—a lyceum-style lecture on the history of inventions, from writing to the development of patent laws. Lincoln had a quirky curiosity about things and processes. "Clocks, omnibuses, language, paddle-wheels, and idioms never escaped his observation and analysis," wrote Herndon (Lincoln never escaped Herndon's observation and analysis). But the lecture on inventions was a failure. Unharnessed from the great issues with which he had been engaged, Lincoln's humor unraveled into whimsy; his interest in history shrank to a harvest of trivia. "That doesn't look much like his being President," wrote one newspaper that reviewed the talk. Lincoln gave it a few times early in 1859, to smaller and smaller audiences, then let his career as a lecturer die.

The newspaper notice of Lincoln's talk was mocking, but was he running, as early as 1859, for president? Of course he was. George Washington had won the first two presidential elections by acclamation, but after his retirement every conceivable politician, and many inconceivable ones, fancied themselves in the role. Still, like any prudent long shot, Lincoln had to be discreet. He could not yet speak about himself; instead he spoke about the founding fathers.

In the spring of 1859 Henry Pierce, a chocolate manufacturer, invited him to a celebration of Thomas Jefferson's birthday on April 13 in Boston. Lincoln had to decline, thanks to the demands of his legal practice, but the letter he wrote Pierce gave him an opportunity to restate his views on the Declaration of Independence and slavery. In his Peoria speech he had compared the Declaration to a sheet anchor. Now he compared its author to Euclid: Jefferson's principles—that all men were equally endowed with certain basic rights—were "the definitions and axioms of free society." He ended with a lofty peroration: "All honor to Jefferson—to the man who, in the concrete pressure of a struggle for national independence by a single people, had the coolness, forecast and capacity to introduce into a merely revolutionary document an abstract truth, applicable to all men and all times." Lincoln had clearly labored over this paean; it was ready to be chiseled in stone—or printed in Republican newspapers, which in fact ran with it.

———

In the fall of 1859 came invitations to address Republicans throughout the Midwest. These Lincoln accepted, regardless of his legal practice. The fall was off-year election season, and he needed to be visible.

Douglas helped him plan his itinerary. The senator had published a defense of popular sovereignty in the September issue of *Harper's Magazine*, and that month Douglas spoke in Columbus and Cincinnati (Ohio was the third most populous state in the country, and a Republican and a Douglas Democrat were running against each other for governor). Lincoln followed Douglas to both cities and rebutted his *Harper's* article; even as the Lincoln/Douglas debates had begun years before their senate race, so now they continued after it.

The opinions of the two men on the future of slavery were unchanged: Douglas was for letting popular sovereignty determine it, Lincoln for containment and ultimate extinction.

The political trajectories of the two men had not changed since the fight over the Lecompton Constitution. In December 1858 southern Democrats had stripped Douglas of his chairmanship of the Committee on Territories as punishment for his aggressive anti-Lecompton stance. If Douglas were to reach the White House, it would have to be with northern support, including the support of Republicans. Although Douglas could scarcely hope for a Republican nomination after the spirited partisan race he had run in 1858, he might still steal the party's followers out from under its leadership. Lincoln was determined to stop him. In a letter to an Ohio politician he called Douglas "the most dangerous enemy of liberty, because the most insidious." In fighting to stop Douglas, he incidentally advanced himself.

At issue once again were the two men's portraits of the founders, and their own self-portraits as founders' sons. Their argument over slavery and politics had become a fratricidal contest over which of them was the Revolution's legitimate heir.

Douglas's article in *Harper's*, "The Dividing Line Between Federal and Local Authority: Popular Sovereignty in the Territories," was long— seventeen and a half double-column pages—but its point was simple: "The ideas and principles of the fathers of the Revolution" were identical to popular sovereignty, as expounded by Douglas. After a long survey of American legislation, going back beyond the founding to colonial times, Douglas distilled his version of the American creed: "The people of every separate political community (dependent colonies, Provinces and Territories, as well as sovereign states) have an inalienable right to govern themselves in respect to their internal polity." That included governing themselves in respect to slavery.

Douglas's founding fathers were permissive parents, as far as white men were concerned. White men should be able to do as they pleased with black men. Lincoln's founding fathers, by contrast, were lawgivers. They believed in sheet anchors and axioms; they laid down the law of liberty, based on human nature.

Lincoln had given the Republicans of Boston the Declaration; he now gave the Republicans of Ohio the Northwest Ordinance. It had, he said, an unimpeachable founding pedigree. The Ordinance had been "made by the very men who were the actors in the Revolution," and it had been ratified as the Constitution "was in process of being framed." What did it show? That when "the revolutionary heroes" considered whether slavery should go into the Northwest Territory, they forbade it. No popular sovereignty on this question for them: "From first to last, they clung to freedom."

In Cincinnati, Lincoln threw out a new idea, tying his belief in liberty to his Whiggish theories of work: "Whereas God Almighty has given every man one mouth to be fed, and one pair of hands adapted to furnish food for that mouth, if anything can be proved to be the will of Heaven, it is . . . that that mouth is to be fed with those hands, without being interfered with by any other man who has also his mouth to feed and his hands to labor with." He went on to add a joke: If God had intended to divide mankind into classes of drones and drudges, he would have given the first class mouths and no hands, and the second hands and no mouths.

This little set piece on hands and mouths was a gloss on Lincoln's moving image, two years earlier, of the black woman whose right to eat the bread she earned with her own hands equaled anyone else's. It was also his gloss on the Declaration of Independence. Jefferson had written that "all men . . . are endowed by their Creator with certain inalienable rights," among them "life, liberty and the pursuit of happiness." At first glance Lincoln's right to eat the bread one has earned may not seem as grand as Jefferson's triad of rights; but bread sustains life, liberty, and any pursuing of happiness anyone might do. Jefferson never worked with his hands, and Lincoln was not a very happy man, so they drew on different life experiences to illustrate their thoughts, but their thinking was essentially the same.

Ironically, Lincoln's test case for liberty evoked agricultural labor— before bakers make bread, farmers have to grow the wheat and millers have to turn it into flour. This was labor Lincoln loathed. But the source of his loathing was the fact that through his twenty-first year he had not been paid; thirty years later, he was able to sympathize with slaves who were in a similar position.

Finally, both Lincoln and Jefferson—though neither of them was a Christian—traced these rights to God.

———

That fall Lincoln got yet another speaking invitation, which he promptly accepted: it was to make his New York debut.

New York was the most populous city in the country. It was already a financial hub, and increasingly a cultural and media hub as well (*Harper's*, the magazine in which Douglas presented his self-justification, was published there; so was Greeley's *Tribune*). Lincoln's invitation, from New York–area Republicans, asked him to come to Brooklyn, across the East River, then a separate city, which was itself the country's third largest. Lincoln's venue was to be Plymouth Church, the pulpit of the Reverend Henry Ward Beecher, an ecclesiastical showman and abolitionist firebrand; the date was set for February 1860. Lincoln bought a new black suit for the occasion for $100, quite a sum. At the last minute the sponsors, hoping to lure a bigger crowd, moved the lecture to Manhattan, to Cooper Union, a free school for the working class.

Lincoln had told his sponsors that he would make a political speech. His mere presence in New York guaranteed that. New York State was the nation's largest, and a bastion of the Republican Party. The party leader there was the senior senator William Seward. Seward had several points in common with Lincoln: he was an ex-Whig; he was funny-looking—short rather than rail-tall, with a big nose and big ears; he was an indifferent dresser (one of his outfits was described as "a coat and trousers made apparently twenty years ago and by a bad tailor at that"). Seward had characterized the future of slavery and freedom in America in a phrase as portentous as the "house divided": the two systems, he said in an 1858 speech in Rochester, New York, were locked in an "irrepressible conflict."

But as of February 1860 Seward's reputation was already made, while Lincoln's was still being made. Seward, who was eight years older than Lincoln, had been a senator for a decade and governor of New York before that. His adviser and right hand was an Albany journalist and wire-puller who had the greatest name that has ever been, or ever will be, in American politics: Thurlow Weed. (*Thurlow*, the last name as first name, suggesting everything that inspires respect, from high ideals to cash on hand. *Weed*, what follows in every politician's footsteps, from backroom deals to stabs in the back.) Seward was the acknowledged front-runner for the Republican presidential nomination. To speak in Seward's back yard was, by definition, a raid. Lincoln would still aim his fire at Douglas, but other Republicans would now suffer by comparison. The better Lincoln looked against Douglas, the better he might look as a possible Republican candidate.

The New Yorkers who saw Lincoln on the Cooper Union stage had the same first impression of him that audiences always had. The adjectives scattered through one man's recollection of him sum it up: "weird . . . long . . . clumsy . . . gaunt." When Lincoln opened his mouth, a western whine came out. His speech, however, was his most carefully wrought so far, one of the best he would ever give. It was also his most thorough account of the founding fathers and their stance on slavery. At Cooper Union he would make his most elaborate case that he was the founders' son.

Lincoln's speech began with a technique borrowed from sermons: the preacher quotes a biblical text, then expounds on it. Lincoln's text came from one of Douglas's speeches in Ohio the past September. "Our fathers," Douglas said then, "when they framed the government under which we live, understood this question just as well, and even better, than we do now." "This question" was the one Douglas had addressed in his *Harper's* article: whether local authority (popular sovereignty) or federal authority controlled slavery in the territories. Douglas naturally thought "our fathers" understood it exactly as he did.

Lincoln announced that he "fully" agreed with Douglas's premise: "our fathers" did indeed understand that question as well or better than anyone in 1860. But he proposed to show that "our fathers" understood it not as Douglas did, but as Lincoln did.

First he defined his terms: for the purpose of answering Douglas's question, the "fathers" were the thirty-nine signers of the Constitution. They had written and endorsed the nation's fundamental law; they were the men who had "framed the government under which we live." Then for the next forty-five minutes Lincoln walked his audience through what exactly these men thought and did.

They had left a legislative trail thirty-six years long. Lincoln began with the Northwest Ordinance. Three fathers-to-be had voted in the old Congress for Jefferson's ban on trans-Appalachian slavery in 1784, and two more for the final bill banning it in the old Northwest in 1787. Then, in 1789, in the first Congress under the Constitution, sixteen fathers (six of them serving as representatives, ten as senators) voted to confirm the Northwest Ordinance; George Washington, the greatest father of them all, signed it into law as president.

In 1798 and 1804 Congress organized territories in the future states of Mississippi and Louisiana, places long marinated in slavery. But Congress nevertheless forbade any slaves to be imported into them from abroad, even though the slave trade was then still legal. Four fathers, all senators, approved these restrictions. Finally, in 1819, the fight over Missouri statehood began. One of the last fathers to hold public office, still serving in the Senate, voted consistently against the expansion of slavery.

Lincoln summed up: of the thirty-nine fathers "who framed the government under which we live," twenty-one had acted to ban or restrict slavery in territories. Some had done so more than once, as different bills came before them at different points in their careers. Sixteen of the fathers had never been in a position to vote on such questions, while two of them—a member of the old Congress in 1784, and a representative in 1819–1820—had indeed voted against restricting slavery in particular territories. But twenty-one out of thirty-nine was, as Lincoln said, "a clear majority."

Lincoln did not stop with this tally. Among the fathers who never voted one way or the other were "noted anti-slavery men": he mentioned

Benjamin Franklin and Alexander Hamilton (who had belonged to manumission societies in their home states) and Gouverneur Morris (who had assailed slavery, the slave trade, and the three-fifths rule in speeches during the Constitutional Convention). Surely, he argued, they would have sided with the twenty-one if they had had the chance.

The Taney Court had maintained in *Dred Scott* that the Fifth Amendment protected property in the territories, including slaves, and therefore that restrictions like the Missouri line were unconstitutional. But Lincoln pointed out that the first ten amendments had been passed by the same Congress that confirmed the Northwest Ordinance. "Is it not a little presumptuous . . . to affirm that the two things which that Congress deliberately framed and carried to maturity at the same time are absolutely inconsistent with each other?"

There was a dry wit in Lincoln's careful parsings—so dry as almost to have evaporated. But the force of the Cooper Union speech came not from humor, but from well-paced repetition. Lincoln turned pedantry into music. He ended his first example, of the three fathers who had voted to restrict slavery in 1784, in this way: "In their understanding, no line dividing local from federal authority, nor anything else, properly forbade the federal government to control as to slavery in federal territory." As the speech marched on, he rang that long formula, sometimes word for word, sometimes with slight variations, a dozen times, like a watchman tolling a bell. Shorter phrases—"our fathers," "the thirty-nine," "the government under which we live"—popped up, time after time, like grace notes.

But maybe the best metaphor for Lincoln's rhetoric at Cooper Union was not music, but wrestling. His absent opponent, Douglas, had unwisely given him a hold; Lincoln gripped him and threw him, again and again and again.

Lincoln devoted the second half of his speech to two appeals and a warning. He urged Republicans to avoid mere passion and ill-temper. He urged southerners to realize that Republicans did not mean to deprive them of "any right, plainly written down in the Constitution." ("Plainly written" was meant to exclude *Dred Scott*, which Lincoln considered a rogue decision.) His warning was that the Republicans would not relent in their efforts to restrict the spread of slavery. They would not relent because that was "the old policy of the fathers," and because that was the right policy. Lincoln's last sentence went straight from the Cooper Union stage to immortality (some typesetter, or perhaps Lincoln himself, capitalized the line when the speech was published): "LET US HAVE FAITH THAT RIGHT MAKES MIGHT, AND IN THAT FAITH LET US, TO THE END, DARE TO DO OUR DUTY AS WE UNDERSTAND IT."

The crowd gave him a long, hat-waving standing ovation. Afterward, the *New York Tribune*'s reporter, asked what he thought of the speaker, replied, stunned, "He's the greatest man since St. Paul."

———

Lincoln concluded his trip east with a swing through New England, to capitalize on the impression he had made in New York, then returned home to cram in some more legal work. His political contest with Douglas would continue through the fall and the presidential election, but Lincoln would give no more major speeches. The back-and-forth of the Lincoln-Douglas debates, which had begun in 1854, was done.

Lincoln had challenged Douglas in his home state, making himself the great Democrat's principal rival, even more than fellow Illinoisan Lyman Trumbull. Trumbull, not Lincoln, had made it to the Senate, but Lincoln, not Trumbull, had fought Douglas on the same podiums, as well as refuting his arguments from Peoria to Cooper Union.

Lincoln had kept Douglas and the national Republican Party apart. The marriage that eastern Republicans had fancied after Douglas denounced the Lecompton Constitution had been forestalled by the 1858 Senate race, while Douglas's seduction of potential Republican voters had been chilled by Lincoln's ongoing criticisms. Horace Greeley registered the change like a weather vane. In 1858 his newspaper had touted Douglas; in 1860 it reported the Cooper Union speech rapturously. Lincoln had gone from being dispensable to being praiseworthy.

Douglas raised Lincoln up to national prominence. Coming from any other state, a one-term congressman and local wheelhorse would have struggled in vain for national attention. As the gadfly of such an important Democrat, Lincoln became important himself.

Illinois also raised Lincoln up to national prominence. The 1856 election showed that Republicans could count on a solid North, Democrats on a solid South. James Buchanan had won the White House by carrying Illinois, Indiana, Pennsylvania, and New Jersey; Republicans would have to carry Pennsylvania plus at least one of the other middle states if they hoped to win in 1860. The Lincoln-Douglas debates had highlighted two contenders from a swing state.

Douglas had made, over and over, a powerful argument. The essence of the American system was self-government. Letting popular sovereignty determine whether slavery should exist in the territories was self-government in action. Douglas saw himself as the champion of the American ideal.

Lincoln had to make a relatively subtle counterargument. Self-government can undermine itself. He had made it most succinctly in Peoria: if a man governs himself, that is self-government, but if he governs another by slavery, that is despotism. Slavery had to be accepted where it was (a further subtlety), but to spread it willfully or allow it to be spread through indifference soiled republicanism.

Lincoln's cure for the disease of self-government was self-government. A towering genius, like Napoleon, might fix a broken system by overturning it and imposing a new one, controlled by himself. Lincoln used the means of ordinary politics, making his case on the hustings to voters in Illinois and, as soon as his speeches were reported and reprinted, throughout the North.

Thus Lincoln the reasoner. But there was another way to settle a disputed question. That was to ask your father. Lincoln had never asked Thomas Lincoln for much of anything. But he had found wiser and better fathers who were as serious, as curious, and as eloquent as he could ever hope to be. They had considered the questions of freedom and slavery, and they had come up with an answer. They believed that all men are created equal, and they meant to put slavery into the course of ultimate extinction.

They had fought for their answer in the Revolution, and they had put their answer into words—in the Declaration of Independence—and into action—in the Northwest Ordinance, in the Constitution (as read by Lincoln), and in other laws. Their answer was Lincoln's answer, not Douglas's.

When Lincoln was a baby, Henry Clay had called for a new race of heroes. Lincoln wanted a new race of heroes, too, so long as they would agree with the old race of heroes. As he put it at Cooper Union, "Let [us] speak as they spoke, and act as they acted."

Ten

THOMAS JEFFERSON AND THE DECLARATION OF INDEPENDENCE. THE TOWERING GENIUS (I)

B UT DID LINCOLN IN FACT SPEAK AND ACT AS THE FOUNDING fathers had? Did he rightly characterize their intentions and their legacy concerning slavery?

Lincoln had prepared for both the opening and closing speeches of his six-year debate with Douglas—Peoria and Cooper Union—by "nosing" in the Illinois state library for facts about the founding fathers. Thanks to modern editions of papers, letters, and diaries, we know much more about the founders than Lincoln did (in some ways, we know more about the founders than they themselves did, since they were not privy to each other's private papers). But by the mid-nineteenth century a fair amount was already on the record.

Lincoln owned a set of *Elliot's Debates*, an 1836 collection of documents about the writing and ratifying of the Constitution. The state library in Springfield owned James Madison's *Papers*, published in 1840, which included his copious notes on the Constitutional Convention. It also owned copies of the debates and proceedings of early Congresses, and the first biographies of Jefferson and Washington. These last were attempts at scholarly work, not tales *a la* Parson Weems, though sometimes the level of scholarship that went into them was not much higher. One early Washington biographer, Jared Sparks, had asked the elderly James Madison about a long unused draft of the First Inaugural Address that he had found in Washington's papers. When Madison (who had ghosted the shorter version that Washington actually delivered) told him the draft was not important, Sparks sliced it into pieces and handed them out to friends as autograph samples.

When Lincoln's Cooper Union speech was published in September 1860 in a pamphlet supervised by Lincoln himself, it appeared with a preface hailing it as a model of "patient research and historical labor" and a long train of historical footnotes. Lincoln had disposed of his own notes by the time the speech went to press, but two young Republican lawyers in New York had compiled a set of their own, which Lincoln glanced over and approved. Though the notes as published were not his research, they represented the kind of research he had done.

He had made a few mistakes. When he delivered the speech, he included among the signers of the Constitution who had voted for the Northwest Ordinance in 1787 Abraham Baldwin of Georgia. Baldwin was simultaneously a delegate to Congress, which then sat in New York, and to the Constitutional Convention, meeting in Philadelphia. Other men with the same double assignment shuttled between the two cities. But Baldwin, once he arrived in Philadelphia in June, stayed put, and thus did not vote when Congress passed the Ordinance in

July. Lincoln's New York assistants caught the error, and the pamphlet version of the speech corrected it.

But Lincoln made two other mistakes that were not caught. He said that George Read of Delaware had agreed to bar the importation of foreign slaves into the Mississippi Territory in 1798. But Read had retired from Congress in 1793. The Read who was serving five years later was Jacob Read, a senator from South Carolina and no relation to George. Lincoln had confused the two; so did his helpers in New York.

To demonstrate Washington's opposition to the spread of slavery, Lincoln referred to a letter he had written to Lafayette in 1798, praising the Northwest Ordinance. The relevant lines were quoted in a footnote: "I consider it [the Ordinance] a wise measure . . . and I trust we shall have a confederation of free states." But this letter to Lafayette is bogus. Washington did write his old friend in 1798, after Lafayette was released from an Austrian jail where he had been held as a prisoner of war (revolutionary France and Europe's monarchies had been fighting for half a dozen years). But Washington's letter was devoted to congratulations on Lafayette's freedom and comments on American politics, with not a word about the Northwest Ordinance.

Lincoln and his footnote-makers may have gotten the supposed Washington letter from a speech Lyman Trumbull had given in the Senate in December 1859. Or they may have spotted it in abolitionist publications, where it appeared earlier in the 1850s. The Washington letter was pure projection: wishing that a great man thought one's thoughts, and believed one's beliefs. (Washington was a common hook for such daydreams: in the 1850s Catholics tweaked the story that he had prayed at Valley Forge; in their version, his prayer was answered by the Virgin Mary.)

These were not gross errors. Both Abraham Baldwin and George Read had voted to restrict slavery during their actual careers in Congress, and thus they legitimately belonged on Lincoln's tally of twenty-one like-minded "fathers." Washington had criticized slavery in letters that were authentic, and Lincoln's young assistants quoted one such in their notes: "There is not a man living who wishes more sincerely than I do to see a plan adopted for the abolition of it," Washington wrote Robert Morris in 1786. If anything these small blunders add the charm of effort to Lincoln's research. He had no staff (except Herndon), and his last-minute helpers in New York worked without search engines. The lawyer-politician and his admirers had to hit the books themselves and root around. The wonder is that they found so much.

More serious than stray mistakes was the tone of special pleading that Lincoln used whenever he discussed the founders and slavery. He was a patriot appealing to the founders, a son appealing to his fathers. But he was also a lawyer making a case. He leaned hard on all the evidence that backed him up, and ignored or hastened over any evidence that didn't.

In his swing through the Midwest at the end of 1859, he described "the early days of the Republic" as an era of wholehearted enthusiasm for liberty: "You may examine the debates under the Confederation, in the [Constitutional] Convention . . . and in the first session of Congress and you will not find a single man saying that Slavery is a good thing."

But this was not true. Lincoln had read in Madison's *Papers* the debates that took place at the Constitutional Convention over the slave trade and the three-fifths rule. This was where he found the blazing antislavery polemics of Gouverneur Morris, the peg-legged delegate from Pennsylvania who had called slavery "a nefarious institution," and "the curse of heaven on the states where it prevailed." This was where he read Madison himself insisting, Virginia slave-owner though he was, that it would be "wrong to admit in the Constitution the idea that there could be property in men" (hence the veiled language the Constitution used to discuss it).

But this was also where he encountered John Rutledge of South Carolina—the lawyer, planter, and patriot who served his state as governor during the Revolution and had his estate confiscated by the occupying British. Rutledge declared at the Constitutional Convention that "religion and humanity had nothing to do" with the slave trade. "Interest alone is the governing principle with nations"—and with states. The people of North and South Carolina and Georgia would be "fools" if they allowed the slave trade to be restricted. Northern states, meanwhile, should welcome the slave trade, since more slave labor "will increase the commodities of which they will become the carriers [merchants]."

Rutledge had not quite said that slavery and the slave trade were good things, but he certainly thought they were good for business. He would not defend them on the grounds of religion and humanity; he simply put interest above religion and humanity. And he insisted that his state and its neighbors would not sign the Constitution unless their interest in the slave trade was protected. (In the end, the Constitution guaranteed the slave trade until 1808—Article I, Section 9—and further stipulated that this provision could not be amended—Article V.) Lincoln admitted in his reckoning of the "fathers" at Cooper Union that Rutledge could not be counted as an antislavery man.

One delegate to the first Congress had gone even further than Rutledge. In February 1789, nineteen years ahead of the constitutional guarantee, Quakers petitioned Congress to end the slave trade (they urged Congress to overlook such "seeming impediments"). They were answered by Rep. James Jackson of Georgia. Jackson had moved to Savannah from England in 1772 at the age of fifteen and had fought in the Revolution. In rebutting the Quakers, he went beyond the letter of the law to defend slavery itself. "Why do these men set themselves up in such a particular manner against slavery? Do they understand the rights of mankind, and the disposition of Providence better than others? If they were to consult [the Bible] they will find that slavery is not only allowed but commended. . . . If they fully examine the subject, they will find that slavery has been no novel doctrine since the days of Cain." Anything supported by both the Bible and Cain must be a good thing.

Jackson's remarks were immortalized when Benjamin Franklin, in his last journalistic spoof, claimed to have found a seventeenth-century speech by a Barbary pirate defending the enslavement of Christians in similar terms: "How grossly are they mistaken in imagining slavery to be disallowed by the Alcoran . . . since it is well known from it that God has given the world and all that it contains to his faithful Musselmen." Lincoln probably never read Franklin's satire, but he might have stumbled across Jackson's remarks when he was hunting for the first Congress's votes on confirming the Northwest Ordinance. Jackson and other southerners were content to keep slavery out of the old Northwest, but they thought, and sometimes said, even in the early days of the republic, that it was a good thing for themselves.

But the most problematic of the founders, for Lincoln, was one of the very greatest: Thomas Jefferson.

———

Jefferson died on July 4, 1826, when Lincoln was seventeen years old. Death linked him with the great event of his life, the Declaration of Independence, which Congress had approved fifty years earlier. George Washington was bound for the pantheon from the moment he became commander in chief. Thomas Paine, after he authored *The Age of Reason*, could only belong to the pantheon of village skeptics. Jefferson's death on the jubilee of his Declaration was his apotheosis. Four months later, in November 1826, his apotheosis took visible form when John Trumbull's heroic painting, *The Declaration of Independence*, was hung in the Capitol Rotunda. In it, Jefferson—taller than his fellow founders, and brighter (he wears a red waistcoat)—hands his immortal document to Congress, and to posterity.

But between 1776 and 1826, Jefferson had had a busy and controversial career. In 1791–1792 he had founded, with the help of James Madison, America's first national political party, the Republicans (under Andrew Jackson they would change their name to the Democrats). Their struggles with their rivals, the Federalists, were as bitter as anything in the history of American politics apart from the Civil War. One story can stand for all: In 1798 a Republican congressman spat in the face of a Federalist colleague on the floor of the House. A few days later, the

Federalist caned the Republican, who defended himself with a pair of tongs from the cloakroom fireplace.

Jefferson's party triumphed, giving the White House to him and to his fellow Virginians James Madison and James Monroe for two terms each—twenty-four years (1801–1825) of government by friends, neighbors, and soul-mates. But the long reign of the first Republican Party was not cloudless. Jefferson's first term (1801–1805) glittered: he cut taxes, enjoyed peace, and bought Louisiana. But his second term (1805–1809) ended in a funk: his efforts to keep America out of renewed European wars by imposing a trade embargo made him odious. Jefferson left the White House in March 1809, when Lincoln was only three weeks old, a worn-out man. His long retirement at Monticello was a period of silent recovery.

In 1829, three years after his apotheosis, the first partial edition of his letters and papers appeared. Before that, stray letters of his had been published by indiscreet correspondents. But the appearance of a mass of his writing, followed over the years by other editions and biographies, took Jefferson out of both the shadows of retirement and the glory of death and revived all the controversies of his life.

In 1870 William Herndon tried to explain to a would-be Lincoln biographer what Lincoln had thought of his great predecessor. "Mr. Lincoln," he wrote, "hated Thomas Jefferson as a man—rather, as a politician, and yet the highest compliment I ever heard or read of his was paid to the memory of Jefferson." By "highest compliment," Herndon meant the paean Lincoln sent the Bostonians who had invited him to celebrate Jefferson's birthday in 1859 ("All honor to Jefferson . . . "). But what of the hatred?

Herndon stumbled at the very start of his sentence, writing first that Lincoln hated the man, then deciding that it was really the politician that he found hateful. But man and politician were fused in people's opinions of Jefferson. Critics and admirers alike had been trying for years to explain his actions in the light of his character; yet both character and actions could defy explanation. It wasn't just that people sometimes disagreed with Jefferson; rather, that Jefferson so often seemed to disagree with himself.

Alexander Hamilton, Jefferson's most eloquent enemy, called him crafty, unscrupulous, dishonest, and "a contemptible hypocrite." Madison, who loved Jefferson above all men, admitted that he shared, with "others of great genius," a "habit . . . of expressing in strong and round terms impressions of the moment." We might love the impressions of some of Jefferson's moments, but then there were the impressions of other, less lovable, moments; and in between were all the moments when he was neither strong nor round, but elusive, maybe even evasive. Who that thought seriously about Jefferson did not hate him, at least a little?

What mattered most to Lincoln, and what was the source of both the hatred Herndon said he felt and the honor he publicly offered, was Jefferson's shifting thoughts about slavery.

———

Early in Jefferson's career, in 1784, he had proposed that the old Congress keep slavery out of the West. Lincoln alluded to Jefferson's proposal in his two historical speeches, Peoria and Cooper Union.

In the same decade, Jefferson had issued an almost biblical warning of what might happen if Congress and the states did not act to end slavery. In 1780 a French friend asked him to write a description of his state; Jefferson's *Notes on the State of Virginia* was published in 1787. There he wrote: "I tremble for my country when I reflect that God is just; that his justice cannot sleep forever; that . . . a revolution in the wheel of fortune, an exchange of situation is among possible events; that it may become probable by supernatural interference! The Almighty has no attribute which can take side with us in such a contest." Lincoln knew of this warning, too, and quoted the opening clause several times.

Jefferson's proposal to keep slavery out of the West reflected the boldness of a revolutionary, and his vision of a race war suggested the foresight of a prophet and the fears of a guilty soul. Yet as the years passed, Jefferson's initiative, if not his apprehensions, seemed to melt away. What happened?

One thing that was widely supposed to have happened was that Jefferson took his slave Sally Hemings as a concubine. The affair was supposed to have begun while he was in France, several years after the death of his wife, and to have produced a handful of children. Federalist journalists made the story a scandal during his presidency. Abolitionists repeated it after his death, more in sorrow than in anger (slavery, in their telling, had corrupted even the author of the Declaration). Foreigners irked by canting Americans thought it was hilarious. The Irish poet Thomas Moore and the English novelist Charles Dickens both mocked Jefferson for dreaming "of freedom in a slave's embrace." In the election of 1860 Democrats would accuse Lincoln of having repeated this crack himself, back in his days as a Whig. Lincoln denied it, and indeed, personal attacks of that sort were not his style; he would needle Democrats for their racial and sexual anxieties, but his own wariness about sex made him slow to defame individuals.

Jefferson's mixed thoughts about slavery could be read in his words, without rummaging in his sheets.

One of his classic mixed messages appeared in an 1814 letter to Edward Coles, the future governor of Illinois. The letter and its publication were tangled up in the story of Coles's career. Coles was the young neighbor and disciple of Jefferson who decided to leave Virginia out of disgust with slavery, and liberate his slaves. Coles wrote Jefferson in 1814 outlining his plans and urging his idol to call for manumission in their home state, so that Virginia might "put into complete practice those hallowed principles contained in that renowned Declaration, of which you were the immortal author." Jefferson wrote back the next month, approving Coles's sentiments and hoping he would stay in Virginia and lead the fight for manumission himself.

Coles would lead a fight for freedom, not in Virginia, but in Illinois, where he moved with his former slaves in 1819. Shortly after they arrived, they faced a campaign to make the new state a slave state.

(The Northwest Ordinance guaranteed its freedom so long as it was a territory, but a state could choose slavery or freedom at will.) Coles ran for governor to keep Illinois free, and after a long struggle he beat the supporters of slavery in his new home.

In 1824 the letter he had gotten from Jefferson a decade earlier appeared in an Illinois newspaper (probably leaked by Coles himself). Jefferson's old letter began with a condemnation of slavery, written in a tone, simultaneously sweet and lofty, that was peculiar to Jefferson at his best. "The love of justice and the love of country plead equally the cause of these people, and it is a moral reproach to us that they should have pleaded it so long in vain." Justice and patriotism pleaded for liberty; so did Jefferson; the ongoing bondage of slaves and the acquiescence of free men were alike deplorable. Here was approval, given in advance, of Coles's course as a liberator and a politician.

But then Jefferson's tone wobbled. "I had always hoped," he continued, "that the younger generation" would oppose "oppression wherever found." Jefferson himself, however, was too old to play any public role. Manumission in Virginia "shall have all my prayers, and these are the only weapons of an old man." Jefferson shifted the responsibility to Coles, and ended with an exhortation from the Bible (Galatians 6:9): "Be not weary in well doing."

Jefferson's letter was reprinted in newspapers and magazines over the years, and finally appeared in a biography in 1858. It was taken as proof of his commitment, even in retirement, to the cause of liberty. But what a feeble and unreliable advocate he had become; his letter amounted to saying, *I'm with you but I won't do anything to show it.*

Back in 1814 Coles had written a reply to Jefferson that was respectful, yet devastating. The old, he argued, were the best leaders in such a cause. "To effect so great and difficult an object great and extensive powers both of mind and influence are required. . . . I looked to you, my dear sir, as the first of our aged worthies, to awaken our fellow Citizens." Then a quiet stinger: Benjamin Franklin was politically active past *your* age. (At the time of the Coles correspondence, Jefferson was

seventy-one; when Franklin had been seventy-one, he had yet to negotiate the Treaty of Paris, sign the Constitution—or mock James Jackson.)
Coles's letters to Jefferson were not published in Lincoln's lifetime, but
his point was obvious from Jefferson's own letter: Jefferson was not too
weary for well doing, he was simply unwilling to do any more good.

Jefferson wrote another ambiguous letter in 1820 in the homestretch
of the Missouri crisis. Jefferson's correspondent this time was John
Holmes, a politician in the first Republican Party. The letter, published
by Holmes shortly after Jefferson's death, became famous for two pul-
sating phrases, almost proverbial in their simplicity: Jefferson likened
the Missouri crisis to "a fire-bell in the night" that "awakened and filled
me with terror"; and he said, of slavery, "We have the wolf by the ears,
and we can neither hold him nor safely let him go."

Jefferson still professed to Holmes a hope that slaves might one day
be free. "The cession of that kind of property, for so it is misnamed"—
slave owner that he was, Jefferson still denied that it was right to call
slaves property—"would not cost me a second thought if, in that way,
a general emancipation and expatriation could be effected." *Free them
and send them somewhere else; I'll even give up my own, if everybody
else does.*

But what to do until then? As of 1820, Jefferson's answer was "diffusion." If slavery were spread over the West, instead of being concentrated in the old South, it would be weakened. Wherever slavery was
thin on the ground (or so went the theory), individual slaves were better
treated and owners felt freer to manumit.

The diffusion theory reflected a truth: slavery was most brutal where
it was most dense, as on the sugar islands of the Caribbean. But it ignored another truth: slavery was devilishly hard to extirpate wherever
it got a foothold. New York State had begun a process of gradual manumission in 1799, but according to its timetable, the state's last slaves
would not be free until 1827.

Diffusion also mocked the early career of Thomas Jefferson. In 1784
he had wanted to confine slavery east of the Appalachians. By 1820 he

was asking for it to be spread to the Rockies. Diffusion was a confession of futility and despair.

Jefferson's letter to Coles was readily available in Lincoln's lifetime. Since Coles was a major figure in the history of freedom in Illinois, it is unlikely that Lincoln would have missed it. It is certain that he knew of the letter to John Holmes, for he quoted the most memorable portion of it—from the "fire-bell in the night" to "the wolf by the ears"—in his 1852 eulogy on Henry Clay, to illustrate the dangers that the Missouri Compromise had averted.

But Lincoln stopped quoting before Jefferson's plea for the diffusion of slavery: he wanted Jefferson showing how momentous Clay's task had been, not Jefferson arguing for a policy that flouted the principle of the Missouri line.

———

Small wonder that Lincoln looked, beyond these fits and starts of a man made even more fitful with age, to the great deed of his first manhood—the Declaration of Independence.

A motion to declare American independence had been made in the Continental Congress in June 1776, after more than a year of revolutionary warfare. It passed on July 2, which John Adams ever after argued should be Independence Day. The Declaration itself was approved two days later. (Adams, as if in defiance of his own argument, would die on July 4, 1826, the same day as Jefferson.)

The task of writing a formal statement had been given to a committee of five: Jefferson, Adams, Franklin, Robert Livingston, and Roger Sherman. The last two let the first three do all the work, and Adams and Franklin, in turn, passed the job to their thirty-three-year-old colleague, suggesting only a few small changes. (Jefferson called the truths "we hold" in his second paragraph "sacred and undeniable"; scientist Franklin made them "self-evident.")

Jefferson felt all the tenderness of an artist toward his composition. From July 2 to 4, Congress made significant cuts to his draft, especially in the long indictment of George III and in the peroration. Jefferson squirmed as his colleagues hacked, which gave rise to one of Franklin's most charming stories. The sage told Jefferson about a man who wanted to open a hat shop, with a sign showing a picture of a hat and the words: "John Thompson, Hatter, makes and sells hats for ready money." After various friends offered their suggestions for tightening the wording of his sign, all that was left was the picture of the hat and "John Thompson." Jefferson had enough humor to tell this story on himself years later; enough pride always to prefer his own first draft.

But Jefferson also maintained that the importance of the Declaration was not owing to his artistry, but to the ideas it set forth, which were not his but everyone's. The Declaration laid out "the common sense of the subject," as he put it in a letter a year before he died, the subject being "our rights" and how Britain had violated them. Jefferson meant the Declaration to be "an expression of the American mind. . . . All its authority rests then on the harmonizing sentiments of the day, whether expressed in conversation, in letters, printed essays, or in the elementary books of public right, such as Aristotle, Cicero, Locke, Sidney, etc." (You have to love the polymath's magisterial "etc.") *Pay no attention to me,* Jefferson was saying, *I was only the oracle of public opinion and eternal truths.*

There was one other feature of the Declaration that made it compelling: all thirteen states, colonies no more, had endorsed it. New York abstained on the July 2 vote for independence because its delegates to Congress lacked instructions from their home government, but as soon as they got them, they, too, signed the Declaration. (This was more unanimity than the Constitution would get at its birth: when George Washington was inaugurated as first president, North Carolina and Rhode Island had still not ratified.)

Jefferson claimed he had expressed the American mind; Congress proved it by signing off on his handiwork—literally. Its members signed off on the sublime rhetoric of his preamble: all the phrases about just powers and the consent of the governed; about self-evident truths and inalienable rights; about the laws of nature and nature's God. They signed off on his assertion that "all men are created equal." Congress, when it was wielding its editorial pen, made only tiny changes to Jefferson's opening section, and no change at all to the declaration of all men's equality. Everyone accepted it, even though every state then permitted slavery. John Rutledge's younger brother, Edward, accepted it; he signed for South Carolina. There it was, in black and white; there it was, for whites and blacks.

Lincoln the artist surely responded to Jefferson's rhetoric. Lincoln liked a fair amount of junk, as many artists do. But he had also been training his ear on Paine and Byron, Shakespeare and the Bible. He would have thrilled to Jefferson's snare drum rolls. But Jefferson could strike up the band even when he was being lazy or fearful (fire-bell in the night, wolf by the ears). Lincoln had reasons besides rhetoric to revere the Declaration.

Lincoln the lawyer and the politician appreciated the force of those thirteen sets of signatures, representing all the states. According to the rules of the Continental Congress, where major decisions required unanimity, that made a contract; according to the ordinary rules of nose-counting, thirteen out of thirteen was a pretty impressive majority.

Lincoln the reasoner seized on the Declaration's self-evident truths. They were the starting point of the American project, and they described human nature. They were "the definitions and axioms of free society," as Lincoln told the Bostonians, and they were—or had been—the axioms of American society. The truths of the Declaration were Lincoln's great backstop against all the founders' miscellaneous utterances that his research had not discovered, or that he, having discovered them, had chosen to minimize. Whatever their stray opinions or their stubborn practice, at the moment of America's creation Jefferson had proposed that all men are created equal, and in Congress assembled all the United States had agreed.

The Declaration had been the high point of Jefferson's life, as he himself acknowledged; it was the first of the three achievements he listed on his tombstone, "because by these, as testimonials that I have

Lincoln read Parson Weems's *Life of Washington* "away back in my childhood." He was inspired by Washington's struggle for liberty . . . *Washington Crossing the Delaware*, by Emanuel Gottlieb Leutze. IMAGE COPYRIGHT © THE METROPOLITAN MUSEUM OF ART. IMAGE SOURCE: ART RESOURCE, NY

. . . less by Washington as a good boy. Shown here: young George, his father, and the cherry tree. COURTESY OF THE EVERETT COLLECTION

Thomas Paine, whose attack on revealed religion, *The Age of Reason*, impressed Lincoln as a young man. Copy by Auguste Millière, after an engraving by William Sharp, after George Romney. © NATIONAL PORTRAIT GALLERY, LONDON

Paine and friend: a hostile view. COURTESY OF THE AMERICAN PHILOSOPHICAL SOCIETY.

MAD TOM in A RAGE

Lincoln honored Thomas Jefferson, despite his contradictions. Jefferson's greatest moment: presenting the Declaration of Independence to Congress. PAINTING BY JOHN TRUMBULL, ARCHITECT OF THE CAPITOL

A PHILOSOPHIC COCK

A not-great moment: Jefferson and Sally Hemings as poultry. *A Philosophic Cock*, by James Akin. COURTESY OF THE AMERICAN ANTIQUARIAN SOCIETY

Joshua Speed, Lincoln's best friend and fellow sufferer from "nervous debility." ABRAHAM LINCOLN PRESIDENTIAL LIBRARY AND MUSEUM (ALPLM)

William Herndon, Lincoln's law partner, disciple, and biographer. SPECIAL COLLECTIONS RESEARCH CENTER, UNIVERSITY OF CHICAGO LIBRARY

Rep. Alexander Stephens gave what Lincoln called "the very best speech of an hour's length I ever heard." He later served as vice president of the Confederacy. PHOTOGRAPH BY MATHEW B. BRADY. © CORBIS

(*Left*) Lincoln's favorite poet was Lord Byron, whose dark moods matched his own. Portrait by Thomas Philips. © BETTMANN/CORBIS

(*Right*) Artemus Ward. Lincoln read Ward and other humorists aloud to his cabinet. COURTESY OF THE HOUSE DIVIDED PROJECT AT DICKINSON COLLEGE

Lincoln's favorite play was *Macbeth*. He read a scene from it after the fall of Richmond. *The Weird Sisters*, by Henry Fuseli. ROYAL SHAKE-SPEARE COMPANY COLLECTION/THE BRIDGEMAN ART LIBRARY

Sarah Bush Lincoln, beloved stepmother, encouraged Lincoln's reading as a boy and feared for his life after he was elected president. NATIONAL ARCHIVES PHOTO 306-PSD-58-14438

Mary Todd Lincoln, wife, shared Lincoln's love of politics and poetry. They also shared difficult temperaments. PHOTOGRAPH BY MATHEW B. BRADY. © CORBIS

Eliza Gurney, Quaker, prayed in the White House that Lincoln might be "strengthened and refreshed" by the river of life. COURTESY OF THE HOUSE DIVIDED PROJECT AT DICKINSON COLLEGE

Lincoln dismissed John Brown as a zealot and a failure. *Tragic Prelude*, by John Steuart Curry. KANSAS STATE HISTORICAL SOCIETY

John Wilkes Booth decided to kill Lincoln after he called for "nigger citizenship" (Booth's words). CHICAGO HISTORY MUSEUM

Lincoln reading the Emancipation Proclamation to his cabinet. This painting was presented to Congress on Lincoln's birthday, 1878. *First Reading of the Emancipation Proclamation of President Lincoln*, by Francis Bicknell Carpenter. US Senate Collection

Icons together. *Washington and Lincoln, Apotheosis.* Library of Congress

lived, I wish most to be remembered." The high point of Jefferson's life became the lodestar of Lincoln's.

Lincoln claimed repeatedly that his political rivals rejected the Declaration; they wanted to "cancel and tear [it] to pieces," as he had put it in his Peoria speech. Very few actually attacked it outright (that was to come), but there were many who reinterpreted it. Perhaps Jefferson's assertion of equality was only racial. Stephen Douglas had argued at the debate at Jonesboro that the equality mentioned in the Declaration applied only to whites, not to Negroes, Indians, Fijians, or Malays. Or perhaps the assertion of equality was merely political. Eleven months after the Cooper Union speech, Jefferson Davis, leaving the US Senate because his state, Mississippi, had seceded, would argue that the equality mentioned in the Declaration applied only to citizens. "The communities" of America "were declaring their independence" in 1776 and stating that all "men of the political community" could aspire to any office. They were laying out the rules of a game in which slaves were not players.

Lincoln dismissed such talk. Jefferson had been writing about men, and he meant all men. Jefferson, it is true, did not want free black men to live in America (he had told John Holmes he was for "expatriation")—a view Lincoln shared. But Jefferson—and Lincoln—did not believe that black men, or any men, could justly be held as slaves.

Lincoln had said of the founding fathers, in his 1859 speech in Columbus, that "from first to last, they clung to freedom." Jefferson proclaimed freedom at the first, in the Declaration, and to the last, he clung to it. Wearily, with bad faith, by his fingernails—but he clung to it. Lincoln, in turn, clung to Jefferson. He did it for his own advantage, to borrow Jefferson's luster, and to wrong-foot the Democrats, Jefferson's political heirs. But he also clung to Jefferson to save him. Sons need their fathers to be at their best; sometimes they need them to be better than they actually were.

Lincoln never spared much thought for Thomas Lincoln, but he gave thought, sympathy, and assistance to Thomas Jefferson.

In Lincoln's long debate with Douglas, there were several noteworthy things he did not say, and arguments he did not make.

He did not dwell on the horrors of slavery. In 1855, he recalled the coffle of slaves he had seen in 1841 on a boat in the Ohio River, chained like fish on a line. Then, in the depths of depression, he had marveled at how happy even slaves could make themselves. Recalling the sight fourteen years later, he described it as a "torment" to him. But this was in a letter to his old friend Joshua Speed; the two were arguing about politics, Lincoln denouncing the Kansas-Nebraska Act, Speed replying as a slave-owning Kentucky Whig. Lincoln's talk about how tormented slavery made him feel was not for publication, and Lincoln did not say such things in front of audiences.

Nor did he arraign the behavior of slaveholders. In his Peoria speech, he had even declared, "They are just what we would be in their situation." Like causes produce like effects. If you are born into a slave society, you will likely support slavery. All the more important, then, to prevent slavery from expanding. Lincoln preferred to focus on the political problem at hand, which was rallying the opinion of the North to a policy of containment. Berating southerners would have been a distraction.

There were other public figures making the arguments Lincoln did not make. In May 1856, just as the Illinois Republican Party was about to hold its first convention, Charles Sumner, a senator from Massachusetts, gave a two-day speech in Congress attacking slavery root and branch. His occasion was the nascent violence in Kansas, where proslavery gangs from Missouri had shot antislavery settlers and trashed Lawrence, an antislavery town. Sumner defended freedom in Kansas in fiery terms; he also excoriated proslavery southern politicians by name, comparing one of his colleagues, Senator Andrew Butler of South Carolina, to Don Quixote (a madman) and slavery to his harlot. Days later, the senator's nephew, Preston Brooks, a congressman from South Carolina, accosted Sumner in the Senate and beat him over the head with a gold-tipped cane until Sumner lost consciousness; a friend of Brooks's, also a congressman, held off onlookers trying to intervene at pistol point. The two congressmen rumbling on the House floor in 1798 had nothing on this.

Sumner was intelligent and eloquent. He was also arrogant, inhumane, and so in love with his own ideas and voice that he could become unbalanced. Brooks was a thug who showed himself to be a coward: he backed out of a duel with a northern congressman, an ally of Sumner's, who was a crack shot.

Two days after the caning of Sumner, John Brown and his sons took five proslavery settlers in Kansas from their homes in the middle of the night and killed them with broadswords.

———

John Brown, born in Connecticut in 1800, was a tanner and wool-dealer by profession, an abolitionist by destiny. The lynching of the abolitionist editor Elijah Lovejoy in 1837 radicalized him; in the 1840s, he became active in the Underground Railroad. Brown came to live in the heart of the movement that Lincoln had always deplored.

Brown was one of many combatants drawn to Kansas. After his quintuple murder, he fought in several pitched battles with marauders from Missouri, acquitting himself well. In 1856, he returned east to raise money for a new plan. He had a network of respectable backers, including the Transcendentalist minister Theodore Parker; he knew the black abolitionist Frederick Douglass, and he visited freed slaves in Canada. Who knew what about Brown's new plan and what they said to Brown about it is still not certain; Brown was intending to liberate slaves in the South.

In October 1859 Brown and eighteen followers seized the federal armory at Harpers Ferry, Virginia (now West Virginia). They rounded up some hostages, including a distant relative of George Washington's who lived in the area, and planned to distribute the armory's weapons to local slaves. But Brown and his men were surrounded, first by militia, then by a party of Marines, and after two days of fighting, he was taken. Brown was tried for murder, conspiracy, and treason against the State of Virginia and hanged early in December.

Brown iconography typically highlights his Old Testament beard. In John Steuart Curry's mural of him in the Kansas State Capitol, his beard mimics the swirls of a tornado filling the sky behind and above him. But his last statement to the court was not stormy, but calm: "[If I] had interfered in behalf of the rich, the powerful, the intelligent, the so-called great . . . it would have been all right; and every man in this court would have deemed it an act worthy of reward rather than punishment." Brown then indicated the court's Bible. "[That] teaches me . . . to 'remember them that are in bonds, as bound with them' [Hebrews 13:3]. I endeavored to act up to that instruction."

Brown became a political lightning rod. Abolitionists considered him a hero and a martyr. In Concord, Massachusetts, the smell of other people's blood filled Henry David Thoreau with rapture: "For once we are lifted out of the trivialness and dust of politics into the region of truth and manhood." Back in the trivialness and dust of politics, Democrats tried to pin Brown on the Republican Party, which tried to have nothing to do with him.

Lincoln's late 1859 swing through the Midwest took him to Kansas, where the subject of Brown was unavoidable. He gave Brown credit for courage, but condemned him as violent, criminal, and insane. He elaborated at Cooper Union. In his passage of reassurance addressed to the South, he denied that the Republican Party had any responsibility for slave revolts, even indirectly. It intended no "interference whatever with your slaves, or with you about your slaves. Surely this does not encourage them to revolt." He added a mild joke: the only way slaves ever even heard of the Republican Party was when they overheard their masters denounce it. Slave revolts, Lincoln went on more sternly, were an inescapable feature of life in slave societies. He mentioned Nat Turner's rebellion in 1831—Had the Republican Party caused that?

Lincoln ended by comparing Brown's effort to failed assassinations: Guy Fawkes's plot to blow up James I, or a recent attempt on the life of Napoleon III: "An enthusiast broods over the oppression of a people till he fancies himself commissioned by Heaven to liberate them. He ventures the attempt, which ends in little else than his own execution." So Lincoln dismissed Brown as a zealot and a failure. So he also managed to equate slaveholders with royalty, a favorite maneuver of his.

Brown was more than an ordinary abolitionist. He was willing to free slaves by force, if necessary, and to do it not just in Kansas, but in the most venerable state in the South. Brown claimed he was not for a general uprising or a race war, but it is hard to imagine a program of armed raids leading to anything else.

Was Brown the towering genius, the Napoleonic destroyer that Lincoln had feared twenty years earlier? If drama belongs to rhetoric, Brown was a rhetorical genius. After six years of speeches, Lincoln had only just come to national attention. With a few bold strokes, Brown had riveted the world.

Brown was outside the channels of ordinary politics. He was not interested in Lincoln or Seward or Douglas, the Senate or the White House; he wanted to free slaves, and he set about it in the most direct way. But the towering genius is not apolitical. He wants a new politics that he controls. Brown hoped to lead a considerable organization, and before Harpers Ferry he even drew up a constitution for it, with an elaborate structure of congress, courts, and cabinet. (His lawyer would introduce it at his trial in an attempt to establish an insanity defense: only a lunatic could have drawn up such a plan.) But Brown's rules were for an underground movement engaged in a guerrilla struggle, not laws for a new America.

Brown was too religious for politics—"commissioned by Heaven," as Lincoln put it. A Puritan, as Thoreau said, more precisely: "He died lately in the time of Cromwell, but he reappeared here." Brown answered his call, and passed into legend.

Temperamentally and philosophically, Lincoln and Brown were strangers: Lincoln was humorous, Brown intent; Lincoln skeptical, Brown pious; Lincoln a lawyer-politician, Brown a lawbreaker and a killer. Lincoln preferred, as he had throughout his long debate with Douglas, to engage with Jefferson and the other founders, not such as Brown. But other candidates for the role of the towering genius would appear during the 1860s.

Eleven

THE ELECTION OF 1860.
THE TOWERING GENIUS
(II)

T HE COOPER UNION ADDRESS KICKED OFF LINCOLN'S RUN
for the White House; the next fourteen months were consumed
with presidential politics and presidential responsibilities. But even in
this rush the founders appeared in his thoughts, speeches, and jokes,
and in the speeches of his rivals; they were by now woven into his life.

———

Presidential contests in Lincoln's lifetime were much shorter than they
are today. The nomination struggles that now take place over a months-
long parade of caucuses and primaries were then compressed into a day,
at worst two, of balloting at political conventions. The campaigns that
followed were also, in one respect, quieter. Would-be candidates might

set themselves up with significant speeches before the contest formally began; Lincoln could point to a string of them going back six years. But once nominations were made, candidates were expected to maintain a dignified silence, while their supporters maintained a raucous hoopla in their behalf.

Despite his new prominence, Lincoln was not among the front-runners for the Republican nomination in 1860. The leader among the leaders was William Seward. Besides a long career and a base in the nation's largest state, Seward was blessed with a winning personality, genial and charming. He was one of those men on whom fortune smiled, and who smiled back. But even the blessed acquire enemies in politics. Horace Greeley, who had long yearned to run for office himself in New York without a hint of encouragement from Seward, had become one such (one reason he had puffed the Cooper Union speech was simply to spite Seward).

Seward was also weighed down by one of his convictions. The Republican Party was a coalition of disparate elements, united by the issue of slavery expansion. As Lincoln had put it in the "House Divided" speech, "we gathered from the four winds." Among the disparate elements were antislavery veterans of the American or Know-Nothing Party, which had flourished and died in the mid-1850s. But Seward was boldly pro-immigrant, going so far in his days as governor of New York to call for state support of Catholic schools. No nativist could ever be comfortable with him.

The opposite drawback affected Edward Bates, an elderly lawyer and politician from Missouri. Bates might give the Republicans clout in the border states, and Greeley (whatever nice things he said about the Cooper Union speech) backed Bates for the nomination for that reason. But Bates had backed the American Party in 1856, and German Americans, who were a mainstay of the Republican Party in the Midwest, would not forgive him for it.

Salmon Portland Chase had been the first Republican governor of Ohio, and Ohio was the third-largest state in the country. Chase was intelligent, energetic, and idealistic—his opposition to slavery had taken him into the Liberty and Free Soil parties in the 1840s, before he became a Free Soil Democrat, then a Republican. But he was both humorless and sharp-elbowed. His rise to office in Ohio had left a trail of bruised competitors. His own state would not be united behind him.

Simon Cameron was a senator from Pennsylvania, the nation's second-largest state. He was a wheeler-dealer, turning alternately—and profitably—from politics to business and back. One deal from the 1830s had given him an unfortunate nickname: he was thought to have cheated Indians whose claims on the federal government he had been appointed to settle, and was known thereafter as the Great Winnebago Chieftain. Pennsylvanians were used to him, and someone like Thurlow Weed could understand him, but ordinary voters outside his home state might look askance.

Years later, Leonard Swett, a veteran of Illinois politics, would attribute Lincoln's success to shrewd positioning: "His tactics were, to get himself in the right place and remain there . . . until events would find him in that place." Certainly Lincoln occupied a surprisingly strong position as 1860 unfolded.

His stature as a politician was noticeable, but not so noticeable as to appear threatening to Seward and the other front-runners. His 1858 Senate race and the Cooper Union speech had put him on the national stage—just. He had the support of those who knew him well—Illinois Republicans were solid for him—and competitors who did not yet know him well did not pay enough attention to him.

He had devoted his energies to slavery expansion, the issue that defined his party—the "question about which all true men do care," he had called it at Cooper Union—without blotting his record with inconvenient positions on other issues. Illinoisans knew he was opposed to Know-Nothingism—in one of his speeches during his 1858 Senate race, he said that all "liberty-loving men," German, Irish, and Scandinavian as well as old-stock Americans, shared the principles of the Declaration of

Independence. But he did not have a record of pro-immigrant policies to match Seward's.

Being from Illinois was one of his strongest attributes. The 1860 census would show that Illinois had become the fourth-largest state in the nation, and Chicago the ninth-largest city (up from twenty-fourth a decade earlier). The Democrats had carried Illinois in the 1856 presidential election, as they had in every contest since statehood. But the Republican and American parties together had outpolled them. If the Republicans could carry the state in 1860, they would have a fighting chance in the Electoral College.

Yet, despite what Swett said, a lot of work went into Lincoln's presidential campaign. Norman Judd, a Lincoln man who served on the Republican National Committee, had lobbied to put the party's convention in Chicago. A home-state advantage was a great leg-up for a candidate. Your operatives knew the setting, your supporters were on the spot to hold rallies and make noise. The other city in the running for the convention had been St. Louis, which would have been a boon to Bates, but the less obvious contender took the prize.

Early in May, before the national convention, Illinois Republicans held a state party convention in Decatur, where Lincoln acquired an image that would serve him through Chicago and beyond: his cousin John Hanks marched into the hall carrying a rail that Lincoln had supposedly split decades ago. Lincoln, who was on the podium at the time, admitted he could not recognize that particular rail, but said he had split "many better ones" in his day. So Lincoln the Railsplitter was born. The drudgery he had fled as a young man now came back to benefit him. His rube/boob persona became heroic; paintings and cartoons showed him with his maul, swinging away. Twenty years after William Henry Harrison's Log Cabin Campaign, Lincoln supporters would run their own version.

The Republican convention ran from May 16 to 18. Candidates in those days might attend state conventions, but they could not, with propriety, appear at national conventions, so Lincoln stayed in Springfield while his associates took care of business in Chicago. They did a superb job. Judd, who was in charge of seating arrangements for the convention, placed the New York and Pennsylvania delegations far apart, so that the Seward and Cameron camps could not easily communicate. Lincoln supporters flooded the city thanks to cut rates offered by Illinois railroads (now friendlier than they had been two years earlier); fake convention tickets were printed for them to ensure that all Lincoln supporters had seats in the spectator galleries.

Lincoln, like all statesmen, solemnly told his minions to make no deals that would bind him later, and his minions, like all minions, did what they had to do. A wonderful story describes Lincoln's floor manager, David Davis, having been reminded in mid-deal of their candidate's prohibition, howling "Lincoln ain't here!" and dealing anyway. Lincoln biographer David Herbert Donald doubts that it is true. But he does concede that Davis promised the Pennsylvania delegation that there would be a spot in the cabinet for Cameron if its votes swung to Lincoln after the first ballot.

The convention made its choice on May 18, its last day. With 233 votes needed to win the nomination, Seward led on the first ballot, with 173½ (states with more delegates than votes cast fractional votes). Lincoln was second with 102. Cameron, Chase, and Bates had about 50 votes each, and there were scattered votes for half a dozen others. On the second ballot Seward rose to 184½, but Lincoln, buoyed by an infusion of Pennsylvanians plus defectors from other candidates, was right behind him with 181. Seward had the lead, but Lincoln had the momentum. On the third ballot Lincoln rose to 231½; a switch of four votes in Ohio put him over the top and triggered a stampede of last-minute conversions.

Lincoln spent the day in Springfield following events by telegram, chatting with cronies, and playing handball in a vacant lot. Christopher Brown, a young lawyer who was one of his handball partners, recalled that Lincoln told one of his off-color jokes to pass the time. This one was about George Washington, the Revolutionary War hero Ethan Allen, and a "back house" (outhouse):

It appears that shortly after we had peace with England, Mr. Allen
had occasion to visit England, and while [he was] there the English
took great pleasure in teasing him and trying to make fun of the
Americans, and General Washington in particular, and one day they
got a picture of General Washington, and hung it up [in] the back
house where Mr. Allen could see it. And they finally asked Mr. Allen
if he saw that picture of his friend in the back house.

Mr. Allen said no, but said he thought that it was a very appropriate [place] for an Englishman to keep it.

"Why?" they asked.

"For," said Mr. Allen, "there is nothing that will make an Englishman shit so quick as the sight of General Washington."

Ethan Allen had been a British prisoner of war for a year and a half
during the Revolution, and for part of that time he was held in England.
But the rest of the story belonged to art rather than history.

It is obvious why Lincoln was telling jokes at such a time. He was
"nervous, fidgety," the young lawyer recalled. When Fate comes to the
front door, some men whistle, some men whittle; Lincoln told jokes.
It is equally obvious why he told this particular joke. If he were nominated, he might sit where Washington sat. And with the country in the
state it was in, that was enough to send any man to the back house.

————

The Democrats had already held their convention in Charleston, South
Carolina, at the end of April, and it was a debacle. The party's rules
required its nominee to win not a majority but two-thirds of the convention's votes—202 out of 303. Since James Buchanan, the incumbent,
had long ago announced that he would serve only one term, Stephen
Douglas was the front-runner. But his fight against the Lecompton
Constitution and his failed dalliance with the Republicans had made
him odious to southern Democrats, and there were enough of these at
the convention to make a two-thirds vote for him virtually impossible.

Southern hardliners, meanwhile, demanded that the party platform call on the federal government to protect property in slaves in the territories. Such a law would give substance to Chief Justice Taney's opinion that the Fifth Amendment sheltered slavery there; it would be *Dred Scott* with teeth, and the end of popular sovereignty. Douglas could not possibly accept such a plank without forfeiting all self-respect.

Douglas led for two days of balloting, hovering between 145 and 152½ votes. A handful of other candidates trailed behind him. Fifty disgruntled southern delegates simply left the convention, awaiting events in another hall in Charleston. After fifty-seven ballots, the exhausted Democrats voted to reassemble in Baltimore in June. There, after two more ballots and more walkouts by southerners, the delegates who remained declared Douglas their candidate. The southerners, meeting in another venue in Baltimore, then tapped the current vice president, John Breckinridge, a thirty-nine-year-old Kentuckian, as theirs. Douglas would stand for popular sovereignty, Breckinridge for expanding slavery into the territories under the aegis of the federal government.

There had been yet another convention in May, mostly of old Whigs, meeting in Baltimore. They called themselves the Constitutional Union Party, and announced that their sole aim was to uphold the Constitution, the Union, and the laws. Noble goals. But what should the laws be? That they would not say. Fanatical in their moderation, they tapped John Bell, a sixty-four-year-old Whig and former senator from Tennessee.

Faced with a split in the Democratic Party, Lincoln seemed bound for victory, unless the plethora of candidates kept him from winning a majority in the Electoral College, which would throw the choice to the House. This had already happened in the election of 1824, and some politicians still active remembered the occasion.

The four candidates divided the national political map on sectional lines. Breckinridge and Bell would make pitiful showings in most northern states; Lincoln would win a mere 1,000 votes each in Virginia and in his birthplace, Kentucky, and was not even on the ballot in any state farther south. Douglas was the only man running nationwide. His campaign was both desperate and heroic. Breaking all precedent, he barnstormed the country, as if he could buck the odds by sheer effort. The other candidates relied on their party's platforms and on their own past statements to make their views known.

Some of the most interesting past statements had been uttered by Bell's running mate, Edward Everett, an old Massachusetts Whig. Everett, a former congressman, governor, and diplomat, had since 1856 served as the self-appointed posthumous spokesman for George Washington. He had crisscrossed the country giving an oration entitled "The Character of George Washington" dozens of times, donating his fees to an association of patriotic ladies who aimed to buy a now-decrepit Mount Vernon from Washington's great-grand-nephew, and restore it. Everett's speech was a charitable enterprise; it was also an effort to summon the nation to Washington's principles, as Everett understood them. "The Character of George Washington" was a much better speech than the one Robert Winthrop had given at the laying of the cornerstone of the Washington Monument. Everett compared Washington intelligently and favorably to other titans of the eighteenth century: the Duke of Marlborough, Peter and Frederick the Great, Napoleon. But Everett's political message for America was the same as Winthrop's: Washington was the icon of unity—unity over everything, unity without content: "O, that from the heavens to which he has ascended, his voice might even now be heard and teach us to unite again in the brotherhood of love, as we are united on one precious remembrance of the past." It was the best that those who merely idolized Washington could offer. It was paltry enough.

Lincoln's near-silence as the campaign proceeded was dictated not only by custom, but also by memories of the blunders of Henry Clay, who had lost a nomination in 1840 and an election in 1844 with his too-clever maneuvers to win southern votes. Now was the time for rallies with rails.

Lincoln did decide to make an important change to his image: he grew a beard. The inspiration is usually assigned to a letter he received in October from Grace Bedell, an eleven-year-old girl in New York State, who told him that "all the ladies like whiskers and they would tease their husband's [sic] to vote for you." We are used to the result, but Grace's advice was unfortunate. Of all the facial hair of the mid-nineteenth century, whose now looks good? Only Ulysses Grant's trim number, and Grant was quite a handsome man to begin with. Shaven, Lincoln's face had acquired an austere plainness like that of a cigar store Indian or an Easter Island head. With a beard he looked like an Easter Island head that had been rolled over the floor of a barber shop.

But the beard served two functions. It made him seem venerable— the admirer of the founding fathers could look even more fatherly than his fifty-one years. The beard was also a way to hide. There was no hiding from what was to come, of course, but whiskers sprouted in midlife can give the bearer an illusion of security.

———

Early signs were good for Lincoln. The practice of holding national and state elections on the same day was not yet universal, so state elections that occurred in October served as weather vanes for the national vote the following month. In October 1860 Republicans did well in Pennsylvania and Indiana. Douglas learned the news while campaigning in Iowa. "Mr. Lincoln is the next president," he said nobly. "We must try to save the union." Whereupon he made a swing through the South, condemning secession.

Lincoln passed the national Election Day, November 6, in Springfield. Everything went as the Republicans had hoped. One hundred and fifty-two electoral votes were needed for victory. Bell carried 12.5 percent of the popular vote and three states—Virginia, Kentucky, and Tennessee—for 39 electoral votes. Breckinridge carried just over 18 percent of the popular vote and eleven states—the remainder of the South plus Delaware and Maryland—for 72 electoral votes. Douglas won almost 30 percent of the popular vote, but his support was so diffuse that he managed to carry only two states—Missouri and New

Jersey—for 12 electoral votes. (He should have gotten 16 electoral votes, but confusion among rival anti-Lincoln slates in New Jersey allowed Lincoln to pick up 4 electoral votes there.)

Two states had joined the Union since the last presidential election, Oregon and Minnesota, and Lincoln carried them both. He carried all the states that John Frémont had—New England, New York, Ohio, and the upper Midwest. Besides his 4 electoral votes in New Jersey, he also carried Pennsylvania, Indiana, and California. He carried Illinois, the first non-Democratic presidential candidate to do so, beating Douglas by almost 51 percent to 47 percent. He won nearly 40 percent of the popular vote nationwide and 180 electoral votes.

If every man who voted for Douglas, Breckinridge, or Bell had voted for only one of them, Lincoln would have lost Oregon, California, and his 4 electoral votes in New Jersey, but he would still have won 169 electoral votes and the White House.

———

Presidents then were inaugurated in March, not January, so the transition to a new administration lasted four months, not two. But then, as now, the mad rush of the presidency began the moment the votes were tabulated. From the day Lincoln became president-elect in Springfield until the end of his life, he was like a man lashed to a locomotive in full view of all he passed, with no chance to get off or even pause.

In some ways, a mid-nineteenth-century president had less to do than a contemporary one. The premodern state was smaller, and the president's role in it was more restricted. Lincoln, to take only one example, would never travel abroad to meet a foreign head of state. Then, however, a president's time was filled with other kinds of business that his successors are spared. Since there was no civil service, every federal job was potentially a patronage appointment, and although cabinet members and lesser functionaries usually parceled such jobs out, the final responsibility rested with the president. The parade of job-seekers began immediately and never ceased.

An object lesson in the politics of patronage was given to Charles Francis Adams, son and grandson of presidents, early in the Lincoln administration. Adams, a Republican congressman from Massachusetts, went to the White House with the new secretary of state to consult about the job he was about to embark upon: minister to Britain. Adams was astonished when Lincoln, after a few words, turned to the secretary of state and boasted that he had just settled a job in the Chicago post office. Lincoln in fact had his priorities straight: patronage was the glue that held a political party together, and a united party was the foundation of a successful administration. (Both of Adams's president forebears, John and John Quincy, had been unpopular one-termers; perhaps they should have paid more attention to post-office appointments.)

Official etiquette in the nineteenth century was simple, and security almost nonexistent, so ordinary citizens as well as office-seekers could see Lincoln in person. The flow of visitors could be regulated somewhat by his personal secretaries—he had two, both young men who had started working for him in Springfield: John G. Nicolay, a German-American journalist, and John Hay, a recent Brown graduate. They would follow him to Washington, where they would be assisted by a tiny White House staff. But the influx with which they contended was endless. Admirers and critics, the prominent and the obscure, the eloquent and the tongue-tied, crackpots and the merely curious, flocked around Lincoln like flies.

Lincoln's first task before his inauguration was to pick a cabinet. (The Republican convention had tapped Hannibal Hamlin, a Maine senator, as his running mate, but nineteenth-century vice presidents had little to do, unless the president died.) Lincoln's first choices for his cabinet, made while he was still in Springfield, were two of the men he had beaten for the Republican nomination, Seward and Bates. Seward, the defeated front-runner, got the most important of cabinet posts, secretary of state (it was he who would accompany Adams to the White House for his lesson in politics). Bates became attorney general.

Later, Chase and Cameron, the other also-rans, were included, Chase as treasury secretary and Cameron as secretary of war.

One slot, postmaster general, went in effect to a family. Francis Blair Sr., a feisty sixty-nine-year-old, was a veteran of the Jackson administration, who in the preceding decade had become a Free Soil Democrat, then a Republican. His personality and his politics were shared by his sons, Francis Jr. (who had argued Dred Scott's case before the Supreme Court) and Montgomery. Francis Sr. and Jr. lived in Maryland; Montgomery was a Republican congressman from Missouri. Hay compared the Blair family to a "close corporation" (the Blairs answered only to each other). Lincoln made Montgomery his postmaster general. By turning to the Blairs, Lincoln repaired his breach with the Whig bugaboo, Andrew Jackson. Jackson's martial firmness, it seemed, could be useful when invoked in causes of which one approved.

Two Republican politicians who had swung their delegations to Lincoln at the Chicago convention—Gideon Welles of Connecticut and Caleb Smith of Indiana—rounded out the cabinet as secretaries of the navy and the interior.

Lincoln, like most presidents, tried to pick a cabinet that balanced regions. The border states (Bates and Blair), the Midwest (Chase and Smith), Pennsylvania (Cameron), New York (Seward), and New England (Welles) were all represented. Only the South was unaccounted for. As the first-time president of a new party, Lincoln also sought a balance of prior party affiliations. Seward, Bates, and Smith were ex-Whigs; Chase, Cameron, Blair, and Welles ex-Democrats. When Thurlow Weed complained that this gave the ex-Democrats a four-to-three edge, Lincoln reminded him that he had forgotten one ex-Whig: "*I* expect to be there."

Harder to balance were the personalities and ideologies of these men. Smith was a cipher and Bates was old, but the others bustled with contending demands and visions. How should the new administration handle southern hardliners? The Blairs, asking themselves *What would Jackson do?*, were for confrontation, the sooner the better. Until southerners experienced a "decisive defeat," wrote Montgomery Blair, they would believe "one southern man is equal to half a dozen Yankees." But Seward, who had coined the phrase "irrepressible conflict," now wanted to repress the conflict; before taking the reins of the State Department, he gave a speech in the Senate calling for conciliation, concession, and extending "the right hand of peace" to a disaffected South. Lincoln reserved that decision for himself.

Seward, meanwhile, would not extend the right hand of peace to Chase. Each man recognized in the other the desire to be first among equals, and Seward went so far as to tell Lincoln, as inauguration day approached, that he could not serve in the cabinet after all (by which he meant he could not serve in a cabinet alongside Chase). Lincoln won Seward back, first by ignoring him, then by asking him to reconsider. Ignoring Seward gave him time to think; asking him to reconsider gave Seward a token of respect. Seward finally agreed to give in and become secretary of state.

One of Lincoln's first jobs for Denton Offut three decades earlier had been to maneuver thirty hogs onto one flatboat. He would face similar tasks many, many times with the members of his cabinet.

The knottiest personal disputes of the next four years would be those that pitted some of these men against Lincoln himself. So many of Lincoln's associates had wanted to be in his place; some of them never acknowledged that he deserved to be in his place. Lincoln believed he deserved it, and this was the bitterest pill the envious had to swallow.

It was "absurd," Hay would write after Lincoln's death, to call him "a modest man." Beneath the self-mocking stories and the rube/boob persona, Lincoln knew he had reached the White House as a result of six concentrated years of thinking and speaking, persuading and working. He, not his rivals, deserved to be the founders' successor, in large part because he, not they, understood the founders better. Of course he had moments of trepidation, when he told Washington-in-the-back-house jokes and tried to hide his face—he would have been insane not to feel them—but he believed that he had earned his moment, and that he was a better man for this crisis than any of the men around him. What

Hay called his "unconscious assumption of superiority" ate at the minds of some of them like a canker. After a brief spell of disappointment, Seward embraced the role of helper, of assistant—of inferiority. Chase never did.

Doris Kearns Goodwin analyzed Lincoln's cabinet as a team of rivals, a phrase that has been picked up by political commentators and management texts as a recipe for success—a model to be emulated. But in 1860 a team of rivals had only bad precedents. Washington's first cabinet, with Jefferson at State and Hamilton at Treasury, was the first and greatest team of rivals. Washington got good service out of both men. But neither he nor they suspected there would be any rivalry when he first appointed them; the two secretaries became estranged only over time, as Hamilton favored commerce and Britain, Jefferson farming and the French Revolution. Their feuding, once it commenced, made life hell for all concerned. Presidents who were less politic or less fortunate had not been able to manage internecine rivalry at all. John Adams presided over a rebellious cabinet that fought him at every turn (they were all Federalists, but who was a better Federalist?); Andrew Jackson's cabinet was wracked by personal quarrels (the secretary of war's wife was thought, by the wives of all the other secretaries, to be a loose woman); Harrison's unlike-minded vice president, John Tyler, single-handedly derailed the Whig Party after Harrison's death. All this was the common lore of American politics; the fate of the Harrison administration was a painful memory for ex-Whigs.

Lincoln was driven to pick a team of rivals by the necessities of a new party in a time of upheaval. To manage them, he had to employ all the arts he had acquired years ago in Illinois, avoiding duels and sharing out congressional nominations—only now he was playing at the highest level, and any mistake could be dire.

———

In the midst of these personnel decisions, Lincoln exchanged some letters with his past.

Alexander Stephens, the Georgia Whig whose philippic on the Mexican War Lincoln had called the best hour-long speech he had ever heard, had continued serving in the House until 1859. He had become a Democrat after the Whigs collapsed, but had maintained his Whiggish nationalism. Lincoln's election had not distressed him. Privately he wrote a fellow Georgian that his old colleague was "not a bad man" and might make an even better president than Millard Fillmore. On November 14 Stephens appeared before the Georgia legislature to argue that "the election of no man, constitutionally chosen, is sufficient cause for any state to separate from the union."

Lincoln felt the lack of a southerner in his cabinet and considered asking Stephens to be secretary of the navy. Perhaps to break the ice after eleven years, Lincoln wrote him from Springfield asking for a copy of his speech to the legislature. Stephens's reply evidently mentioned the peril facing the country.

Peril indeed. On November 9 the South Carolina legislature had resolved that the election of "Abram [sic] Lincoln" was an act of "open and avowed hostility" to the slaveholding states. Six weeks later, on December 20, a state convention declared that "the union now subsisting between South Carolina and other states, under the name of 'The United States of America,' is hereby dissolved."

States had challenged the federal government several times in American history. During the administration of John Adams, Virginia and Kentucky, led by James Madison and Thomas Jefferson, had called on the states to interpose their authority against the Alien and Sedition Acts, laws the Republicans considered unconstitutional. During the administration of James Madison, Federalists returned the favor, calling a convention of New England states in Hartford, Connecticut, to condemn the War of 1812. Both episodes had stopped at the stage of posturing, thanks to changes in the political scene: the Republican Party had managed to beat Adams in the election of 1800 and repeal the odious acts; the Federalists collapsed after Madison's war ended in victory at the Battle of New Orleans.

During the Nullification Crisis of 1832, South Carolina had asserted a right to nullify the tariff, a federal law. In his eulogy for Henry Clay, the man who had resolved that crisis, Lincoln simply assumed that South Carolina was peculiar, calling it a hotbed of "political eccentricities and heresies." But never had that state gone so far as secession.

On December 22 Lincoln wrote Stephens, assuring him that the incoming administration had no intention of interfering with the slaves of southerners: "The South would be in no more danger in this respect than it was in the days of Washington." But Stephens wanted more. Both North and South were being driven by "passions," he wrote back on December 30, yet no one was trying to allay them. He gave John Brown's raid on Harpers Ferry the year before as an example: it had filled the South with fear, yet it had not been condemned by "any of the leading members" of the Republican Party. Stephens wanted Lincoln as president-elect to do so. He ended with a Bible verse, Proverbs 25:11: "A word fitly spoken by you now would be like 'apples of gold in pictures of silver.'"

The problem with Stephens's plea was that Lincoln had already answered it. He had called John Brown violent, criminal, insane, and a failure. He had assured the South, as recently as Cooper Union, that Republicans intended no interference "whatever" with their slaves. He had said in the "House Divided" speech that the nation could not endure half slave and half free, but he had explained subsequently that its time of full freedom might take a century to arrive. Asking him to repeat what he had already said was a tic, a nervous ritual. Lincoln had his own Bible verse to characterize such requests, which he had given to another anxious southern correspondent, a minister in Tennessee: "If they hear not Moses and the prophets, neither will they be persuaded though one rose from the dead" (Luke 16:31).

Stephens's last-minute plea ignored the issue that did separate Lincoln and the South. Slavery was not a good thing protected by the laws, and disallowed only in certain states; it was a bad thing, to be discouraged by the laws and guaranteed only in certain states. Lincoln spelled it out in his letter of the 22nd: "You think slavery is *right* and ought to be extended, while we think it is *wrong* and ought to be restricted. That I suppose is the rub."

Lincoln and Stephens wrote no more, but Stephens would soon have another chance to express himself publicly on the peril facing the country.

The New Year came. South Carolina had accompanied her November 9 resolutions with an appeal for "the cooperation of her sister slaveholding states." In January 1861 five states answered South Carolina's call: Mississippi seceded on the 9th, Florida on the 10th, and Alabama on the 11th. Alabama's ordinance of secession gave as a justification "the election of Abraham Lincoln . . . by a sectional party avowedly hostile to [our] domestic institutions." Georgia followed on the 19th, and Louisiana on the 26th.

South Carolina was no longer an outlier, but a leader. The South felt a sense of encirclement that few in the North, and almost no one in the Republican Party, understood. The House had had a majority of free-state congressmen for years. With the admission of Kansas as a free state on January 29, in addition to California, Minnesota, and Oregon in the 1850s, the Senate's balance of free and slave states had vanished forever, unless there was sweeping American expansion in Central America and the Caribbean. Now an antislavery northern party was about to move into the White House, from which position it could begin slowly reshaping the courts. Since the South stood alone in fact, perhaps its only safety was to make a formal break.

On January 31 Lincoln visited his past, going to Coles County, Illinois, to see his stepmother. Sarah Bush Lincoln was then seventy-two years old. Years later, she would say that she had not wanted her stepson to be president. "When he came down to see me after he was elected . . . something told me that something would befall Abe and that I should see him no more." She recollected her fears after he had died; very likely his death altered her recollection. But Lincoln lived in a superstitious world. In the White House his wife would consult mediums who contacted the spirits of the dead; that was rather modern in the mid-nineteenth century, almost scientific. Lincoln, for all his skepticism, bore traces of an older world of folklore. He believed in the efficacy of mad stones (hairballs from the innards of deer that reputedly cured bites and poisonings); he examined disturbing dreams for portents. Perhaps his stepmother felt some unease, which events chanced to confirm.

Back in Springfield Lincoln rented his house, wrapped up his law business, and bade farewell to the loyal Herndon. He left town by train on February 11, the day before his fifty-second birthday; it was cloudy and wet. "I go," he said in brief remarks, "to assume a task more difficult than that which devolved upon General Washington." No joking about back houses; this was serious—serious enough to invoke God. "Unless the great God who assisted him shall be with me and aid me, I must fail. . . . Let us all pray that the God of our fathers may not forsake us now."

Lincoln's trip to Washington was deliberately indirect. In twelve days he passed through seven states—Illinois, Indiana, Ohio, Pennsylvania, New York, New Jersey, and Maryland. There was some relaxation—he saw a new Verdi opera, *Un Ballo in Maschera* in New York—and some alarm—he hurried through Maryland in the dead of night to frustrate a supposed plot to assassinate him in Baltimore. But his primary purposes were dramatic and political. He spoke repeatedly, not saying anything new, or even much at all, but enough to secure his base and to reassure all who needed, and would accept, reassurance.

In the most historic spots he recapitulated his many efforts to connect himself to the founding fathers. On February 21, in Trenton, New Jersey, he recalled what Parson Weems had taught him about Washington's desperate battle there: "I recollect thinking then, boy even though I was, that there must have been something more than common that those men struggled for." This was his answer to the Washington idolaters, Robert Winthrop and Edward Everett, whose Washington fought merely for unity. Lincoln's Washington fought for liberty.

On February 22, in Independence Hall in Philadelphia, Lincoln recalled a founding document: "I have never had a feeling politically that did not spring from the sentiments embodied in the Declaration of Independence," he said. This was permissible hyperbole; although he had not referred to the Declaration in any serious way before his 1852 eulogy for Henry Clay, he had referred to it repeatedly since then. "What great principle," he went on, "kept this Confederacy so long together[?] It was not the mere matter of the separation of the colonies from the mother land; but something in the Declaration giving liberty, not alone to the people of this country, but hope to the world for all future time." This was his answer to Jefferson Davis and Stephen Douglas. The Declaration was not only an act of separation or a declaration of equality for white people. It was both of those things. But America's claim to independence, and the white man's claim to equality, rested on all men's equal right to liberty.

———

Lincoln arrived in Washington on February 23. On the same day, Texas voters ratified an ordinance of secession.

Meetings, receptions, discussions, rumors, crowds; all the madness of Springfield repeated and magnified by the normal hubbub of the capital and the abnormal shriek of a country splitting. Lincoln stayed at the Willard Hotel until he could move up the street into the White House.

Inauguration day was March 4, which began under clouds but cleared up in time for the ceremony. Lieutenant General Winfield Scott, still in active service at age seventy-four, had posted sharpshooters on nearby rooftops and watched the proceedings with his staff from a carriage stationed in a side street, ready for any emergency. If any rebels showed their heads, he had assured Lincoln that he would "blow them to hell."

Lincoln gave his Inaugural Address on a platform at the East Portico of the Capitol, the preferred location for inaugurations for the previous twenty years. He was introduced by an old political colleague, Edward

Baker, who had moved to Oregon and become a senator. He felt some confusion on rising to speak, in setting aside his top hat and cane, gaudy and unfamiliar appurtenances for him; Stephen Douglas, who sat on the podium, took them from him.

Lincoln's address, at 3,600 words, was rather long for an inaugural, but the state of the nation demanded it.

He began by declaring what he had written privately to Stephens: slavery was safe in the South. To prove it, he quoted himself from the Lincoln-Douglas debates in 1858: "I have no purpose, directly or indirectly, to interfere with the institution of slavery in the states where it exists. I believe I have no right to do so, and I have no inclination to do so."

He then addressed the secession crisis. He started by saying that he held "the union of these states" to be "perpetual." He offered several reasons, one from logic, one from law, and a number from history.

Lincoln the logician argued that no government ever provided for its own dismemberment. Leagues and alliances might dissolve, but they were not governments. "Perpetuity is implied, if not expressed," by the nature of government itself.

Lincoln the lawyer added that if government were a mere contract, would not all the parties have to consent to its dissolution?

Lincoln the historian traced the Union back through the Revolution to its earliest stirrings. The Union had come into being in the First Continental Congress, in 1774; it was "matured" by the Declaration and "further matured" by the Articles of Confederation, the country's first constitution, which had been in force from 1781 until 1788. (The Articles had asserted that "each state retains its sovereignty, freedom and independence," but they had also several times described the confederation as "perpetual.") He ended with the Preamble to the Constitution, which looked to a "more perfect" union. "But," he noted, "if destruction of the union . . . be lawfully possible, the union is *less* perfect."

This risked being arid, but it was very Lincolnian: trying to nail down principles, axioms, starting points.

Lincoln touched on several specific issues, trying, with varying degrees of success, to be mollifying. Some of the seceding states had complained of the difficulty of retrieving fugitive slaves, as guaranteed by the Constitution (Article IV, Section 2). Lincoln honored the guarantee. But he asked if there might not be "safeguards" (i.e., trials) to ensure that free blacks were not wrongfully seized by slave-catchers. Henry Clay had wanted such a provision in the federal fugitive slave law that was part of the Compromise of 1850, but it had not been incorporated into the final bill. No secessionist now would accept such a thing.

Lincoln proposed "to hold, occupy and possess the property and places belonging to the government." In an early draft, he had said he would "reclaim" property that had fallen to secessionists. Since that would have committed him to a battle over every post office in the Deep South, he took that pledge out. The final version would be sufficient cause for disagreement.

He iterated his views on the Supreme Court and the *Dred Scott* decision. The Supreme Court, he said, had the final word on cases brought before it, and its judgments were entitled to "very high respect and consideration" thereafter. But the people should not defer in every subsequent case or policy decision to "that eminent tribunal." Chief Justice Taney, about to turn eighty-four, and looking like "a galvanized corpse," sat on the podium behind Lincoln. He kept his thoughts to himself.

Lincoln mentioned a proposed constitutional amendment that was being discussed in the corridors of the Capitol as a possible compromise. It would be the Thirteenth Amendment, and it would declare that the federal government could never interfere with slavery in the states where it existed. Lincoln said he believed that was "implied constitutional law already," and so he had no objection to putting it in writing.

As he concluded he called on God. Lincoln asked Him to speak not through Bible verses, and certainly not through direct commands *a la* John Brown, but through politics and political history. "If the Almighty Ruler of nations . . . be on your side of the North, or on yours of the South," His will would "surely prevail by the judgment of this great tribunal, the American people." This was more facile than Lincoln's invocation of God as he left Springfield three weeks earlier. Then he had admitted that he needed God's help. Now he pretended that God might go either way, although—if God truly spoke through the American people—He had already voted for Lincoln.

Lincoln ended not with God, but with an appeal to the founding fathers. Logic, law, history, politics, and theology were all very well. But Seward, after reading an early version of the speech, had urged Lincoln to add a last paragraph of emotion and poetry, and offered his own draft. Lincoln had polished Seward's words, and read his own version now: "I am loath to close. We are not enemies, but friends. We must not be enemies. . . . The mystic chords of memory, stretching from every battle-field and patriot grave, to every living heart and hearthstone all over this broad land, will yet swell the chorus of the union when again touched, as surely they will be, by the better angels of our nature."

A *chord* (spelled with an *h*) now means three or more notes played together. Chords in music are the building blocks of harmony (or the weapons of dissonance). But Lincoln used *chords* in an older sense, to mean the strings of an instrument. His instrument was the remembering mind, which clung to the founders and the Revolution, to all that they had fought for and all that it meant. This was not the poetry of the Lyceum Address, in which the founders were dead, but the poetry of Lincoln's plea to the court for Rebecca Thomas, the old widow; the poetry of all his rhetoric about the Fourth of July, the Declaration, and the Battle of Trenton. See what they did for us, see what we have: their sacrifices made our peace and prosperity, their labor gave us our lives.

The chief justice administered the oath of office, and Lincoln became the sixteenth president. Not enough angels would touch his chords.

———

Before the war began there came another notable speech, by Alexander Stephens.

Stephens attended the January convention called by the State of Georgia to decide whether or not it should secede, where he argued to the last for patience and compromise. But when the convention voted to leave the Union, Stephens supported his state and secession. He served in a provisional Confederate congress that met in Montgomery, Alabama, in February, and was chosen by it to be the new Confederacy's vice president. Jefferson Davis of Mississippi, former congressman, senator, and secretary of war, was chosen as president. Davis had been a lifelong Democrat; Stephens would represent former Whigs.

On March 21 Stephens spoke to a reception in his honor in Savannah. His remarks appear to have been impromptu, but Stephens, as Lincoln long ago observed, was a ready speaker and an intelligent man, and he rose to the occasion.

He praised the new Confederate constitution. It had, in his view, all the virtues of the American Constitution—and indeed borrowed much of its language, including the Preamble (with a reference to "Almighty God" added) and the first eight amendments of the Bill of Rights (relocated into the main body of the document itself). But the Confederate constitution also had several new structural features, which Stephens considered improvements: a man could serve in the congress and the cabinet simultaneously, making the Confederate system more like Britain's, which Stephens admired; the president was limited to one six-year term, which removed the temptations of electioneering.

Stephens then mentioned yet another improvement—"though last, not least." The constitution had "put to rest, *forever*, all the agitating questions relating to our peculiar institution—African slavery as it exists among us—[and] the proper *status* of the negro in our form of civilization."

The Confederate constitution, unlike the American one, openly mentioned "slaveholding," "slaves," and "negro slavery": although it forbade the foreign slave trade, it committed the new government to protecting property in slaves in all its territories. (The seven seceded states had as yet no territories, unless they could establish a claim to New Mexico, but Cuba would be a likely target for expansion.) But Stephens did not bother about these details. No less than Lincoln, he had an instinct to dig up the root, and he now set about doing it.

Slavery, he said, "was the immediate cause of the late rupture and present revolution." He invoked Jefferson, who had feared that slavery might break the country up (it would be "the knell of the union," as he wrote John Holmes in 1820). "He was right," Stephens said simply. "What was conjecture with him is now a realized fact."

Stephens stayed with Jefferson for a moment more. "The prevailing ideas entertained by him and most of the leading statesmen at the time of the formation of the old constitution were that the enslavement of the African was in violation of the laws of nature; that it was wrong in principle, socially, morally, and politically. It was an evil they knew not well how to deal with, but the general opinion of the men of that day was that, somehow or other in the order of Providence, the institution would be evanescent and pass away." This could almost have been a paragraph in one of Lincoln's speeches. Lincoln believed that Jefferson and the other founders had taken concrete steps to hasten slavery's passing, allowing the slave trade to be banned after twenty years, and blocking slavery from expanding into the old Northwest. But Stephens and Lincoln agreed that the founders had thought that slavery was evil and had hoped that it would end.

Stephens went on. "Those ideas"—the ideas of Jefferson and his fellow statesmen—"were fundamentally wrong. They rested upon the assumption of the equality of races. This was an error. . . . Our new government is founded upon exactly the opposite idea; its foundations are laid, its corner-stone rests upon the great truth, that the negro is not equal to the white man; that slavery—subordination to the superior race—is his natural and normal condition." The reporter who covered Stephens's speech for a local newspaper noted that at this point, there was "Applause."

Lincoln had labored to depict himself as the loyal son of the founders. Stephens portrayed himself as the wiser son—wiser than Lincoln, wiser than the founders themselves.

Stephens elaborated on his newfound wisdom: "This, our new government, is the first in the history of the world based upon this great physical, philosophical and moral truth." Slavery had been universal in the ancient world, but in those societies white men had enslaved other white men, which was wrong. The Confederate states put equally free white men above equally unfree black men, which was right: "This truth has been slow in the process of its development, like all other truths in the various departments of science." Stephens cited other discoverers of great truths: Galileo, Adam Smith, William Harvey. All faced skepticism, all prevailed. Galileo put bodies in the hand of gravity; Smith put the economy under the invisible hand of the market; Harvey showed that blood moved at the pulse of the heart. The Confederacy put the Negro where he belonged. "He, by nature, or by the curse against Canaan, is fitted for that condition which he occupies in our system."

The curse against Canaan is described in Genesis 9:21–27: Noah cursed his son Ham for looking at his nakedness, and condemned Ham's son Canaan to servitude. Genesis goes on to say that Canaan and his descendants lived between Sidon and Gaza—roughly modern Israel—though American slave-owners liked to think they populated Africa, and thus supplied their chattel.

Stephens drew on another Bible verse to wind up his thought: "This stone which was rejected by the first builders 'is become the chief of the corner'—the real 'corner-stone'—in our new edifice." Again the reporter noted "Applause."

Verses about the once-rejected stone occur throughout the Bible. In the Book of Psalms, the "stone which the builders refused" is King David. In the New Testament the stone is Jesus or His followers. All these stones became cornerstones. David was hunted by Saul, then crowned. Jesus was crucified, then rose from the dead. Christians are tempted and tried, yet win salvation. Similarly, slavery had been viewed by Jefferson and the other founders with embarrassment and dismay, but the Confederacy proudly made it the cornerstone of society.

Stephens's paean to slavery was the inversion of the Henry Clay paragraph that Lincoln loved so. Clay found the desire for freedom in the human heart, he heard it celebrated by the cannons that mark the Fourth of July, and he saw it working its way in the modern world. Stephens found slavery in nature; it triumphed over Jefferson and his mistaken Declaration, and it formed the basis of Stephens's new country. With a few brisk arguments, the rhetorical equivalents of a sweep of the hand, Stephens corrected the founding and disposed of all the political foreground of the past thirty years (tariffs, Texas, popular sovereignty, the power of the Supreme Court). What counted was slavery. The founders were wrong about it; later Americans had talked around it; only the Confederacy put it in its proper place.

The "Corner-Stone" speech—it took its name from this masterful passage—was clear, direct, and logical, purged of the rant and sentiment of so much midcentury rhetoric. Lincoln was right to have admired the man who was capable of delivering it. Was Stephens then the towering genius, the new Napoleon that Lincoln had imagined in 1838? John Brown had been outside politics, a crackpot and a terrorist. Stephens was a statesman who had risen to new eminence in a new cause.

But Stephens was no Napoleon. He was hobbled, in the first place, by his office: a Confederate vice president, it turned out, would be no more potent than an American vice president. He would wield power only if his president died, and although Jefferson Davis was plagued with health problems, from malaria to eye trouble, he succumbed to none of them. Stephens could not even offer advice, for he served a president with whom he disagreed. He would clash with Davis on a range of issues, from economic policy to military strategy, and he failed to get his way almost every time. He never imagined getting his way by impeachment or (Napoleon's method) by a coup. He gave an inspired speech, and left it at that.

The conclusion of the "Corner-Stone" speech was desultory, touching on future prospects and the latest news. As of March there were still eight slave states in the Union, more than the seven that were out of it, but Stephens expected North Carolina, Tennessee, Arkansas, Virginia, Kentucky, and Missouri to join the Confederacy soon.

Stephens discerned the threat of "coercion" in Lincoln's Inaugural Address, though he allowed that it had not been followed up "so vigorously as was expected. Fort Sumter"—a fort in Charleston Harbor, still held by US troops—"it is believed, will soon be evacuated." In the meantime, he urged all good Confederates to "keep your armor bright and your powder dry."

"Enthusiastic cheering" was noted by the reporter.

———

Lincoln had committed himself in the final draft of his Inaugural Address to holding such government property as was still in its possession. This included two forts on islands off the Confederate mainland—Fort Pickens at the mouth of Pensacola Bay in Florida, and Fort Sumter. Fort Pickens was the more defensible of the two; Fort Sumter could not hold out against determined enemies, and South Carolina was determined to take it.

The fate of Fort Sumter had been a theme of cabinet discussions since the lame-duck days of the Buchanan administration. Buchanan's position on the slow-motion dissolution of the Union was that states had no power to leave, but neither did the federal government have any power to compel them to remain. As December 1860 wore on, however, unionist hardliners in his cabinet—including the new attorney general, Edwin Stanton, the Ohio lawyer who had snubbed Lincoln during the McCormick patent case—had convinced Buchanan to reinforce Fort Sumter. In January 1861 the administration sent an unarmed supply ship, which the South Carolinians drove off with shore batteries.

The problem became Lincoln's with his inauguration. Stephens's prediction, in the "Corner-Stone" speech, that Fort Sumter would soon be evacuated, was not unreasonable: he was responding to the uncertain mood of the new administration, which reflected the mixed counsels of the cabinet and Lincoln's slowness in deciding what should be done. (Well might Lincoln hesitate; any misstep, and maybe every possible step, meant war.) Seward, who thought a show of mildness would strengthen unionist sentiment in the Upper South and border states, was initially in favor of letting Fort Sumter go. The Blairs were for confrontation. The new administration was hobbled by ordinary confusion, magnified by the extraordinariness of the circumstances. The commander of a ship assigned to resupply Fort Pickens was reassigned to resupply Fort Sumter, but, disbelieving his order—it was signed by Seward, not Lincoln—he sailed for Fort Pickens anyway.

Seward added a political wrinkle with an April 1 memo to Lincoln complaining that the administration was "without a policy either domestic or foreign" and offering to shape one himself. It was Seward's bid to be an American prime minister, a president-by-proxy. Lincoln in reply reminded Seward who the president was, and the secretary of state never made such suggestions again. Perhaps Seward had unconsciously been looking for some sign of authority from the top.

Early in April, Lincoln decided to resupply Fort Sumter, simultaneously informing the governor of South Carolina that he was sending "only provisions." This had no more chance of success than Buchanan's doomed attempt in January, but notifying the rebels ahead of time changed the political dynamics. If there was fighting, it would be on their heads.

On April 12, the Confederates bombarded the fort, which surrendered the next day. The only deaths had been caused by misfiring cannon on each side. "After all that noise," wrote Mary Chesnut, a South Carolina diarist, " . . . sound and fury signifying nothing." Admirers of *Macbeth*, like Lincoln, knew that after the "sound and fury" line is delivered, many things happen.

PART THREE

Twelve

1861–1863:
WAR, EMANCIPATION

L INCOLN HAD SAID WHEN HE LEFT SPRINGFIELD THAT HE
faced a task greater than George Washington's. The fall of Fort
Sumter had made his task greater still. Secession had led to an act of
war, which would be followed by others. On April 15, 1861, Lincoln
issued a proclamation asking for 75,000 militia from the loyal states to
suppress the rebellion.

Americans had fought wars before, against Britain, France, Mexico, and Indians, and they had fought each other in various domestic
commotions (most recently in Kansas). They knew from Plutarch
and Shakespeare of the civil wars of ancient Greece and Rome and
medieval England. But an American Civil War—a rebellion of one-
third of the country against the rest of the Union—was a new thing in
American experience.

Yet even in this strange landscape Lincoln would look to the founding fathers—not for precedents, since there were hardly any, but for principles.

———

One founder who supplied a seeming precedent was George Washington, who had suppressed a rebellion in his second term.

In July 1794 distillers in southwestern Pennsylvania had balked at paying an excise tax on their whiskey. The crisis came when the federal revenue collector for that part of the state fought a gun battle with a company of local militia, in which several persons were killed. The countryside erupted. Angry westerners raised a rebel flag, robbed the mails, and held a protest meeting, 7,000 strong, outside Pittsburgh.

Washington gave the rebels time to cool off while simultaneously mobilizing the militias of four states. In September he sent more than 12,000 men over the Alleghenies. The passage of time and the show of force together stilled the uprising. When the troops Washington dispatched reached their destination, they found no one in arms. About a hundred men were arrested; two were convicted of treason and sentenced to death; Washington pardoned them both.

The affair acquired a faintly comical name—the Whiskey Rebellion. But Washington took it seriously—the force he sent over the mountains was four times larger than the one he had led across the Delaware for the Battle of Trenton. Sixty-seven years later, Lincoln took the Whiskey Rebellion seriously enough to echo Washington's language in his own call for militia on April 15. Washington and Lincoln defined rebellion in the same way: "The laws of the United States . . . are opposed and the execution thereof obstructed . . . by combinations too powerful to be suppressed by the ordinary course of judicial proceedings." They both urged rebels "to disperse and retire peaceably to their respective abodes." These were phrases lifted from the Militia Act of 1792, which had defined when and how the president could summon state militias for federal duty.

More important was the similarity of what Washington and Lincoln thought was at stake and what they hoped to accomplish: Washington said he was acting to uphold "the essential interests of the Union" and "the very existence of Government"; Lincoln said he was defending "the existence of our National Union, and the perpetuity of popular government."

Yet the resemblances between Washington's response and Lincoln's only highlighted how unalike their respective rebellions were. Washington faced armed resistance in a corner of one state. Lincoln took office with seven states missing. In 1794 the passage of time had worked in Washington's favor. In the spring of 1861 it seemed to be running against Lincoln. On April 17, two days after his call for militia, Virginia passed an ordinance of secession. Over the next month, Arkansas, Tennessee, and North Carolina followed, making eleven out of thirty-four states that had left the Union.

Lincoln would have to find his own way through an immensely greater problem than Washington's.

———

Like any president, Lincoln brought a mixture of skills to the task before him.

Some thought he had no skills at all. After Lincoln won the Republican nomination, the New York diarist George Templeton Strong wrote that his only qualifications for high office seemed to be that "he cut a great many rails, and worked on a flatboat in early youth; all of which is somehow presumptive evidence of his statesmanship."

And who could say that Strong was mistaken? Lincoln was indeed one of the unlikeliest executives ever to reach the White House. Most of his predecessors had had some experience managing men before they became president: Washington, Jackson, Harrison, and Taylor had been generals; Jefferson, Monroe, Van Buren (briefly), and Polk had been governors; all the southern presidents were plantation owners. Lincoln's few political offices had been legislative. He had never managed anything larger than a two-partner law firm, and he had done that by stuffing papers in his hat. His aides and the mere pressure of business imposed some order on him, but he rebelled against every attempt to make him act with more system. "He would break through every regulation as fast as it was made," wrote John Hay, who devised many.

This style of management—or anti-style—suited a nature that was self-directed, self-willed, solitary. Everything Lincoln had learned, and much of what he had done, he had learned and done by himself. So why submit to the schedules and strictures of other men?

As with management, so with advice. Lincoln listened to everyone, then went his own way. "I have sometimes doubted," wrote Leonard Swett, one of his Illinois cronies, "whether he ever asked anybody's advice about anything." Humor and anecdotes helped him deflect anyone who became too pressing. Swett left a succinct description of how Lincoln turned people aside: "He told them all a story, said nothing, and sent them away."

Lincoln's political skills, however, were of the highest order, and the presidency is, after all, primarily a political office. The Constitution describes it as the repository of "the Executive power." But politics is older than all constitutions and works its way into every branch of government—executive, legislative, and judicial.

Lincoln was adept at sensing the mood of the country (at least that part of it that had not seceded). He did this by attending to his correspondents and to his callers. He might ignore their suggestions and refuse their requests, but he noted what they said. The hordes of petitioners, favor-seekers, well-wishers, would-be counselors, old ladies, clergymen, and disgruntled military officers who wrote him or trekked to the White House to see him were a four-year immersion in popular sentiment. There were no pollsters then to ask people questions; people came straight to Lincoln, by mail or in person, and spoke their minds.

He kept tabs on his team of rivals, observing their rivalries with each other and with himself. He might not take their advice, but he took their temperature. He always knew better what they were thinking than they knew what he was thinking; if they schemed against him, he generally had a better sense of their chances of success than they themselves had.

On one occasion, circumstances forced his hand on a high-level personnel decision: in January 1862, he had to dismiss Simon Cameron for incompetence and waste; the Great Winnebago Chieftain was simply not up to running the War Department. Lincoln replaced him with Edwin Stanton, impressed with his energy and intelligence, despite their awkward personal history. (Stanton would do an excellent job, and become devoted to Lincoln.) In every other controversy over cabinet personnel, whether caused by critics demanding a secretary's head or by a secretary himself threatening to resign, the man in question stayed or left as Lincoln himself wished.

Another requirement of the presidency almost as important as political skill is that the president should look the part. George Washington, tall, graceful, strong, light-footed on the dance floor—and a centaur when he rode—had set the highest standard for his successors.

Lincoln's appearance gave his enemies much to work with. His gangliness and his newly hirsute face suggested the higher primates. During the McCormick reaper case Stanton had called him a "long-armed ape," and after his election critics nationwide took up the theme. A South Carolina newspaper called him "the Ourang Outang at the White House." George McClellan, commander of the Union armies, called him "a well-meaning baboon" and a "gorilla." Another Union officer fretted that when Lincoln reviewed the troops, he "grinn[ed] like a baboon." Ape imagery had political resonance, since it was routinely used to degrade black people. If Lincoln, as an enemy of slavery, was their presumptive friend, it could be used to degrade him too. A century and a half later the African-American writer Toni Morrison would call Bill Clinton the first black president (this was before Barack Obama got the job). But she was wrong: Lincoln was.

Lincoln did have a way of showing himself to advantage, however. That was through the camera's lens. The day of his Cooper Union address, he had gone to the studio of Mathew Brady, on Broadway, to have his picture taken. Brady was America's premier photographer, and the image he made—Lincoln standing beside a "pillar" (actually a prop), with his left hand resting on a stack of books—would be the first view most Americans had of him. This was the clean-shaven Lincoln, before Grace Bedell wrote her letter. It was reproduced in lithographs, engravings, and small photographs during the 1860 campaign.

Even after Lincoln grew his beard, cameras looked, as they often do, beyond such an obvious feature to highlight others. The camera loved the bones of Lincoln's cheeks, and the nose like a prow. But photographs inevitably alighted on his deep-set eyes ("his eyebrows," wrote Herndon, "cropped out like a huge rock on the brow of a hill"). Because he had to hold still for the long exposures of the day, his photographed eyes lacked the sparkle they showed when he laughed. But at rest they conveyed seriousness, sometimes sadness. They were the visible symbol of that strain of his personality that treasured dark poetry and skirted (or plunged into) depression.

Lincoln the mature politician usually guarded his sadness; literature offered a safe and circumscribed outlet for it. But close observers spotted it. Seward noticed this quality in Lincoln even before his inauguration: "The President," he told a dinner party, "has a curious vein of sentiment running through his thought." By "sentiment" he meant tender emotion rather than sentimentality. Then Seward added that it was Lincoln's "most valuable mental attribute." Valuable not for an executive, but for a leader in time of war.

The way Lincoln reached people who never met him, or who wanted more than his picture, was through his words. Presidents then spoke less often than they do today; the Whig Party in which Lincoln had grown up, ever reacting against the example of Andrew Jackson, believed that presidents should speak even less than they did. But thanks to the troubled times in which Lincoln served, he spoke and wrote for public consumption more than was then normal.

A president typically gave an Inaugural Address and annual messages to Congress (these, unlike modern State of the Union addresses, were delivered in writing, not in person). A president might also send messages to Congress on special occasions. In his proclamation of April 15, 1861, Lincoln called on Congress to assemble for a special session on July 4 to consider the crisis of disunion. When it met, he gave it a lengthy written overview of the rebellion so far and his thoughts on what should be done.

Lincoln made remarks to delegations of citizens who visited him and to revelers in the streets outside the White House celebrating Union victories. Occasionally he even traveled to nearby Maryland or Pennsylvania for ceremonies—fairs to raise money for treating wounded soldiers, the dedication of a cemetery—at which he would speak briefly. He was invited once to return to Springfield for a Republican rally, but rejected the idea as too time-consuming.

He made good use of an old practice. The founders had occasionally written letters, nominally personal, which they expected to be circulated among interested parties or even published. Jefferson surely knew that something as eloquent as his letter to John Holmes on the "fire-bell in the night" would be widely read as soon as he was dead, if it was not leaked to the newspapers beforehand. Lincoln used the technique to deal with one of his knottiest problems—suspending the writ of habeas corpus.

The US Constitution (Article I, Section 9) allows habeas corpus to be suspended during rebellions and invasions so that alleged wrongdoers can be arrested and tried by military tribunals rather than ordinary courts. In April 1861, to combat saboteurs, Lincoln suspended habeas corpus along the rail line connecting Washington and Philadelphia. In September 1862, to allow the army to arrest anyone interfering with recruitment, he suspended it nationwide.

In 1863 a military tribunal went too far. Clement Vallandingham, a vociferous antiwar Democrat from Ohio, gave a speech denouncing the war as "wicked, cruel and unnecessary," fought "for the freedom of the blacks and the enslavement of the whites." The army arrested him for discouraging enlistments—Who would volunteer to fight to free blacks and enslave whites?—which only made him a martyr. Lincoln ordered Vallandingham released and exiled to the Confederacy, but he realized he needed to do more to undo the damage.

He got his chance when a New York Democrat, Erastus Corning, sent him a letter protesting Vallandingham's treatment. Lincoln's reply, a copy of which he mailed simultaneously to the *New York Tribune*, carefully explained the constitutional justification for suspending habeas corpus—something the administration had not yet done at length. He also went after Vallandingham. He used pathos, contrasting the politician's fate with that of ordinary folk: "Must I shoot a simple-minded soldier boy who deserts, while I must not touch a hair of a wily agitator who induces him to desert?" He used humor, comparing rebellion to sickness and military tribunals to medicine, arguing that there was no chance of the remedy outlasting the disease: Would anyone "contract so strong an appetite for emetics during temporary illness as to persist in feeding upon them during the remainder of his healthful life?" The letter, reissued as a pamphlet, sold 500,000 copies and finished Vallandingham as a political leader. The Democrat left the Confederacy to run for governor of Ohio from Canadian soil, and was crushed.

Lincoln's joke about feeding on emetics was in his best debater's style: Paine on the platform, winning arguments by getting laughs. As a rule, however, Lincoln as president saved the jokes for personal interactions, to distract and to lighten his own mood. He loved other people's jokes as much as his own. His favorite humorist was David Ross Locke, a journalist with the *Toledo Blade*, who wrote under the persona of Petroleum Vesuvius Nasby. Locke's creation had the opinions of Clement Vallandingham and the vocabulary—elaborately misspelled—of a tavern-keeper. "There is now 15 niggers, men, wimin and childern . . . in Wingert's Corners [Nasby's fictional hometown], and yesterday another arrove. I am bekomin alarmed, fer if they inkreese at this rate, in suthin over sixty yeres they'll hev a majority in the town." Lincoln thought Nasby was hilarious, and he would regale callers and his cabinet with his latest grotesqueries.

For his public pronouncements, however, Lincoln generally wrote and spoke seriously. He held the highest office in the land at the worst moment of its history, and he suited his rhetoric to his place and time. His style was direct, sometimes tinged with poetry; occasionally, when reaching for an effect, he overreached, yet he regularly managed to tap what Seward had called the vein of sentiment.

The conclusion of his second Annual Message to Congress, given in December 1862, showed him finding his range. His topic was how the end of the war might be hastened by ending slavery; Lincoln wanted to impress Congress with the magnitude of the question and the weight of their shared responsibility, and he finished with three rhetorical strokes, like chimes. "The dogmas of the quiet past are inadequate to the stormy present." This was an attempt at loftiness—a failed attempt. There was a little too much horsehair stuffing in it. After a few beats, Lincoln tried again: "*We* cannot escape history." This was better, a statement as simple as it was sweeping. Then, after a few more beats, bull's-eye: "We shall nobly save, or meanly lose, the last best, hope of earth." This was as lofty as Henry Clay at his most eloquent; it was sweeping, surveying all of history; the cluster of monosyllables, varied by only two adverbs, seems as plain as dirt, but there is gold dust in it: the sliding *l*s, the very intonations of loss, are stopped by the sharp almost-rhyme of *last/best*.

Words alone do not win wars or lead men, but what words could do, Lincoln's would.

———

Lincoln's task as the Civil War unfolded was twofold: to preserve the Union and to fulfill the goals of the Republican Party.

Preserving the Union was his duty under the Constitution. The oath of office, prescribed in Article II, Section 1, bound him to "preserve, protect and defend the Constitution of the United States." Fulfilling the goals of the Republican Party was the condition under which he had won his office. Although the founding fathers professed to dislike parties—Madison, in the *Federalist*, called them "factions," and Washington

in his Farewell Address warned against them—they themselves created
the first two-party system (Republicans vs. Federalists) almost as soon
as their Constitution went into effect. In seventy-one years of presidential elections, parties large and small had come and gone, and in
one case changed names (Jefferson's Republicans becoming Jackson's
Democrats). But parties themselves had become an inescapable feature
of American political life—the mechanisms by which leaders acquired
office and the people expressed their will.

Lincoln might have saved the Union immediately after his election
simply by abandoning the principles on which he and the Republican
Party had run. There were various efforts to urge him to do just that.
One compromise proposal, floated in December 1860 by John Critten-
den, an old Whig senator from Kentucky, would have pushed the Missouri line to California by constitutional amendment, and made this
amendment unchangeable. Lincoln had begun his rise to the White
House by fighting to restore the Missouri line—but that was the old
line, dividing slavery from freedom in the former Louisiana territory. An
extended line, crossing the continent and graven into the Constitution,
would be an incentive, Lincoln wrote, to grabbing "all [territory] south
of us, and making slave states of it"—Central America, the Caribbean,
whatever might be won in a new Mexican War. "A year will not pass,"
he predicted, "until we shall have to take Cuba" to satisfy slaveholders.
Indeed, expansion into the subtropics was the only way an outnumbered
South could recover parity in the Senate. But Republicans, as Lincoln
wrote Alexander Stephens, thought slavery was "*wrong* and ought to be
restricted." On any proposal to let it grow into new territories, Lincoln
was "inflexible."

———

Lincoln's first task, saving the Union, was simultaneously military and
political.

The Confederacy had reason to think it could win on the battlefield.
Its subculture was more bellicose than that of the North. This bred an

arrogance that Montgomery Blair, who partook of it, defined when he wrote that southerners believed that any one of them equaled half a dozen Yankees. But even arrogance could work to the Confederacy's advantage, since attitude and audacity often do carry the day. The situation of the Confederacy was favorable. Like the United States during the Revolution, it would be fighting a protective war, repelling the incursions of invaders. The defensive always has a natural advantage in war.

The Union had advantages of its own. Unlike Britain in the Revolution, it did not have to send attacking armies across an ocean. The enemy was always a few marches away. The Union would be better armed than the South, thanks to its superiority in manufacturing, and it would be better served by its more numerous railroads. Most important, it was more populous. Lincoln had made this point in 1859 in a speech in Cincinnati, addressing the Kentuckians who lived just across the Ohio. "Why, gentlemen, I think you are as gallant and as brave men as live; . . . but man for man, you are not better than we are, and there are not so many of you as there are of us."

The grand strategy devised by the aged Winfield Scott, known as the Anaconda plan, proposed to blockade southern ports, split the Confederacy into two unequal parts by taking control of the Mississippi River, and press in from the perimeter of the larger portion on different fronts simultaneously. Scott knew his business; this is in fact what the Union would do over the next four years.

But political accident gave northeastern Virginia special prominence. After Virginia seceded, a grateful Confederacy moved its capital from Montgomery to Richmond. Virginia was no longer the largest state in the Union, scarcely the largest in the Confederacy. But it was the oldest, the most eminent, the nursery of presidents and of liberty. By moving to Richmond, the Confederacy appropriated Virginia's luster.

The proximity of Richmond and Washington—the two capitals were only ninety-five miles apart—made voters and politicians on both sides avid for quick victories. The proximity was deceptive, because many winding rivers lay between the two cities. The proximity was doubly deceptive, because the primary goal in war is not the conquest of capitals, but the destruction of the enemy's ability and will to fight. Yet since losing a capital necessarily entails a loss of morale and prestige, focusing on Washington and Richmond made some sense after all, especially since both the Union and the Confederacy were republics, in which popular sentiment and the election calendar always had to be considered. If people and politicians thought the capitals were important, then they became so. Thus the Virginia theater was crucial for both sides.

From its site on the Potomac, Washington stared Virginia in the face. A rebel flag flying over the Marshall House, a hotel in Alexandria, could be seen from the White House with a spyglass. In May 1861 Union troops took Alexandria; one of their officers, Elmer Ellsworth, a dashing young Illinoisan who had studied law under Lincoln in his Springfield office, and accompanied him on his preinaugural train trip, sprang up the hotel stairs to tear down the disloyal banner. The manager shot him dead (and was killed in turn by a Union man). Lincoln wrote Ellsworth's parents: "In the untimely loss of your noble son, our affliction here is scarcely less than your own."

Everyone knew there would be more deaths to come, though no one suspected how many. What came at the end of July was a full-dress battle twenty-five miles southwest of Washington. The Union called it Bull Run, after the nearest stream, the Confederates Manassas, after the nearest crossroads. If Scott had been even ten years younger and fifty pounds lighter, he might have led the Union troops himself. Instead the Union advance was commanded by Irvin McDowell, one of his former staff officers. After initial setbacks, the Confederates rallied. The Union retreat became a rout, with exhausted, disorderly soldiers straggling back to Washington. A total of almost 900 men from both sides were killed, and almost 3,000 wounded—small numbers compared to the hecatombs of Napoleon or Marlborough. But the battle was one of the bloodiest fought so far in North America. (By way of comparison, 24 men had died altogether at the Battle of Trenton, and just over 300 at the Battle of New Orleans.)

The war in Virginia became a series of offensives and counteroffensives. The names of the major engagements were once known to every schoolchild and are still sacred to reenactors, history buffs, and patriots: Seven Days', Second Bull Run, Antietam, Fredericksburg, Chancellorsville. They were, with one exception, a procession of Union defeats incurred by a rotating cast of commanders.

Scott retired at age seventy-five in November 1861, and was succeeded by George McClellan, forty years his junior, who had won plaudits by defeating the rebels in Virginia's Appalachian northwest (the future state of West Virginia). McClellan's plan for winning the war was to land on the Virginia coast and approach Richmond from the southeast, moving up the long peninsula between the York and the James rivers—hence the name by which his effort is known, the Peninsula Campaign. McClellan was an excellent organizer who was always popular with his men. But in the Seven Days' Battles (June 25–July 1, 1862), the Confederates, though they lost more men than he did, managed to stop him short of Richmond.

The Confederates then made their own move north, nearly destroying an army under John Pope at the Second Battle of Bull Run (August 28–30). They decided to swing northwest into central Maryland, but McClellan, restored to grace after his stalemate on the peninsula, stopped their advance at Antietam (September 17).

McClellan's failure to pursue the enemy after this near-victory ended his period of grace, and the Union's next efforts to take the war south again were led by other commanders, disastrously. Ambrose Burnside (whose whiskers were the model and namesake of sideburns) got as far as Fredericksburg on the Rappahannock River, where he suffered fearful casualties (December 11–15). The next spring, at Chancellorsville (May 1–4, 1863), only a few miles from the site of Burnside's defeat, Joseph Hooker was beaten by Confederate forces half as strong as his.

Union generalship on the Virginia front was certainly inadequate. (One Union general knew it: Burnside, a modest man, had refused two offers to take a commanding role before—unfortunately—accepting.)

At the same time, the Confederates could not mount a successful offensive of their own, and they, too, were bleeding.

The Anaconda plan worked better in the West. By the spring of 1862 the Union had managed to clear western Tennessee, with victories at Fort Henry (February 6), Fort Donelson (February 16), and Shiloh (April 6–7). At the southern end of the Mississippi, New Orleans, the largest city and greatest port in the Confederacy, fell on May 1.

In faraway London, Charles Francis Adams's son Henry, who had accompanied his father as his personal secretary, found himself surrounded by Confederate sympathizers: the light-headed and the fashionable, always willing to shed tears for distant underdogs. The Union capture of New Orleans fell on them, Henry wrote, like a "blow in the face on a drunken man."

———

Lincoln had poked fun at his meager military experience for years; it was one element of his rube/boob persona: "[I never] saw any live fighting Indians," he said of his days in the Black Hawk War, "but I had a good many bloody struggles with the mosquitoes." Now he took his responsibilities as commander in chief seriously. He borrowed a textbook from the Library of Congress entitled *Elements of Military Art and Science*, by Henry Halleck, an officer who would later become chief of staff for the entire army, and studied it. He followed his generals' actions minutely and corresponded with them anxiously, careful to couch most of his ideas as advice rather than orders. Sometimes his advice was worthless. He ended the letter in which he congratulated Hooker on replacing Burnside with this imitation gemstone: "Beware of rashness, but with energy, and sleepless vigilance, go forward, and give us victories." It was like telling an investor to buy low and sell high. In fairness to Lincoln, his opposite number, Jefferson Davis, despite far greater experience (colonel in the Mexican War, secretary of war under Franklin Pierce), gave orders and advice that were consistently worse.

The longer arc of Lincoln's relationship with his commanders was sound: he supported them until they failed unignorably, then he sought new ones.

Supporting them often required a vast patience. The egos of military men (never small) had been piqued by the career of Napoleon. Perhaps they could win as many victories as he had. Perhaps they could, as he had, become more than military men. McClellan, who was nicknamed the Little Napoleon—he was of average height, but youth, slimness, and attitude gave him a bright, bristling appearance—wrote early in the war: "I almost think that were I to win some small success now I could become Dictator or anything else that might please me." Hooker, on the eve of his elevation, said that "nothing would go right until we had a dictator, and the sooner the better."

McClellan made his remark about a dictator in a letter to his wife; Hooker spoke his to a reporter. Lincoln knew about Hooker's remark, and knew McClellan well enough to know his frame of mind (it was not hard to discern). He correctly judged that their talk was bluster, not actual disloyalty—these were not towering geniuses—and he let them try to do their jobs. "I will hold McClellan's horse," he said, "if he will only bring us success." He joshed Hooker about his dictator talk in a letter: "Only those generals who gain successes can set up dictators. What I now ask of you is military success, and I will risk the dictatorship."

And yet once these men failed, Lincoln cast them aside and looked for others. When he found generals who won, he stuck by them. The first Union victories in western Tennessee were won by Ulysses Grant, a thirty-nine-year-old whose early military career had been marred by drinking. But the two-day Battle of Shiloh was almost lost through his overconfidence: not believing the enemy to be near, he had not ordered his men to entrench, and the Confederates nearly drove them from the field. On the second day, he saved all with a ferocious counterattack. The casualties on both sides, however, were terrible (over 1,700 Union soldiers were killed, and more than 8,000 wounded; Confederate losses were similar). A storm of criticism beat on Grant, but Lincoln would not dismiss him: "I can't spare this man; he fights."

———

As the war widened, Lincoln had to preserve the Union politically.

His first task was to stop the hemorrhaging of states. After the last four states had seceded in April and May 1861, four slaveholding states still remained in the Union: Delaware, Maryland, Kentucky, and Missouri. Missouri stayed loyal, though it was so plagued by pro-Confederate guerrillas and quarrels among its own unionists that Lincoln, in a moment of irritation, compared it to the tree stumps in the fields of his youth that were so deeply rooted that he could not dig them up or burn them out, but only plow around them. Delaware, small and isolated, would have to do whatever Maryland did, and Maryland had enough unionists and enough Union troops in regular transit that it, too, stayed loyal.

Kentucky was critical. If it seceded, the Union anaconda would have to swallow the Ohio River before it could begin on the Mississippi. "To lose Kentucky," Lincoln wrote, "is nearly the same as to lose the whole game." At the end of May 1861, Kentucky declared itself neutral. Lincoln, without conceding that a state had any power to do such a thing, bided his time. Confederate troops moved into the western end of the state in September, which allowed local unionists to depict them as aggressors. Thereafter, despite numerous battles and raids, the state was officially in the Union camp. Throughout, Lincoln took counsel from his old friend Joshua Speed, who was now living in Kentucky, and from his own sense, as a native son, of how important and how delicately balanced the state was.

Lincoln's very sensitivity to Kentucky could be used against him, however. Benjamin Wade, a Republican senator from Ohio, disliked Lincoln for his caution, and believed that Lincoln's Kentucky roots were the source of it: Lincoln, he said, was "poor white trash." Vilification was one of the few race-blind enterprises in America: Lincoln could simultaneously be a degraded white man and a degraded black man.

Lincoln welcomed the support, so far as it was offered, of unionist Democrats. Most northern Democrats were incensed by the fall of Fort Sumter, none more so than Stephen Douglas. Lincoln's longtime rival had wanted him to call up 200,000 militia in April 1861 instead of 75,000. A high-strung temperament and years of hard drinking had undermined Douglas's health, however, and he died, at age forty-eight, in June. Lincoln ordered the White House to be draped in mourning for thirty days.

One southern Democrat shared Douglas's unionist passion. Senator Andrew Johnson of Tennessee, a former tailor, was a self-made populist. Although he was proslavery, he was virulently anti-secession. His opinion of his fellow southerners as the nation came unglued was that they "ought to be hanged for all this." Johnson had to flee his state when it seceded, but he would return as military governor.

Lincoln's support among Democrats waxed and waned with the tide of battle and with their opportunities to find partisan advantage. Democrats looked for weapons to attack their Republican rivals in the Constitution (by defending habeas corpus) and in the gutter (by upholding racism). Lincoln, for his part, looked to the Democrats for occasional allies and for opportunities to sow confusion. When New York elected a Democratic governor, Horatio Seymour, in 1862, Lincoln reached out to him, suggesting that if he supported the war zealously he might be the next president. Was Lincoln offering Seymour a promise of future support, or the appearance of a promise, to lull him? Bait, or bait in a trap? Seymour responded cautiously. Soon enough, ordinary partisanship resumed, and the two leaders were fighting openly.

Lincoln's main support in running his administration, and therefore in keeping the country together, was his own party, the Republicans. They commanded majorities in both houses of Congress throughout his administration (though Democrats made gains in the midterm elections of 1862, after it became clear that the war would not be won quickly). But dominance can be a temptation to disagree—there are so many of us, we can afford to fight among ourselves. Lincoln had to employ all his talents to keep Republicans in good spirits and away from each other's throats.

One of his most magnanimous acts was to defend Simon Cameron after he was eased out of the cabinet as secretary of war. Lincoln made him minister to Russia in February 1862 as consolation. But in Cameron's absence, a House committee investigating the War Department issued a damning report, detailing bad contracts that had been hastily issued in the first days of the war, and calling for Cameron to be censured. Lincoln wrote Congress saying that he and the rest of the cabinet were "at least equally responsible" for Cameron's mismanagement: the times had required stopgap measures, and everyone in the administration had approved them. Cameron was overwhelmed with gratitude. "Very many men in your situation," he wrote Lincoln from St. Petersburg, "would have permitted an innocent man to suffer." And very many more men would have permitted an incapable one to take all the blame. Cameron would never forget Lincoln's generosity, and Lincoln would be able to call on him later.

In December 1862 Lincoln had to frustrate a power play by his treasury secretary, Salmon P. Chase, and the Republican Senate caucus. After the disappointing midterm elections and the debacle of Fredericksburg, there was a powerful desire to find a scapegoat. Chase and his congressional friends settled on Secretary of State William Seward, whom they accused of running the administration himself, and of running it into the ground. When Seward learned of their charges, he wrote Lincoln offering to resign.

Lincoln did not want to be seen as Seward's tool, and he did not want senators dictating his cabinet—especially not senators who were in cahoots with one of his own secretaries. He wrong-footed Chase by inviting a committee of unhappy senators to present their complaints about the administration to a meeting of the entire cabinet (minus Seward). When secretary after secretary assured the senators that Seward was no dark mastermind, and that all of them had the president's ear, Chase buckled. Confronted by the unanimous testimony of his colleagues, he was not bold enough to be the only man in the room to criticize Seward.

After the meeting, Chase's Senate allies scorned him for his failure to speak up. Why had he said one thing to them, and another in front of the full cabinet? One angry senator offered a pithy explanation: "He lied." Chase, mortified, offered to resign himself. Lincoln then wrote to both Seward and Chase, asking them to stay at their posts (both, after all, were competent men). Seward agreed happily, Chase morosely. Lincoln kept the secretaries he wanted, kept a congressional faction at bay, and kept himself in charge. Sometimes a leader must manipulate men in secret; sometimes he must manipulate them openly, to show his mastery.

These intra-Republican fights were about more than personalities. The Republicans, like any major party, embraced different shades of opinion. In Lincoln's cabinet, Caleb Smith (who would resign in December 1862 from ill health) and Edward Bates tended to favor moderate courses; so did the Blairs, despite their combative natures. Seward continued to take the moderate tone he had assumed before Lincoln's inauguration. His moderation was the effect of his congenital optimism. Once the war began, he was convinced that the victory of the Union and the destruction of slavery were assured: Why push too hard at an open door? Chase and his congressional friends—Charles Sumner, Benjamin Wade—thought of themselves as Radicals, as did Stanton.

Lincoln mastered tendencies as well as men. He managed to place himself in the center of Republican opinion and to keep its factions, if not happy—there were almost always some Republicans who were unhappy about something—at least not rebellious. One newspaper described Lincoln's maneuvers this way: "The art of riding two horses is not confined to the circus."

———

As he worked to preserve the Union, Lincoln simultaneously advanced the Republican Party's goals—in his terse summary to Alexander Stephens, "We think [slavery] is wrong, and ought to be restricted."

On the question of slavery's expansion, Lincoln had told his fellow Republicans that he was "inflexible." He was in fact a bit flexible: he was willing to allow slavery in the New Mexico territory—the present state plus Arizona. But he opposed any deal that would give slavery a free field in Central America or the Caribbean. The secession of the South and its congressmen, coupled with Republican dominance of the White House and Capitol Hill, put the territorial question to rest after forty years of contention: in May 1862 Congress formally ended slavery in all the territories.

Lincoln showed his belief in the wrongness of slavery in other ways. In December 1861 he called for diplomatic recognition of Liberia and Haiti. Liberia was a project of the American Colonization Society, and Haiti had been liberated in an eighteenth-century slave revolt, the largest in modern history. Diplomatic recognition of these countries was a symbolic statement about slavery, and even race; one Democratic newspaper worried about "strapping negro" ambassadors coming to Washington.

Slavery itself was abolished in the District of Columbia, a goal Lincoln had discussed as long ago as 1837. In the summer of 1862 Congress passed a bill emancipating the District's slaves immediately and compensating owners. Lincoln, who had long favored compensation, preferred gradual, not immediate, emancipation, and worried what effect the bill might have in the border states. But he signed it anyway.

The foreign slave trade had been illegal since 1808, and had been equated with piracy, a capital crime, since 1820. Yet, although America maintained an Atlantic naval squadron to seize slave ships, only one American had ever been convicted of the crime, and he had been given a light sentence and a fine (the latter pardoned by President Buchanan). In November 1861 Captain Nathaniel Gordon, a slaver from Portland, Maine, who had been captured off the Congo River with a shipload of almost nine hundred slaves bound for Cuba, was tried in New York City and sentenced to death. Lincoln gave him a two-week stay of execution to prepare his soul, but warned him to "relinquish . . . all expectation of pardon by Human Authority." In February 1862 Gordon was hanged.

Lincoln continued to pursue the idea of colonization, which was, in his own mind, part of the solution to the problem of slavery. In his speech on the *Dred Scott* decision, he had compared blacks to the Jews of the Bible, destined for their own homeland; the land he had in mind as president was not Liberia but Central America. The Chiriqui coast on the Isthmus of Panama seemed to be a likely spot; it was supposed to have coal mines, and the isthmus was a busy trade route. The Blairs were enthusiastic supporters of colonization; they envisioned outposts of free blacks as vanguards of American influence in the Caribbean Basin. Lincoln and the Blairs contemplated a black-only version of the slave owners' dream of southern expansion.

In August 1862 Lincoln asked to meet a delegation of free black men from Washington, DC, picked by their churches, to push his Central American scheme. While calling slavery "the greatest wrong inflicted on any people," he said that free blacks could not hope to be treated as equals in America: "[I] present it as a fact with which we have to deal. I cannot alter it if I would." So why shouldn't they move elsewhere? He tried to inspire them by comparing the hardships of emigration to George Washington's trials during the Revolution—"yet [Washington] was a happy man, because he was engaged in benefiting his race." He ended with auctioneer's patter. "Could I get a hundred tolerably intelligent men" to try it? "Can I have fifty? If I could find twenty five . . . " Lincoln's auditors, who had no desire to live anywhere but where they now did, said nothing critical to the president's face, but none accepted his offer. (And just as well—Chiriqui's coal proved to be too low-grade to be usable.) Colonization was, as it had always been, a nonstarter. Still, the meeting was noteworthy in one respect: it was the first time a president had received a delegation of blacks in the White House.

———

All these things might have been done by a peacetime president with firm convictions and a solid congressional majority. But Lincoln had to apply the principles of his party to the institution of slavery in wartime.

What should be done with the slaves of rebels? With escaped slaves? What, if anything, should be done with the slaves of those who had remained loyal?

At the beginning of the war, Lincoln named John Frémont, the first Republican presidential candidate, commander of the Western Department with responsibility for Missouri. In August 1861 Frémont declared martial law in the state and freed all slaves belonging to Confederate sympathizers. Lincoln did not want generals making policy, and he particularly did not want them making policies that freed slaves while nearby Kentucky, a slave state, still hung in the balance. If Frémont needed the labor of rebels' slaves, Lincoln wrote, "he can seize them and use them; but when the need is past, it is not for him to fix their permanent future condition. That must be settled according to laws made by law-makers, and not by military proclamation." When Frémont became entangled in a charge of graft, Lincoln took the opportunity to reassign him.

But another general suggested a policy that Lincoln permitted. Benjamin Butler was a Democratic politician from Massachusetts; at the endless Democratic convention of 1860, he had voted consistently for Jefferson Davis for president. But after secession he stayed loyal to the Union. In the spring of 1861, as the commander of a Massachusetts regiment occupying Fort Monroe at the mouth of the James River, on the coast of Virginia, he found himself dealing with slaves who were fleeing from rebel lines. Their owners applied, under a flag of truce, to reclaim them as fugitives. Butler refused, calling them "contraband"—goods that could be seized in time of war—and asked for further directions from Washington. Lincoln, amused, nicknamed the policy "Butler's fugitive slave law." It was an inversion of the fugitive slave law that would have turned the Union Army into one vast underground railroad if universally applied. Lincoln let Butler's action stand, but let other Union commanders decide the fate of runaways as they wished.

Lincoln's reaction to Frémont had been correct: the law had to be settled by lawmakers, in Congress, in the states, and by himself as president. In the first fifteen months of the war, Congress passed two laws aimed at slavery in the Confederacy. In the summer of 1861, the Confiscation Act declared any property used for Confederate military purposes—including slaves—forfeit; any slaves who had been laboring for the rebel army who were captured by Union troops, or who fled to Union lines, would automatically be freed. In the summer of 1862, a second Confiscation Act freed any rebel-owned slaves who fell into Union hands, whether they had been employed for military purposes or not—in effect, legalizing Butler's contraband policy.

Lincoln meanwhile tried to induce the loyal border states to abolish slavery within their own borders. Almost half a million slaves lived in Missouri, Kentucky, Maryland, and Delaware (3.5 million lived in the Confederacy). Lincoln wanted the border states to free their own slaves—for a price.

Some of the founders had wondered how much it might cost to free all of America's slaves. In 1819, when there were 1.5 million slaves in the country, James Madison calculated that it would cost $600 million to free and deport them; five years later, Thomas Jefferson estimated that it would cost $900 million. But these had been the speculations of old men (Jefferson had already told Edward Coles that emancipation was the task of the young). Now the pressure of war made the question of compensated emancipation urgent.

Lincoln believed it was wrong to hold men as property, yet under the existing evil of slavery they were indeed held that way. Their owners, he felt, should be recompensed for lost assets. Offering money would also, obviously, make slaveholders more willing to act. In March 1862 Lincoln asked Congress to offer compensation for any border states that would undertake emancipation. In July he appealed to a delegation of border-state politicians to endorse such a process. Slavery, he told them, was doomed "by mere friction and abrasion" if the war continued. How much better to end it now, and get paid in the bargain. Ending slavery in the border states would also deprive the Confederacy of all hope of ever peeling them off from the Union. Lincoln made a separate appeal to Delaware, as a small and easy test case, offering to pay $719,200 over thirty-one years to liberate its 1,800 slaves by 1893.

Lincoln found no takers. As a Kentuckian, he sympathized with the border states, but he also projected too much of himself onto them. He had come to hate slavery; surely, he thought, they would, too. But the time was not yet.

———

But Lincoln had another plan in mind. On July 22, 1862, he broached it with his cabinet, reading the draft of a proclamation. It endorsed both the second Confiscation Act and Lincoln's plans for compensation, but added a new idea: as of the coming New Year, all slaves in the Confederacy would be declared free. When the cabinet recovered from its surprise, most of the secretaries approved the plan. But Seward argued that it would look desperate unless it were issued after a victory. The Peninsula Campaign had just ground to a halt. Perhaps John Pope could give the Union better news.

While waiting for better news, Lincoln was attacked by Horace Greeley in an August 20 editorial in the *New York Tribune*, entitled "The Prayer of Twenty Millions" (approximately the population of the loyal Union, minus the border states). "The Union cause has suffered," wrote Greeley, "from mistaken deference to Rebel Slavery." Slavery was the root of the conflict, Lincoln should dig it up. Greeley urged him to enforce the second Confiscation Act zealously.

Lincoln answered with a letter, printed by Greeley, which appeared to dismiss his concerns. "My paramount object," Lincoln wrote, was "to save the Union, and . . . *not* either to save or to destroy slavery. If I could save the Union without freeing *any* slave I would do it, and if I could save it by freeing *all* the slaves I would do it; and if I could save it by freeing some and leaving others alone I would also do that." A hasty reader might have focused on Lincoln's first hypothetical—saving the Union without freeing any slaves. But the third hypothetical—saving it by freeing some—was what he actually intended with his yet-unissued proclamation. He used his reply to Greeley to slip the thought into the public's mind.

The news from John Pope at the end of August was the Second Battle of Bull Run. Not until Antietam on September 17 did the Union win something like a victory. Five days later Lincoln met with his cabinet.

He began with a reading from a humorist, not Petroleum V. Nasby this time, but Artemus Ward (the penname and persona of another Ohio journalist, formerly with the *Cleveland Plain Dealer*, Charles Farrar Browne). Ward, a P. T. Barnum–like showman, was exhibiting a wax model of the Last Supper in Utica, New York, when an "egrejus ass" in the audience attacked the figure of Judas. "'Judas Isscarrot can't show hisself in Utiky with impunerty by a darn site!' with which observashun he kaved in Judassis hed." Why did Lincoln read that particular story at that particular time? Judas was the icon of betrayal for all of Christendom. Who was Judas in September 1862? Democrats (and of course Confederates) would accuse Lincoln of betraying the order of nature with the drastic step he was about to take. But Lincoln believed that rebels and faint-hearts before them had already betrayed the founders by embracing or shrugging at slavery ("Our republican robe," he had said at Peoria, "is soiled, and trailed in the dust"). Assuming that Lincoln was not Judas, was he fighting treachery effectively—or only behaving like an "egrejus ass"? Like many a comic, Lincoln expressed his anxieties in disguise.

Lincoln then turned to his proclamation. Now was the time to issue it. "I made the promise to myself" before Antietam, he said. (Chase, who recorded the scene in his diary, noted that Lincoln hesitated at this point, then added: and "to my Maker.")

Lincoln read his draft. As of January 1, 1863, all slaves "within any state, or designated part of a state, the people whereof shall then be in rebellion against the United States shall be then, thenceforward, and forever free." On the New Year Lincoln would indicate what states or parts of states qualified. The remainder of the proclamation endorsed compensation, colonization, and the second Confiscation Act. The entire cabinet approved, except for Montgomery Blair, who was worried that the proclamation would hurt Republicans in the November elections.

In his slow and sidling way, Lincoln had nevertheless jumped ahead of the ongoing conversation on slavery. The Union would, he hoped, still use monetary inducements to end slavery in the loyal states: as late as December 1862, he asked Congress to ratify a constitutional amendment that would provide for buying out the slaves of all the states by 1900 (Congress would not act on this suggestion). But after the New Year the Union would consider slavery ended in the Confederacy.

Southern newspapers accused him of trying to stir up a race war. Lincoln had never feared such a thing, and he did not fear it now. John Brown had not stirred up a race war, because, as Lincoln put it at Cooper Union, the slaves thought he was crazy. The second Confiscation Act already gave Confederate-owned slaves an incentive to flee if they could. Lincoln's proclamation told them that if they sat tight, then whenever the Union armies arrived, their freedom would arrive also.

The language of his September message, called the Preliminary Emancipation Proclamation, and of the Final Emancipation Proclamation on January 1, was dry and muted; the final version contained only one small flourish about "the gracious favor of Almighty God," and the roll—like "found" poetry in legalese—of "then, thenceforward, and forever." Lincoln kept to legalisms because of the nature and scope of what he was doing. The Emancipation Proclamation was a war measure: "a fit and necessary war measure for suppressing . . . rebellion," as the final proclamation put it. But his only power to issue it derived from his powers as "Commander-in-Chief . . . in time of actual armed rebellion."

The possibility that the federal government might use its war powers to free the slaves had been raised as early as the founding. In 1788, Patrick Henry, in a last-ditch effort to prevent Virginia from ratifying the Constitution, warned the Virginia ratifying convention that the language of the Preamble would allow Congress to free slaves in wartime to fight as soldiers. "Have they [i.e., Congress] not power to provide for the general defense and welfare? May they not think that these call for the abolition of slavery?" James Madison, champion of the Constitution against Henry's attacks, scoffed: "Such an idea never entered into any American breast, nor do I believe it ever will." Yet in the 1830s and 1840s such an idea entered into the breast of John Quincy Adams, who argued, during his postpresidential career as a congressman, that in the case of an invasion or a slave uprising, either of them large enough to require federal action, Congress could free slaves under its war powers.

Patrick Henry's prophecy was recorded in *Elliott's Debates*, which Lincoln owned. John Quincy Adams's speculations were common knowledge among Republicans: Charles Sumner had asked Charles Francis Adams to reprint his father's speeches during the run-up to the election of 1860. Lincoln's only innovation was to do the deed as president. But he could only do it as commander in chief, fighting a rebellion. Hence his legalistic language.

Hence also the geographical limits of the Emancipation Proclamation. Lincoln freed slaves who were as yet out of the control of the Union. A map of the territory the Emancipation Proclamation did not cover was almost a map of the progress of Union armies as of January 1863. New Orleans and the parishes of southeastern Louisiana, occupied in May 1862, were exempt, as was southeastern Virginia (the Union's base for the Peninsula Campaign). Andrew Johnson, who had been appointed the Union's military governor of Tennessee in March 1862, had procured an exemption for his entire state. The proclamation, of course, did not apply to the loyal states of Missouri, Kentucky, Maryland, or Delaware—or to the northwestern counties of Virginia, which were forming themselves into a new, unionist state, West Virginia. They were not in rebellion. Lincoln's powers as commander in chief extended to the entire Union (in suspending habeas corpus, for example). But not his powers as commander in chief to free the slaves of rebels.

Even so, the Emancipation Proclamation represented a dramatic extension of the Republican Party's program. In 1861 Lincoln and his party thought slavery was wrong and ought to be restricted. By 1863 they thought it was wrong and ought to be ended by fiat wherever rebels still held sway. The change had come under the pressure of war. Events, as Lincoln would say in 1864, had controlled him. But he had taken advantage of events.

To his cabinet, Lincoln attributed the timing of the Emancipation Proclamation to a promise he had made to his Maker. But the proclamation also allowed him to reverse a despairing judgment he had once made of himself. In 1841, in the depths of his depression over his then-broken-down courtship of Mary Todd, he had told Joshua Speed that "he had done nothing to make any human being remember that he had lived." Over two decades later, when Speed was visiting Washington, Lincoln reminded him of that conversation and said, "with earnest emphasis," that thanks to the Emancipation Proclamation, he would at last be remembered.

Thirteen

PREAMBLE TO THE CONSTITUTION

L INCOLN'S POLICIES COULD NOT BE GUIDED BY THE
founders, because the founders had never grappled with a national rebellion or a national project of emancipation. But Lincoln continued to be guided by their principles, which he found incarnated, as he had
in the 1850s, in the Declaration of Independence and the US Constitution.
During the first two and a half years of his presidency, he turned particularly to the Preamble to the Constitution, especially its first three words,
"We the People," which seemed to him to express a truth about the American Union as potent as the declaration that all men are created equal.

———

Lincoln kept no journals, and his letters were mostly businesslike, but
some of his private thinking about the founding documents has survived
on paper.

Before his inauguration, in January 1861, he sketched some thoughts about the relationship between the Declaration and the Constitution. His stimulus, ironically, was the last letter from his old colleague Alexander Stephens, who had asked him at the end of 1860 to criticize John Brown's raid: "A word fitly spoken by you now would be like 'apples of gold in pictures of silver.'" Stephens was quoting Proverbs 25:11: advice, supposedly from Solomon, about how to behave prudently at a royal court. "Put not forth thyself," Solomon said (25:6); speak only words that fit the time and place, then they will be golden. Lincoln ignored Stephens's appeal, but took up his verse. Stephens had wanted assurances for an unassurable South; Lincoln wanted to arrange his ideas about how America was organized and why.

The Declaration of Independence, he wrote to himself, expressed the "principle of 'Liberty to all.'" This was the principle that had animated the Revolution. "No oppressed people will fight and endure, as our fathers did, without the promise of something better than a mere change of masters." Lincoln would say this publicly a month later when he recalled Parson Weems and the Battle of Trenton in his speech to the New Jersey state senate.

In his memo to himself, he turned to Proverbs. "The assertion of that *principle*, at *that* time, was *the* word '*fitly spoken*' which has proved an 'apple of gold' to us. The *Union* and the *Constitution* are the *picture* of *silver* subsequently framed around it. . . . The *picture* was made *for* the apple—*not* the apple for the picture." The Declaration was the end, the Constitution the means. Did that make the Declaration more important than the Constitution? Practically, there was no difference. Lincoln added: "So let us act that neither *picture* [n]or *apple* shall ever be blurred or bruised or broken." Declaration and Constitution, one and inseparable.

Lincoln made another private précis of his thoughts about liberty and the Constitution, less intellectual but equally felt, in a letter to John Clay, the youngest of Henry's sons. In August 1862, Clay, a Kentucky loyalist, sent Lincoln his father's snuff box. Lincoln thanked him for the memento and for his assurances that he remained loyal to the Union. John also sent greetings from Lucretia Clay, Henry's eighty-one-year-old widow. The thought of the old woman touched a chord in Lincoln, as it had when the old woman was Rebecca Thomas, the Revolutionary War widow he had defended in court. "In the concurrent sentiments of your venerable mother," Lincoln wrote, "so long the partner of [Henry's] bosom and his honors, and lingering now, where he *was*, but for the call to rejoin him where he *is*, I recognize his voice, speaking as it ever spoke, for the Union, the Constitution, and the freedom of mankind." Lincoln had received a gift, and he gave a gift back: the gift of right remembrance. As he had with Jefferson, Lincoln honored the best of Clay—not his power or his fame or even his eloquence, but his twin devotion to freedom and to the Constitution.

There was another noteworthy point about this brief exchange: the vividness of the dead. Henry Clay was still alive, somewhere; speaking through his widow and his son, he was still alive here and now. The dead were not gone, but communicated with the living.

Alexander Stephens and Henry Clay's family made different choices, but they provoked the same thought in Lincoln—the Declaration, the document of liberty, and the Constitution, the document of law, were indissolubly linked.

———

Lincoln did not keep these thoughts to himself. He cited both founding documents as touchstones in numerous public utterances. He could be elusive when he was saying what he was doing, as his letter to Horace Greeley on emancipation showed, but he was forthright when he was saying why.

Lincoln's first extended public expression of his thinking after he became president came in his Special Message to Congress on July 4, 1861. The Special Message was given to the session of Congress he had summoned in his proclamation after the fall of Fort Sumter. (Congress would ordinarily have reassembled after a long summer break in

December. But the president was empowered—Article II, Section 3—
to convene it on "extraordinary occasions.") In the message Lincoln reviewed the course of events so far—the fall of Fort Sumter, Virginia's
secession, the neutrality of Kentucky, the first suspension of habeas
corpus. He called for 400,000 men and an outlay of $400 million. (By
war's end, the Union would have enlisted many, and spent far more.)

But, in the crush of politics and the approach of war, Lincoln also
devoted a great deal of time to the Declaration and the Constitution.
Doing so was not a formality, or a bit of historical decoration. He wanted
to show that his course and the country's destiny depended on the
founding documents.

He derided the Confederacy for rewriting them. "Our adversaries,"
he wrote, "have adopted some Declarations of Independence, in which,
unlike the good old one, penned by Jefferson, they omit the words 'all
men are created equal.' . . . They have adopted a temporary national
constitution, in the preamble of which, unlike our good old one, signed
by Washington, they omit 'We, the People,' and substitute, 'We the dep-
uties of the sovereign and independent states.'" The Confederates had
forgotten the documents, the authors, the signatories, and the principles; they had "press[ed] out of view the rights of men, and the authority
of the people."

Lincoln quoted the provisional constitution of the Confederacy,
which had been adopted in Montgomery in February, rather than the
final Confederate constitution, adopted in March, which did indeed
begin: "We, the people of the Confederate States, each state acting in
its sovereign and independent character." Was the omission of "We, the
People" in the preamble of the first a mere oversight, corrected in the
preamble of the second? Or was the final Confederate constitution still
weighted toward the states, rather than the people? Lincoln believed
the latter.

There was no possibility of mistaking the rebel declarations of independence. Georgia's, the longest, mentioned at the tail end the state's
desire "to seek new safeguards for our liberty, equality, security and

tranquility." But the context made clear that what Georgia wanted to guard was the liberty to own slaves and the state's equality with its Confederate peers.

The Confederacy professed to honor the founding fathers in its own way. Its vice president, Alexander Stephens, had offered a dramatic new direction for the new country in the "Corner-Stone" Speech: repudiate the founders openly, tell all the world they were wrong about slavery, and correct their error. Stephens's audience applauded him, but the Confederacy was not willing to be so radical. When it issued postage stamps, it put Jefferson on one (10 cents) and Washington on another (20 cents). Jefferson Davis, meanwhile, decorated the 5-cent stamp. Confederates, too, wanted to be founders' sons. Lincoln would have deplored their hypocrisy. The Confederacy put the founders on its letters, but it did not read or heed their words. The Confederates were not just rebels, but vandals, effacing ideas as they destroyed the country.

———

The Special Message was most important for developing a new thought, derived from the Preamble to the Constitution, specifically its invocation of "We the People."

The final draft of the Constitution, including the Preamble, had been produced in September 1787, the home stretch of the Constitutional Convention, by a five-man Committee of Style. The committee included two of the convention's most notable younger members, James Madison and Alexander Hamilton. But by Lincoln's day it was known that the committee member who did the writing was Gouverneur Morris, the peg-legged delegate from Pennsylvania.

In the Cooper Union address, Lincoln had called Gouverneur Morris a noted antislavery man. His denunciations of slavery and the slave trade at the Constitutional Convention were incendiary (he called slavery "the curse of heaven" and the slave trade a "defiance of the most sacred laws of humanity"). Morris was notable for many other qualities, good and bad. He was handsome, intelligent, witty, and independent-minded; he was also arrogant and impatient, easily moved to scorn or boredom, and not shy about saying so. Although Morris's leg had been amputated after a carriage accident, rumor had it that he had injured it by jumping out of a lover's window (after his amputation, his friend John Jay wrote that he might better have "lost *something* else"). Morris's defects (and some of his virtues) prevented him from having the successful political career that Jefferson had, and thus ensured that he would not be identified with the founding document he had drafted, as Jefferson was with the Declaration.

Morris brought his best qualities to bear in writing the Preamble. He worked from a draft, assembled by a Committee of Detail, which had gathered all the decisions the convention had made over a summer of orating and dickering. The Preamble of this preliminary draft was merely a list of states, and a decree: "We the people of the States of New Hampshire, Massachusetts, Rhode-Island," and so on, north to south, ending in Georgia, "do ordain, declare and establish the following Constitution . . . "

In place of this, Morris wrote a one-sentence paragraph that was a trim little essay about the purposes of government—forming a more perfect union, establishing justice, and the rest. But he began his version of the Preamble by cutting out the states entirely and leaving only "We the People of the United States."

He did so in part to finesse an awkward fact: Rhode Island had refused to attend the Constitutional Convention, and two of New York's three-man delegation had gone home in disgust in July, leaving behind only Alexander Hamilton, who, though he would sign the document when it was finished, felt he could not speak for his state by himself. The convention could not honestly list thirteen states at the head of its Constitution when only eleven were represented there.

"We the People," however, was more than a verbal fix. It identified those whom the Constitution would benefit and empower. All the jockeying and balancing at the Constitutional Convention had been done to design a government that would justly express the people's will.

Time and again the delegates had said so. Madison, the great analyst of the Constitution's checks and balances, said that all the Constitution's intricate defenses "against the inconveniencies of democracy" were "consistent with the democratic form of government." Hamilton, the arch-elitist of the Constitutional Convention, who gave a day-long speech advocating life terms for senators and the executive, nevertheless insisted that even a constitution containing such features would still be republican because under it all officeholders were chosen "by the people, or [by] a process of election originating with the people." Later he said that his fellow delegates "were now to decide forever the fate of Republican government."

Morris put the people in the Preamble twice more, by implication. The last of the purposes of government he listed was securing the blessings of liberty "to ourselves and our posterity" (to the people of the present and of the future). Then, finally, at the very end of his long sentence, its subject found its verb: "We the People . . . do ordain and establish" the Constitution. The people must act—they must ordain and they must establish—so that they and their descendants might benefit.

The Committee of Style submitted Morris's draft of the Constitution to the convention on September 12, 1787; there followed five days of last-minute arguments and adjustments. None of the delegates, however, raised any questions about the new Preamble or its new opening. All of this, by Lincoln's adulthood, was on the record, in Madison's *Notes*.

So when Lincoln in the Special Message wrote of "the People," he was following in the Preamble's spirit, as well as echoing its words. He called the United States "a constitutional republic, or a democracy—a government of the people, by the same people." The "power which made the Constitution," he wrote further on, "speaks from the preamble, calling itself 'We, the People.'" Again he wrote, of the impending struggle, "This is essentially a People's contest." It was a contest between those whose preamble still honored the people, and those whose preamble had demoted them.

If suppressing the rebellion was a People's contest, what was at stake?

One of the stakes that Lincoln discussed in the Special Message was economic. It was a matter that was dear to him: all people had a right to work for themselves. Lincoln had won the right when he stopped being hired out by Thomas Lincoln as a farmhand. A black woman would enjoy the right when she could eat the bread she made with her own hands. "The Union," Lincoln wrote, was fighting "to elevate the condition of men—to lift artificial weights from all shoulders—to clear the paths of laudable pursuit for all." Lincoln's Union was a Union of self-made Lincolns and self-made black women.

But the idea of a People's contest had a political as well as an economic meaning. In Lincoln's view the American republic was democratic in spirit, and this had consequences for his administration and for the prosecution of the war.

In the Special Message he off-handedly equated a constitutional republic with a democracy ("a constitutional republic or a democracy"). This was sloppy political science. Not all republics in history had been democratic, and not all democracies maintained their republican forms for long. The founding fathers were well aware of the excesses and failures of democracy in the ancient world. The modern world had seen a sinister innovation in democratic governance, the despotic plebiscite: one man, one vote, one time. This was how the Bonapartes, Napoleon and his nephew Napoleon III, had cemented their power in France.

Yet for all its dangers democracy was ingrained into American habits and institutions, and the American republic had become more democratic over time. National political parties were a democratic innovation almost as old as the Constitution itself; the Twelfth Amendment, passed in 1804, assumes their existence by instituting the two-man ticket of a presidential candidate and a running mate (the tickets have always been picked by parties). In Lincoln's lifetime the first Republican Party had changed its name to the Democratic Party, and Andrew Jackson, the incarnation of its new identity, was a populist. Jackson was the bogeyman of Lincoln's youth, but two of Lincoln's favorite presidential candidates, William Henry Harrison in 1840 and himself in 1860, had won the White House with populist campaigns.

The voice of the people was filtered in a variety of ways, according to the Constitution—the Senate preserved the equality of states; two houses of Congress, and an executive limited the powers of each; and judges were chosen by elected representatives, not elected themselves. Lincoln the conservative lawyer/politician approved all these mechanisms. But in democracies, elections have consequences, and Lincoln meant to follow them out. The Republican Party, playing by the rules, had been the people's choice in 1860. No possible coalition of its enemies could have kept it out of the White House. The people had spoken, and Lincoln meant to do what he had told them he would do until they spoke differently. Thus he and the Republicans had made no preinaugural compromises surrendering their views; nor would they back down until the people rebuked them at the polls. It was up to "the people themselves," he wrote in the Special Message, "and not their servants [to] reverse their own deliberate decisions."

There was one other meaning of a People's contest, and that was moral. The people had a responsibility to correct their own mistakes. This was one of the reasons why Lincoln pushed so steadily for compensating slave owners: not just to bribe them to free their slaves, not just to ease their pain for the loss of their property, but to spread their pain among all who had ever profited from slavery. He did not mention this reason in the Special Message. But in 1862, when he asked Congress for a constitutional amendment that would free all slaves by 1900 with compensation, he stated it plainly: "When it is remembered how unhesitatingly we all use cotton and sugar, and share the profits of dealing in them," who could say "that the south has been more responsible than the north" for maintaining slavery? If both were responsible, "is it not just" that slavery be ended "at a common charge"?

Acting to repair your own mistakes was Lincoln's version of popular sovereignty.

Lincoln returned to his idea of the People's contest again and again. He recalled it in July 1862 when he asked border-state politicians to accept compensation for the end of slavery: "I beseech you . . . as you would perpetuate popular government for the best people in the world." In September 1862 a delegation of ministers from Chicago asked him to issue an Emancipation Proclamation. He was only waiting for a victory to do it, but he told them, with some tartness, that the Union "already ha[d] an important principle" for which it was fighting: "Constitutional government is at stake."

The almost-victory at Antietam, which allowed Lincoln to issue the Emancipation Proclamation, had been followed by defeats and stalemates. In Virginia there were the debacles of Fredericksburg and Chancellorsville. In the west, Ulysses Grant bent his energies to reducing Vicksburg, midway between Memphis and New Orleans, one of the Confederacy's last bastions on the Mississippi River. After months of attacks, feints, and efforts to dig new channels through the bayous, he had managed by May 1863 to lay the city under siege. But it still held out.

In the east, the Confederates decided once again to move north. In June 1863 they crossed the Potomac into Maryland and then kept moving on into south-central Pennsylvania. Lincoln tapped a new commander, George Meade, to meet them. On the first of July the Union and Confederate armies collided at Gettysburg, a town forty-five miles southwest of Harrisburg. After three days of fighting, the invaders withdrew, beaten.

The convergence of a victory at Gettysburg, another victory at Vicksburg (which finally surrendered to Grant), and the Fourth of July made a banner day for the Union—and an unmissable opportunity to draw historical parallels and political lessons. When Lincoln addressed a happy throng that had gathered outside the White House on the evening of July 7, he did not let the opportunity pass. "How long ago is it?—eighty odd years—since on the Fourth of July, for the first time in the history of the world, a nation . . . declared as a self-evident truth that 'all men are created equal.'" He rang the changes on the date, and on the Declaration of Independence. On July 4, 1826, the Declaration's "two most distinguished" signers, Jefferson the author and John Adams the doughty advocate of independence, were taken by "Almighty God . . . from the stage of action," Lincoln said. "And now, on this last Fourth of July just passed . . . a gigantic rebellion, at the bottom of which is an effort to overthrow the principle that all men were created equal," had suffered twin defeats. Lincoln's survey of famous Fourths was like a three-act play: 1776, the Declaration; 1826, the apotheosis of its signers; 1863, the confounding of its enemies. The founding fathers had gone, but their handiwork remained unconquered.

"Gentlemen," Lincoln concluded, "this is a glorious theme, and the occasion for a speech, but I am not prepared to make one worthy of the occasion." That would come later. So he praised the Union Army, and asked the bands that had come along with the crowd for music.

———

Like many victories in the Civil War, the Union's victories on July 4, 1863, were incomplete. The fall of Vicksburg was indeed a triumph—a key step in accomplishing the Anaconda plan. After the fall of Port Hudson in Louisiana on July 9, the Union commanded all the lower Mississippi, from the tip of Illinois to the Gulf of Mexico, and the Confederacy was cut in two. Intelligent Confederates recognized the magnitude of the loss. Diarist Mary Chesnut was traveling by train when, she said, "a man came in, stood up, and read from a paper, 'The surrender of Vicksburg.' I felt as if I had been struck a hard blow on the top of my head."

After Gettysburg, however, Meade's army had been too battered to pursue the surviving Confederates, who retired to Virginia. So the battle, though important, was not final, but one more episode in the grind of the eastern theater.

The casualties at Gettysburg were the worst of the war so far: more than 3,100 Union men killed (joined by 4,700 Confederates). The bodies, hastily buried on the battlefield, had been dug up, here and there, by grieving relatives or hungry hogs. "Arms and legs and sometimes heads" protruded from unquiet graves. An interstate commission organized a reburial and planned a ceremony in November to dedicate the cemetery. The oration was to be delivered by Edward Everett, George Washington's rhapsode and losing vice-presidential candidate in 1860, still at sixty-nine years old one of America's greatest orators. Lincoln was invited to give "a few appropriate remarks" after Everett finished.

Everett spoke for two hours and he spoke well. He surveyed the causes of the conflict, gave a detailed account of the battle, and looked forward to victory and reconciliation. His language was more chaste than that of Henry Clay and his peers, the generation of orators just before his. Some of his small touches were almost austere, as when he described, before Pickett's charge, "the awful silence, more terrible than the wildest tumult of battle." Or he could be blunt as a bat, as when he explained why he called the war a rebellion. "I call the war which the Confederates are waging . . . a 'rebellion' because it is one, and in grave matters it is best to call things by their right names."

Everett, like Lincoln, was mindful of the founding fathers. His greatest speech had been in praise of Washington, and he praised him again at Gettysburg as "our Washington . . . the founder of the American Union," who with "more than mortal skill" had built "a well-compacted, prosperous and powerful State." But in this speech Washington was no longer the smooth icon of unity. He had antagonists, anti-Washingtons: the leaders of the Confederacy, whom Everett in his angriest language called "bold, bad men . . . who for base and selfish ends rebel against beneficent governments. [They shall] inherit the execrations of the ages."

In a letter written the day after the ceremony, Lincoln told Everett he had particularly liked two passages of his speech. One had praised the nurses of the wounded: "brethren and sisters of Christian benevolence, ministers of compassion, angels of pity, hasten[ing] to the field and the hospital, to moisten the parched tongue, to bind the ghastly wounds."

Everett began by mentioning nurses of both sexes, though he went on to single out the women. When Lincoln complimented the passage, he wrote as if it had been entirely about "our noble women." Lincoln relied rather little on female figures in his rhetoric; he did not depict America or liberty as a she, as Parson Weems had done. But particular women, including Lucretia Clay and Rebecca Thomas, or even specific imagined women, such as Everett's nurses or the black woman who ought to be free to make her own bread, drew his attention and sympathy.

The other passage that Lincoln liked concerned the Preamble to the Constitution, which Everett noted did not mention the states "by their names" at all, but derived its authority from "the People of the United States." So Lincoln had been saying for over two years.

Lincoln's address (the program called it *Dedicatory Remarks*) lasted three minutes. This was to be the speech worthy of the glorious theme that he had imagined when he had answered the serenaders outside the White House on July 7. He did not jot it down on an envelope in the train coming to Gettysburg, as legend has it, but prepared it carefully beforehand. In it he would try to explain, in an epitome, the purpose of the war, at what, he hoped, was its turning point. He would do that by linking the war to America's history and purpose. He would crown and compact all he had been saying about the founding fathers since his Peoria speech, in 1854, or his eulogy for Henry Clay in 1852. He would give a better answer to the questions he had raised about the founders' ongoing relevance at the Springfield Young Men's Lyceum in 1838.

The Gettysburg Address is not quite the modern ideal of plain prose, as expounded by George Orwell in his essay "Politics and the English Language," written in 1946 and still canonical. For Orwell, English words derived from Anglo-Saxon were simple and therefore virtuous, while words of Latin origin were complicated and lent themselves to trickery. But, as Garry Wills noted, Lincoln used Latinate words when he felt like it—"'conceived in liberty,' not born in freedom; . . . 'dedicated to [a] proposition,' not vowed to a truth." It is hard to say, at

this point, whether the glacid sheen of his address is inherent or con-
ferred by so many repetitions. By making it concise, Lincoln certainly
made it repeatable.

He began, as he had begun his reply to the serenaders four months
earlier, with the Declaration of Independence. Now at Gettysburg he
had done the math ahead of time. Instead of asking, as he had at the
White House, "How long ago is it?—eighty odd years," he said, "Four
score and seven years ago . . . " He risked the mental gymnastics his
listeners might perform—$((4 \times 20) + 7)$ from 1863 equals 1776—to gain a
rhyme and an alliteration, three *ors*, three *fs*: "*four* sc*ore* and seven years
ago our *f*athers brought *f*orth . . . "

He also gained a biblical echo. "Four score" appears in various lists
and enumerations in the Old Testament. It is also used in giving men's
ages, most famously in Psalm 90, which was supposed to have been
written by Moses. Verse 10 is about the span of human life: "The days of
our lives are threescore years and ten; and if by reason of strength they
be fourscore years, yet is their strength labour and sorrow; for it is soon
cut off, and we fly away."

In his eulogy for Henry Clay, Lincoln had equated Clay's life with
the life of the country. Clay was seventy-five years old when he died
in 1852; the country was seventy-six. The country was older now, but
eighty-seven years, though longer than the life span envisaged in the
psalm, remained within the range of ordinary human possibility. Chief
Justice Roger Taney was still sitting on the bench at age eighty-six.

The psalm was about death ("soon cut off, and we fly away")—an
appropriate thought for the dedication of a cemetery. Everyone buried
and reburied there had been cut off sooner than seventy or eighty
years, and violently; but even the happiest civilians would join them,
in time.

But the one metaphor Lincoln would allow himself was not about
death but life—specifically, birth.

He described two births in his address. The first was in 1776, when
the nation was "conceived in Liberty." The Declaration of Independence

was the birth certificate. Lincoln quoted his favorite phrase—"all men are created equal"—to make the allusion, and the principle he found so important, absolutely clear.

There followed a mention of the war and the battle. Everett had described both in detail, so it was fitting of Lincoln not to try to match him. But he did dwell on the motives of the Union men who had fought at Gettysburg. Lincoln had given one other important speech about a battle—the Battle of Trenton, which he had recalled in his remarks to the New Jersey Senate in 1861. Then he had said, after summarizing Parson Weems's account, "there must have been something more than common that those men struggled for." He had stated what that something was: "this Union . . . and the liberties of the people." But the men who had fought at Gettysburg had also been struggling for something more than common. "The brave men, living and dead, who struggled here," Lincoln said, had been devoted to "that cause." What was "that cause"? To prove that a nation conceived in liberty could "long endure"—that it could face down a rebellion in eleven states, and that it could maintain its principles while doing so. The Battle of Trenton had been refought and re-won at Gettysburg.

Lincoln's speech at Trenton in 1861 had not been all about the battle or the past. He had said that there was an important task facing the living: Union and liberties must "be perpetuated in accordance with the original idea for which that struggle was made." At Gettysburg in 1863 Lincoln saw a similar task for the living. They had come to dedicate a cemetery. But "it is for us the living, rather, to be dedicated here to the unfinished work."

The unfinished work would be another birth—the second of the address. "[Let us] here highly resolve . . . that this nation, under God, shall have a new birth of freedom."

New birth of freedom is a portentous phrase that in the years since Lincoln uttered it has tempted opportunists and alarmed the timorous. What exactly did it mean? Was it open-ended? Could it be stretched to include anything at all—communism, for instance? One of Lincoln's foreign admirers during the Civil War was Karl Marx, the German communist who earned a little money by writing articles on European politics for Horace Greeley's *New York Tribune*, and on American politics for European newspapers. Marx had hailed the Emancipation Proclamation in *Die Presse* of Vienna as "the most significant document in American history since the founding of the Union, and one which tears up the old American Constitution." Marx hated slavery in the nineteenth century, yet he would be one of the fountainheads of slavery and mass murder in the twentieth. Inspiring words are potent, sometimes dangerous things; they can inspire idiots and devils as well as good men. John Brown read the Bible.

But Lincoln tried to be a careful writer and speaker. He generally meant what he said, and said only what he meant. If he had intended to write a blank check at Gettysburg, he would have called for "a birth of new freedom" (or "a birth of new freedoms"). What he did call for was "a new birth of freedom." His freedom was the old freedom, the freedom of "our fathers." It was what they had envisioned in 1776, a lifetime ago.

Their freedom needed a second birth because of the slaughter and strain of war. And it needed a second birth because the first birth had left a birthmark—the cancer or wen of slavery. (Lincoln did not say such a thing at Gettysburg, and he said it only from time to time, because of the risk of seeming to criticize the founding fathers, whom he considered helpless in dealing with slavery, rather than negligent or malicious.) What he did say at Gettysburg was that the men of the present should preserve, and revivify, what "our fathers" had done; the men of the present could complete their fathers' unfulfilled intentions.

This was Lincoln's final correction of his youthful mistakes in the Lyceum Speech. Then the novice lawyer and closet Paine-ite had honored the fathers, but dismissed them (with poetic regret) as dead. They were still dead—dead as Henry Clay; dead as all the reburied corpses at the battlefield. But if dead men have lived with a purpose, it can live after them; they can live on in it. We the living can share their purpose, which has become ours.

Lincoln closed by referring to the Preamble. He had fit two founding documents into an address of 272 words: neat work. He took the language of his Special Message of 1861—"a government of the people, by the same people"—polished it, and made it the last of the high resolves that end the address: "[Let us] here highly resolve . . . that government of the people, by the people, for the people, shall not perish from the earth." The reporter from the Associated Press who covered the speech noted here that there was "long-continued applause."

By framing these words in this way, Lincoln drew one more implication from the Preamble. Principles, even great ones, are not self-enacting. If government of, by, and for the people was not to perish, it was up to the people to resolve to sustain it. They had to ordain and establish it, as they had done in the Constitution. But then they had to vote wisely in its elections. They had to fight for it, if necessary. This was the value—the purpose—of pictures of silver: they preserved the apples of gold.

Lincoln often said that he respected the people. He pretended to be one of them, for political effect; and despite his intelligence, pride, and ambition, he remained one of them, roaring over Petroleum V. Nasby and Artemus Ward while auditors who were less easily amused ground their teeth. In the Special Message of 1861, Lincoln had praised "the patriotic instinct of the plain people," who "understand, without an argument, that destroying the government which was made by [George] Washington means no good to them." Perhaps Lincoln said too much. Maybe the people did understand, by instinct, their best interests. But they were not always motivated to act on what they knew. They needed arguments; they needed jokes (that were pointed); they needed inspiration. They needed leadership.

Lincoln told Speed that, thanks to the Emancipation Proclamation, he would be remembered. But he would never have been able to issue the proclamation (or defend the Union) if he had not won elections, united a party, made his case. He did it by hard work and dirty work: watching for opportunities, stroking egos, greasing wheels, all the back-room deals and open maneuvers of politics. But he made his mark as a politician mostly by communication. He would never have been able to do anything memorable and right if he had not said so many memorable, true words.

Fourteen

1864–1865: WAR, DEATH

WHEN LINCOLN GAVE THE GETTYSBURG ADDRESS, THE Civil War had lasted two years and seven months, as long as the entire War of 1812, nearly as long as the Mexican War. Gettysburg and Vicksburg had felt like turning points, the beginning of the end, but how long would the end take? What sort of end would it be—a new birth of freedom, or some haggard compromise?

And what of the ongoing cost—in lives, and in scars on the lives of the survivors? In 1864 Lincoln began to speak of "this terrible war," and it was certainly the most terrible in American history so far.

As Lincoln labored under the shadow of these questions, and tended to his daily military and political tasks, the founding fathers did not vanish—they were by now inseparable from his vision and his program—yet they would shrink, and make way for another Father.

——

The obvious military course for Lincoln and his generals was the one they in fact followed, the Anaconda plan: squeeze the encircled heart of the Confederacy until it gave out.

There was a setback in September 1863. A Union army, trying to push into Georgia from southeastern Tennessee, was beaten at Chickamauga and forced to retreat to Chattanooga. Ulysses Grant, summoned from his headquarters at Vicksburg to retrieve the situation, was given control of almost all the Union armies west of the Appalachians. At the battle of Chattanooga at the end of November, Grant defeated the Confederates, allowing the Union to resume its forward march.

This was now Grant's moment. In March 1864 he was called to Washington and given command of all Union armies, east and west. Lincoln told him that "all he wanted or had ever wanted was some one who would take the responsibility and act." Grant put his longtime comrade William Tecumseh Sherman, whose features were as harsh as Grant's were satisfying, in his place in eastern Tennessee, and made his own headquarters with the Union army in northeastern Virginia. Grant's assignment to Sherman was to take Atlanta, a hub of the Confederacy's railway network; his assignment to himself was to beat the enemy armies defending Richmond.

Their efforts were bloody and for a long time fruitless. Starting in early May at a point near Chancellorsville, Grant fought a month-long campaign—with major battles at the Wilderness, Spotsylvania Courthouse, and Cold Harbor—which left him a few miles east of Richmond without, however, breaking the Confederate line. In June he crossed the James River and moved south to attempt a siege of Petersburg, a railway junction vital to the Confederate capital's communication and supply. Meanwhile, Sherman fought a series of battles from May through the end of the summer that took him from the northwest corner of Georgia to the outskirts of Atlanta.

The pressure of two simultaneous campaigns was designed to prevent the Confederacy from shifting troops to reinforce either. The fighting bled the enemy, but the Union bled even more: by the beginning of September, Sherman had lost 4,000 killed, Grant more than 7,000. ("I have always regretted that the last assault at Cold Harbor was ever made," Grant would write tersely in his memoirs.) Grant had nevertheless kept a Union army in Virginia despite its losses, not retreating north to lick its wounds, while Sherman had gained a foothold in the Confederacy's largest state.

Lincoln encouraged his commanders' aggressive temperaments. In a note to Grant in August he urged him to "hold on with a bull dog grip, and chew and choke as much as possible."

————

Politically, Lincoln sought to achieve the Republican Party's goals, to manage its feuds, and to lead it to victory.

By 1863 Republicans had shifted from a policy of containing slavery to dismantling it. The most tangible step toward the new goal was the enlistment of black men in the armed forces. This had been happening on the sly since 1862, in Kansas and South Carolina. "This must never see daylight," Stanton warned the Union general who was doing the enlisting in South Carolina, "because it is so much in advance of public opinion."

But by January 1863 Lincoln felt that public opinion had advanced sufficiently to enable him to declare, in the Emancipation Proclamation, that freed slaves could be "received into the armed service of the United States." The announcement encouraged free blacks in the North to sign up; the war was now manifestly their fight, too. Lincoln defended the policy in a letter he sent to be read to a Republican rally in Springfield in September 1863. Addressing a hypothetical critic of black soldiers, he used his best platform sarcasm: "You say you will not fight to free negroes. Some of them seem willing to fight for you; but no matter . . ." With a straight face he said the opposite of the truth, for it mattered a great deal. Black soldiers performed every task, from humdrum guard duty to desperate combat. By the end of the war, about 10 percent of all the men who served in Union ranks were black.

George Washington had commanded black soldiers in the Revolution, and one icon of his career recorded the fact. Emanuel Leutze's grand painting, "Washington Crossing the Delaware," which had been exhibited in New York City and the Capitol Rotunda in the 1850s, showed a black oarsman in the main boat (probably from the 14th Massachusetts, a regiment recruited from Marblehead sailors, mostly white but including blacks and Indians as well). When Washington fought for liberty at Trenton, there were free black men at his side.

But the military soon thereafter became all white: the Militia Act of 1792 specified that its provisions applied to "free able-bodied white male citizen[s]." Andrew Jackson had enlisted blacks to help him defend New Orleans, but that was an emergency measure.

Black soldiers in the Union Army from 1863 on would serve under white officers in segregated units. Still, they earned one of the highest marks of citizenship—fighting for the common defense.

———

In tandem with the national rebellion, little rebellions broke out continually in the Republican Party—trivial by comparison, but requiring Lincoln's attention and care to snuff out. The Republicans who were most unhappy most of the time were the Radicals. Everything that Lincoln did they wished he had done the day before, and they were certain that if they themselves had been in a position of authority they could have done it.

Perhaps they would get their chance in the 1864 election. Five of the first seven presidents (Washington, Jefferson, Madison, Monroe, and Jackson) had served two terms. But since Jackson left office in 1837, no president had. It was not for lack of trying: Van Buren and Pierce had sought reelection, and Tyler and Fillmore, the two vice presidents promoted by death, had tried to be elected in their own right. But all had failed. The presidency seemed to have fallen into a pattern of rotation.

The Republican most eager to replace Lincoln was Salmon P. Chase. He had a political machine ready-made: 10,000 Treasury Department employees, who could be turned into campaigners, augmented by the 2,500 salesmen who reported to Jay Cooke, the financier in charge of selling war bonds. But Chase moved too soon. In February a committee of his supporters sent a circular condemning Lincoln and praising Chase to one hundred leading Republicans. It was supposed to be confidential, but there is no such thing as a confidential message with one hundred recipients. The main effect of its public exposure was to stimulate a rash of endorsements for Lincoln.

John Frémont, the first Republican presidential candidate, lent himself to another Radical rebellion in the spring. He and Lincoln had clashed three years earlier over his premature emancipation order in Missouri and allegations of corruption, and Frémont cherished their disagreements as grievances. A convention of four hundred Radicals met in Cleveland at the end of May and nominated Frémont for president.

Lincoln, mindful of the political limitations of both men—Chase was tone-deaf, Frémont self-infatuated—watched their efforts but chose to let each fall of its own weight. He did not even bother to be vengeful. When Chase offered his resignation after his circular had been exposed, Lincoln refused to accept it, just as he had after Chase's failed cabinet intrigue in 1862. Lincoln's response to the Cleveland convention, when a friend spoke to him of it, was to read aloud a passage from the Bible describing David, the future king of Israel, hiding from the wrath of Saul, the king he would replace, in a cave: "And every one that was in distress, and every one that was in debt, and every one that was discontented, gathered themselves unto him; and he became a captain over them: and there were with him about four hundred men" (1 Samuel 22:2). Four hundred men might be enough for a king on the run; not enough for a presidential campaign.

Lincoln did have allies, and they labored for his renomination with his blessing. Simon Cameron got all the Republicans in the Pennsylvania state legislature to sign a letter urging Lincoln to run again—an important endorsement in the nation's second-largest state. So Lincoln's magnanimity to his disgraced former secretary of war was repaid.

The Republican convention, meeting in Baltimore June 7–8, nominated Lincoln on the first ballot (22 of out 506 votes were cast for Grant, against his wishes, but they switched to Lincoln at the end of the roll call to make the choice unanimous). The convention assumed the name National Union Party in the hope of attracting war Democrats. With the same end in mind, it tapped former Democratic senator Andrew Johnson, the military governor of Tennessee, to run with Lincoln, instead of his incumbent vice president, Hannibal Hamlin.

Lincoln seems to have been indifferent to the switch in running mates. Even without the benefit of foreknowledge, this was an odd thing to treat casually. Two presidents (Harrison and Taylor) had already died in office. Lincoln had supported both of them, and the misbehavior of one of their successors (Tyler) had crippled Lincoln's old party, the Whigs, in the moment of its first great success.

Johnson was a patriot and a brave man, and by 1864 he had abandoned his support of slavery in favor of emancipation, but he boiled with resentments. A conversation he had with Charles Francis Adams Jr., another of the diplomat's sons, as the South was seceding, in which Johnson discussed his rebellious Senate colleagues, captured his tone. He began with David Yulee of Florida: "Miserable little cuss! I remember him [when I was] in the House—the contemptible little Jew—standing there and begging us—yes! begging us to let Florida in as a state. Well! We let her in, and took care of her, and fought her Indians; and now that despicable little beggar stands up in the Senate and talks about *her* rights." He moved on to Judah Benjamin, of Louisiana: "There's another Jew—that miserable Benjamin! He looks on a country and a government as he would on a suit of old clothes. He sold out the old one; and he would sell out the new if he could in so doing make two or three millions." This was an old anti-Semitic trope: the shiftiness of Jews, epitomized by the fact that many of them were tailors, a profession that follows fashion. Yet Johnson had been a tailor himself: hatred was fueled by self-hatred. He finished with Louis Wigfall of Texas: "a damned blackguard" who "hadn't a cent." (Wigfall was a bankrupt. But

Johnson himself had been poor once—more self-hatred.) "The strongest secessionists never owned the hair of a nigger." This was the man who was now supposed to help Lincoln lead the Union to victory and then, if that happened, help him bind the nation's wounds.

Yet men rarely count on their own deaths; the vice presidency was (and remains) a constitutional oddity—necessary, but most of the time, inconsequential. So the ticket of Lincoln and Johnson would face the voters.

———

Lincoln's worst political problem was not Republican infighting, but war fatigue. The hopes roused by Grant's ascent had shriveled in the months-long stalemate.

In August, Thurlow Weed wrote Seward that a Lincoln victory was "an impossibility." Republicans considered desperate scenarios: If Lincoln lost New York, Pennsylvania, and Illinois, he could still win by three electoral votes; if Nevada, which was enjoying a silver rush, became a state in time for the election, his margin would be six votes.

Late in August Lincoln wrote a brief memo to himself sketching what he would do if he lost: since he believed it would be impossible, with a Democratic administration, to save the Union, he would try to work with the Democratic president-elect to save it in the four months before the inauguration. It was a desperate thought—Why would the victor cooperate with his defeated opponent? But it salved Lincoln's honor—*I will have done all I could*—and allayed his fears of approaching impotence—*I will try to do something*. He brought the memo, folded, to a cabinet meeting and asked his secretaries to sign it, unread, so that he could prove his intentions later on. Lincoln was a master of small-group theatrics, but the tone of melodrama and self-pity in this little show suggests his alarm and foreboding.

The Democratic convention, which met in Chicago from August 29 to 31, gave the Republicans their first sign of hope. The nomination

went to George McClellan on the first ballot. The Little Napoleon
seemed like a good candidate: he had always been popular with his
troops, taking good care of them everywhere but on the battlefield. He
also had ample reason to dislike Lincoln. But McClellan wanted to win
the war. The convention, however, was dominated by peace Democrats
who cheered when the band in the hall played "Dixie." The platform
they wrote called for "immediate efforts" to end the fighting. McClellan
refused to run on it, though he accepted the nomination. In attacking
Lincoln from different directions at once, the Democrats gave the impression of fighting each other.

One thing on which war Democrats and peace Democrats could
agree was racism. Democratic campaign pamphlets called Lincoln
"Abraham Africanus," whose first commandment was, "Thou shalt have
no other God but the negro." One Democratic cartoon showed white
Republican men dancing with fleshy black women in low-cut gowns
(the reader knew what would happen next). Racial manners and mores
were different then: the letters and casual conversation of every white
politician of the day, the most Radical Republicans included, could
be culled for racist remarks and expressions. But the Democrats said
theirs in public; they were proud to say them. Racism was both a campaign plank and a policy position; the Democrats were the party of
negrophobia.

Two days after the Democrats adjourned, Atlanta fell. Finally the
direction of the war could be measured in something more dramatic
than attrition. The Confederacy had already been severed along the
Mississippi. Sherman was now poised to sever it again, between the
Carolinas and the Gulf states.

The tangible victory changed the dynamic of the election even more
than the dynamic of the war. In one stroke the administration was transformed from a quagmire to a success. Lincoln tended to every detail
that might make success complete. In September, as a sop to the Radicals, he asked Montgomery Blair to resign as postmaster general; the
Radicals should have the satisfaction of feeling that, even though they

could not lift Chase or Frémont to the White House, they could drive a Blair from the cabinet. The Blairs accepted the dismissal with good grace: their view was, anything to get Lincoln reelected. The following month, Chief Justice Taney went to his reward, age four score and seven years. Chase yearned to succeed him, but Lincoln, who wanted Chase's support on the hustings, withheld nominating him until after the election.

Soldiers were an important part of the Republican coalition—McClellan was popular with the troops, but Lincoln, it turned out, was even more popular, mental and moral leadership trumping military command. Everything was done to get out the soldier vote. Since Indiana law did not allow troops to cast absentee ballots, Sherman gave his Indiana regiments furloughs for the bellwether state elections in October.

Cash flowed to civilian poll workers. Days before the election, Weed, hopeful once more, wrote Lincoln that "every ward" in New York and Brooklyn had been "abundantly supplied with 'material aid.'"

Election Day was November 8. Twenty-five states voted. Lincoln won every state he had carried in 1860, except for his share of New Jersey's electoral votes. Three new states had joined the Union since the 1860 election—Kansas, West Virginia, and Nevada (under the wire, on October 31); Lincoln won these, too. He also carried Missouri and Maryland, for a total of 212 electoral votes. McClellan took Delaware, Kentucky, and all of New Jersey, for 21 electoral votes. Lincoln's victory in the popular vote was equally lopsided—55 percent to 45 percent (he carried Illinois by nearly the same margin). No one in the Confederacy, of course, participated, which skewed the results. But Lincoln would have won even if every Confederate state had voted and McClellan had carried them all; Lincoln's popular vote, over 2.2 million, was 350,000 more than he had received in 1860.

After all the intrigue and jabber of a capital city, and all the fears and qualms of a campaign, Lincoln's endless White House sessions with ordinary folk, retold by them to the folks back home, and his written and spoken words, often eloquent, always clear, had brought him to this point. He was the symbol of the Union and of its cause. Despite all the distractions and sufferings of wartime, voters recognized it.

Tradition forbade Lincoln from campaigning himself, though he did make brief remarks to Union regiments that marched to the White House to be reviewed before being mustered out. In these he explained—less resoundingly than at Gettysburg, but no less earnestly—what the Union was fighting for. "Nowhere in the world," he told the 148th Ohio, was there "a government of so much liberty and equality"; it was the people's duty to transmit it "to our children and our children's children forever." This was a thought he had been turning over in his mind from the Lyceum Address ("the perpetuation of our political institutions") to the Gettysburg Address ("shall not perish from the earth"). As he had for a decade, he looked back to the founding fathers, for it was their handiwork that Americans had to transmit: "We are striving to maintain the government and institutions of our fathers." But in these remarks Lincoln also, at long last, included his actual father. Thomas Lincoln had a role to play in the American system, too. "The present moment," Lincoln said, "finds me at the White House, yet there is as good a chance for your children [to be there] as there was for my father's. . . . To the humblest and poorest amongst us are held out the highest privileges and positions."

His father had given him life, and under the system of the founding fathers, that was opportunity enough for any man to rise as high as he could.

———

Lincoln's reelection and the renewed impetus given to the war effort were stages in the fulfillment of his life's work. What about death's work?

Lincoln's grandfather had been killed by Indians; Lincoln himself had seen the bodies of men who had been scalped in the Black Hawk War. In his domestic life, he had lost a mother, a sister, a fiancée, and a young son to various diseases, all before reaching the White House. Such brushes with death were common enough in early nineteenth-century America.

The destruction of the Civil War was uncommon. After Lincoln's death, William Herndon, ruminating on his friend's intellectual preoccupations, came up with a homely phrase. Lincoln, he wrote, tended to ignore individuals "unless they should concretely appear and tap [him] on the shoulder and say, 'Here we are again.'" The war gave many taps on the shoulder—especially the shoulder of the commander in chief.

Lincoln's former law student Elmer Ellsworth had been killed in Alexandria in May 1861, in one of the first engagements of the war. In October 1861 another Illinois friend, Edward Baker, was killed in the Battle of Ball's Bluff, a sharp engagement in the lull before the Peninsula Campaign. Baker had been Lincoln's peer in Illinois Whig politics; he was the namesake of Lincoln's second son and the man who had introduced the president-elect to the crowd from the podium at his first inauguration. Lincoln said Baker's death struck him "like a whirlwind from a desert"; at the funeral, he wept "like a child."

William McCullough was the court clerk in Bloomington, Illinois, on Lincoln's old circuit. When the war began, he asked the president to help him join an Illinois cavalry unit. He needed presidential help because he was fifty years old and had lost an arm in a farm accident. Lincoln intervened for his old friend. In December 1862, in the early days of the Vicksburg campaign, McCullough was killed in a cavalry skirmish in northern Mississippi. Lincoln wrote a letter of condolence to McCullough's daughter Fanny. "In this sad world of ours, sorrow comes to all; and, to the young, it comes with bitterest agony, because it takes them unawares. The older have learned to ever expect it." Only time, he wrote, would ease the pain. But time now brought only more deaths.

The powers-that-be in Washington were not insulated from battle. Simon Cameron, when he was secretary of war, lost his brother James at the First Battle of Bull Run. William Seward's third son, William Jr., had a horse shot out from under him during a cavalry battle in Maryland (he escaped with nothing worse than a broken leg). Edward Bates had one son in the Union Army, one in the Missouri militia, one at West Point, and another in the Confederate Army. Deaths in the family crossed political lines. Mary Lincoln lost two half-brothers and a brother-in-law fighting on the Confederate side. When she invited Emilie Helm, her widowed sister, to the White House, Lincoln was criticized for it: in the minds of his enemies, he could be by turns a black man, white trash, and a rebel sympathizer.

As the commander in chief, Lincoln was exposed to losses beyond those of family and friends. At the end of 1864, he wrote a letter, which has become one of his most famous, to Lydia Bixby, a Boston widow who, he had been told by the military, had lost the shocking total of five sons. There is some dispute about whether the Bixby letter was actually written by Lincoln, or for him by John Hay. Whoever was the wordsmith labored under the futility of his own words: "I feel how weak and fruitless must be any words of mine which should attempt to beguile you from the grief of a loss so overwhelming. But I cannot refrain from tendering to you the consolation that may be found in the thanks of the Republic they died to save." Lincoln, it turned out, had been misinformed. Mrs. Bixby had lost two sons in battle; one was honorably discharged, one deserted, and one either deserted or died in a Confederate prison. But wasn't the loss of two (possibly three) sons grievous enough? The loss of one?

Sometimes the specter of loss came almost literally close enough to tap Lincoln on the shoulder. Noah Brooks was a young journalist who had met Lincoln in Illinois in the 1850s, then covered his presidency for a California newspaper. One day he accompanied Lincoln on a visit to a soldiers' hospital in Washington. Ahead of them, as they made their rounds, a "well-dressed lady" was distributing tracts. After she had moved on, "a patient picked up with languid hand the leaflet dropped upon his cot, and, glancing at the title, began to laugh." When Lincoln and Brooks came up to the man, Lincoln gently reproved him: "That lady doubtless means you well, and it is hardly fair for you to laugh at her gift." The soldier explained why he could not help it: "She has given me a tract on 'The Sin of Dancing,' and both of my legs are shot off."

The story has the shape of a joke—one of Lincoln's, perhaps. But this joke was on Lincoln himself. And on the legless soldier, of course.

Joshua Speed witnessed one of Lincoln's close encounters with the war, not involving death, only military justice and the helplessness of those caught in its meshes. But Speed was acute enough to understand its impact.

Late in the war, Speed came to Washington to see the president. Lincoln asked him to sit in his office until he was done with visitors. At last only "two ladies in humble attire" were left. One was the wife of a man who had been arrested for resisting the draft in western Pennsylvania, the other the mother of another resister. "They both commenced to speak at once," and Lincoln asked for their written petition.

"We've got no petition," the older one said. "We couldn't write one, and had no money to pay for writing one. I thought it best to come and see you."

Lincoln called for the relevant administrator and told him that, after thinking over the matter—it was evidently an ongoing case—he had decided to pardon all the accused. ("I believe I will turn out the flock," was how he put it.)

The younger woman fell to her knees in gratitude, but Lincoln told her to get up. "Don't kneel to me, thank God and go." Then the older woman bade him farewell: "Good-bye, good-bye, Mr. Lincoln. I shall never see you again till we meet in Heaven."

Lincoln "instantly took her right hand in both of his and following her to the door . . . said, 'I am afraid with all my troubles I shall never get there. But if I do I will find you. That you wish me to get there is the best wish you could make for me.'"

Finally the two old friends were alone. "Lincoln," said Speed, "with my knowledge of your nervous sensibility, it is a wonder that such scenes as this don't kill you."

Lincoln answered that that scene was the only thing he had done all day that had given him any pleasure.

Lincoln and Speed had been the closest of friends twenty-five years earlier. Marriage and distance had parted them, then politics had parted them still more: in the 1850s, Speed could not understand Lincoln's vehemence in opposing the expansion of slavery, while Lincoln could not understand Speed's failure to understand. Once the Union fell apart, their differences shrank away; Speed and his brother James were Lincoln's eyes and ears in problematic Kentucky. In December 1864, after Edward Bates had resigned as attorney general, for reasons of age and ill health, Lincoln picked Speed's brother to replace him.

One of the bonds uniting Lincoln and Speed at the height of their friendship had been women and distress—women they had distressed, women who distressed them. Here, in the president's office, was another tableau of Lincoln, Speed, and two distressed women, purged of any question of sex or marriage. It could have been a sentimental scene rendered by a period artist—a print by Currier and Ives, or one of John Rogers's mass-produced statuary groups—with a title such as "Mercy in War-time," or "The President's Good Deed."

And surrounding the entire scene, like the throb of steam engines, was each man's awareness, Lincoln's especially, that this drama of mercy was an eddy in a rush of conquest, resistance, liberation, injury, imprisonment, illness, and death. A fatalist, such as Lincoln professed to be, must have smiled at the tininess of the pleasures that even he, the commander in chief, could snatch from the torrent.

Alongside the war and its inspiring, lurid, brutal movements of men and ideas, Lincoln's domestic troubles seem inconsequential. Yet they troubled him. In February 1862 his third son, Willie, had died of typhoid fever, age eleven. Mary Lincoln despaired, convinced that God had taken Willie as punishment for her political ambition. Lincoln believed that he communed with his dead son in dreams; Mary tried to contact him through spiritualist mediums.

Before and after her child's death, Mrs. Lincoln was an unfortunate
first lady. Yearning to cut a figure in Washington society, she splurged
on clothing and furniture, ran into debt, and had to be bailed out by
Congress. Washington society, unimpressed by her accoutrements,
rejected her as an anxious parvenu. More serious were her migraine
headaches—a torment that only those who suffer from them can comprehend. In a memorable image, she compared hers to an Indian pulling
the bones out of her face. These daily burdens added their weight to the
burdens that came with Lincoln's job.

He could think of the death and destruction of the war as being in
the service of a cause. Still it was terrible ("this terrible war," he called it
in an 1864 letter to Eliza Gurney, a Quaker who visited him in the White
House). Lincoln had compared slavery to a disease in his Peoria speech.
The founding fathers had hidden it "away in the Constitution, just as an
afflicted man hides away a wen or a cancer, which he dares not cut out
at once, lest he bleed to death." Now that it was being cut out, many
Americans were bleeding to death.

There are two wrong ways to write about war. One is to treat it as
wholly glorious, noble, or purposeful. Propagandists embrace this error,
and orators are tempted by it; even a text as chaste as the Gettysburg
Address could be so misheard—not, presumably, by many in its first
audience, in a newly made cemetery where coffins were still stacked,
but by those removed from the event by time or lack of imagination.

The other wrong way to write about war is to treat it as wholly
meaningless—empty carnage. One of the modern pioneers of that
error was Lord Byron, who devoted a canto of *Don Juan* to the battle
for Ismail, an Ottoman town captured by Russia in 1790:

> *Thus on they wallowed in the bloody mire*
> *Of dead and dying thousands, sometimes gaining*
> *A yard or two of ground, which brought them nigher*
> *To some odd angle for which all were straining;*

At other times, repulsed by the close fire,
   Which really poured as if all hell were raining,
Instead of heaven, they stumbled backwards o'er
A wounded comrade, sprawling in his gore.

Each error speaks for a truth—noble causes sometimes require the last full measure of devotion, and war is hell—but the truths are only true when held simultaneously in the mind. Lincoln's intellectual and rhetorical gifts showed him the purpose of the war; his nervous sensibility (Speed was more right about Lincoln's sensitivities than Herndon) showed him the horror.

————

As 1864 drew to a close, Grant was still investing Petersburg, trying to encircle it. Six days before the election, Sherman had begun to march from Atlanta to Savannah and the Atlantic coast.

Two political dramas played out over this military one. In 1861 the newly elected Lincoln had indicated that he favored a proposed Thirteenth Amendment declaring that the federal government had no power to end slavery in the states. (Lincoln believed that was implied constitutional law, so why not put it in the Constitution?) A last-ditch compromise proposal, it crumbled along with the country. Now, as the war finally seemed to be ending, there was a push, from abolitionists and Radical Republicans, for a different Thirteenth Amendment, one which would end slavery by constitutional mandate.

Charles Sumner proposed a text based on the French Revolution's Declaration of the Rights of Man and the Citizen: "All persons are equal before the law, so that no person can hold another as a slave." The Senate Judiciary Committee, wiser than he was, instead echoed the Northwest Ordinance, the founding document that had shaped the lives of millions of Americans, including the Lincolns: "Neither slavery nor involuntary servitude, except as a punishment for crime . . . shall exist within the United States." The amendment did not forbid holding "persons . . . to labor," it forbade "slavery": the institution was first named in the Constitution as it was being ushered out of it. The Senate approved the Thirteenth Amendment by the necessary two-thirds margin in April, and the Republican (or National Union) convention endorsed it in early June. But on June 15, the amendment fell short in the House.

The November elections gave the Republicans increased majorities in Congress, but they would take their seats no earlier than March 1865 (and then only if Lincoln called a special session). A renewed push for a Thirteenth Amendment came in the lame-duck session of the same Congress that had failed to approve it.

The wen or cancer of slavery was being cut out by war. Everywhere the Union armies penetrated—Sherman took Savannah just before Christmas—slaves were being freed under the provisions of the Emancipation Proclamation. No conceivable replacement for Chief Justice Taney (least of all Salmon P. Chase, who finally got the job in December) would lead the Court in undoing the proclamation with some *Dred Scott*–like decision.

Yet the Emancipation Proclamation was a war measure only. Legal challenges and delays could proliferate in peacetime. Slavery still lingered in the loyal border states (though Maryland had abolished it in November 1864, and Missouri was moving to do the same). Anyone with a legalistic mind, which included Lincoln, would want the matter resolved, before the war ended, if possible.

Lincoln lobbied to pass the Thirteenth Amendment. He used persuasion, calling on former Whigs to honor the spirit of Henry Clay (Clay the master legislator, or Clay the lover of freedom? There was no difference now, since both qualities pulled in the same direction). He used more tangible inducements, too: one congressman who changed his vote became ambassador to Denmark.

At the same time, Lincoln was fielding a peace initiative from the Confederacy. Lincoln himself had encouraged it, allowing Francis Blair Sr. to go to Richmond in January 1865 for an unofficial talk with Jefferson Davis, a prewar friend of Blair's. While the Civil War raged,

Napoleon III had put a puppet of France on the throne of Mexico; Blair's idea was that there should be an American truce, during which the Union and Confederate armies would join in driving the French out. Davis was sufficiently interested to send peace commissioners to negotiate with Lincoln.

Rumors of the talks reached Congress and threatened to delay the Thirteenth Amendment: Was peace at hand? What would be the terms? How would they affect the status of slavery? On January 31 Lincoln sent a note to the floor manager for the amendment in the House stating that there were no Confederate peace commissioners in Washington, "or likely to be in it." The amendment got the necessary two-thirds in the House that day and went out to the states for ratification.

On February 3 Lincoln and Seward met the Confederate peace commissioners on a ship off Hampton Roads, Virginia. (Lincoln had told the House the truth, literally—Hampton Roads was not Washington.)

The three-man team Davis had sent included Lincoln's old friend Alexander Stephens. Stephens's tenure as vice president of the Confederacy had been an ongoing quarrel with his president. (One example will serve for many: In 1861 Davis had embargoed the South's cotton, to show European governments what they would suffer if the North prevailed. Stephens had argued for shipping it out and using it as collateral to buy weapons. Stephens, the economically sophisticated ex-Whig, was correct.) Stephens became an early leader of the Confederacy's peace faction, looking for chances to negotiate a settlement. Now his path had crossed Lincoln's once again. The two had shared a moment of history, by then more than sixteen years past, and still shared a lingering respect for each other.

Both sides ached to stop the fighting. The war was clearly coming to an end, but there was still no telling how far off the end was. Sherman, after taking Savannah, had swung north. Ultimately he and Grant would link up. But perhaps the shrunken Confederate armies in northern Virginia and the Carolinas would link up first. Typical of the ongoing grind of war was a battle at the Salkehatchie River in South Carolina, west of Charleston, the day of the Hampton Roads Conference. One of the Union generals involved was Francis Blair Jr., son of Lincoln's negotiator. The conflict delayed Sherman's advance for one day. Eighteen Union men and eight Confederates died. It was a small engagement as such things went, but it had killed more than five times as many men as had supposedly been lost to Lydia Bixby.

Yet neither the memory of old ties nor the pressure of new deaths could save the conference. The two sides could not even agree on the terms under which they met. Davis looked for peace between "the two countries." Lincoln sought peace for "the people of our one common country." The Mexican plan, which was Blair's idea, not Lincoln's, went nowhere. The parties adjourned without result.

Lincoln presented one idea that he had floated at the Hampton Roads Conference to his cabinet on February 5. It was his old vision of compensating slave owners for the loss of their slaves. His latest version of the plan was to offer $200 million to the Confederate states if they gave up before April 1, plus another $200 million if the Thirteenth Amendment was ratified by July 1. Lincoln was willing to pay for peace; since the war was costing $3 million a day, he argued that his plan might actually save money. Lincoln was also willing to acknowledge northern complicity in slavery. "If it was wrong in the South to hold slaves," he had said at Hampton Roads, "it was wrong in the North to carry on the slave trade." The cabinet, believing that the way to end slavery was to win the war, opposed him unanimously, and he folded up his proposal.

The fighting continued.

Fifteen

GOD THE FATHER

L INCOLN'S LIFE, LIKE ANY MAN'S, CAN BE READ AS A SERIES
of engagements with his fathers.

Thomas Lincoln, who had been unsuited to his son in so many ways,
and not acknowledged by his son even in the ways that he had been
suitable—Thomas had given Abraham life, and shown him how to tell
a story, win a wrestling match, and decline a drink—was finally mentioned by him in a few late speeches to homeward-bound troops.

The fathers that Lincoln took to heart and that showed him how
to be a great man were the founding fathers, surrogates plucked from
reading and history. As a boy he was thrilled by George Washington
and his struggles for liberty. As a young man he was thrilled by Thomas
Paine's skepticism and his laughter. As a middle-aged man, however
much he disliked Thomas Jefferson's late-life cowardice, Lincoln
found the perfect expression of America's essence in the Declaration of Independence—logical, beautiful, and universally endorsed
("*We* hold these truths . . . "). But Lincoln loved everything about the

founding fathers: the Constitution and its Preamble, the Northwest Ordinance, the Revolutionary veterans and their widows. What he did not love he made lovable, or ignored. He brought the founding fathers back to life; he labored to have their principles recognized, by political rivals and crowds of listening voters. He enlisted them in the fights of his time, from prairie elections to multi-thousand-men battles. He enlisted them in his own rise to power, which would (he hoped) be power to do good.

But these same fathers had harbored a wen or a cancer—slavery. They had not known what to do with it. They had blocked its expansion, by declaring the old Northwest off-limits to existing slaves, and they had cut off its supply, by making it possible to end the importation of new slaves. Perhaps slavery would then wither away. But the wen or cancer lived and thrived; it became a national disease. The slave trade never resumed officially, but slavery had expanded into new American states and territories, first to Louisiana, then to Missouri, then to Texas, then to New Mexico, then to Kansas and Nebraska (that last leap had been blocked, barely; but then, what about Cuba? and Central America?). And now Americans, from simple soldier boys to fifty-year-old one-armed men, were dying by fives and by thousands to cut out the wen or cancer—the founding fathers' untended deadly legacy.

Where could Lincoln turn for help? To himself, of course, and to his friends, allies, cronies, and instruments. The first is the resource of every man, the others are the resource of every politician.

But there was another father for this extremity: God the Father.

Thomas Lincoln and his wives were Baptists. Abraham had gone with them to their church services to hear the preaching, and had amused his playmates afterward by imitating it. Once Lincoln had left the nest, Paine told him not to bother with all that; it was contradictory and ridiculous: Jesus was a bastard and the Bible was full of holes. Lincoln saw the contradictions and joined in the laugh. But Paine had his own God, who was loving and beneficent, speaking through nature and our reasoning faculty. That was not quite Lincoln's experience. God, or someone or thing equally potent, had swept away his seeds, his mother, his sister, and his sweetheart. God put poison in cow's milk that turned tongues brown; He gave women delirium and diarrhea then rained on their graves.

There was much to be said for God, even so. He inspired great writing, a matter of first importance for a man like Lincoln. Paine, always doubling down, mocked the Bible's style along with its content, calling Paul's epistles "quibble, subterfuge and pun"; the Book of Jeremiah an "incoherent bombastical rant"; and the Book of Judges "paltry stories." The only biblical writing Paine liked was in the Book of Job, and he thought that had been lifted from a non-Jewish source. A man with Lincoln's ear would easily have heard how ludicrous Paine's literary judgments were. Paine was a great writer when it came to polemics, whether earnest or knock-about, but the King James Bible—the Bible of Lincoln's world—touched chords beyond Paine's ken.

One of Lincoln's favorite phrases came from one of the books Paine specifically scorned, Judges 5:20: "The stars in their courses fought against Sisera." (Sisera was the Canaanite general who had been defeated in battle and then killed by Jael, the wife of Heber, as he slept.) Lincoln, ever impressed by the unwinding of causes and forces, would naturally be moved by the spectacle of inevitability bearing Sisera down. But he also had to be entranced by the startling image and the sumptuous language. There is a tide in the affairs of men, says Shakespeare's Cassius; the tide of the Book of Judges was in the heavens. The tolling r's—*stars, their, courses, Sisera*—resembled the r's that rolled out the Gettysburg Address—*four, score, years, our, fathers, forth*.

The translators of the King James Version had breathed the same air as Shakespeare, and their Bible was as great a source of incident and character as Shakespeare's plays. Some of its images and expressions were so vivid that they had become free-floating proverbs detached from their original context. The metaphor of the house divided was used by Jesus (Matthew 12:25, Mark 3:25, Luke 11:17) to rebut those who accused Him of performing miracles with diabolical assistance: devils, argued Jesus, cannot cast out devils, for how can a house divided against itself stand? The powers of Hell work in concert. But Lincoln, and most people who employed the image, used it to evoke the perils of disunity in a good cause.

One description of Lincoln's Bible reading, recorded decades after the fact, but first seen with eyes of innocence, came from Julia Taft Bayne, the daughter of a Washington patent officer, who as a teenager had played with Willie and Tad Lincoln in the White House. She recalled that Lincoln's Bible lay on a table in the sitting room, "and quite often, after the midday meal, he would sit there reading, sometimes in his stocking feet with one long leg crossed over the other, the unshod foot slowly waving back and forth. . . . He read it in the relaxed, almost lazy attitude of a man enjoying a good book." She had been an observant girl, but even as an old woman Mrs. Bayne did not fully understand what she had observed. Many people read carelessly or casually, like people grabbing a bite to eat; what they read stays with them as long as what they have eaten. But a storyteller, a displaced poet, a man stooped under his burdens, will absorb a book, even one that he is enjoying, in a different spirit.

The accident of Lincoln's name thrust him into the Bible. Most presidents had had common religious or royal first names. By 1860 four Jameses, three Johns, and one George, Thomas, Andrew, Martin, and William had held the office. Long handling had worn away any special meaning these names had once possessed, like faces on old coins. Franklin and Millard were last names as first names. Zachary carried a more pungent biblical flavor; in various spellings it was the name of an evil king, a minor prophet, and the father of John the Baptist. But Abraham is the first of the patriarchs, the father of Israel. During the war, "Father Abraham" became a popular nickname for Lincoln— partly jocular, partly a play on his beard (patriarchs should always be bearded); more and more, as time passed, a recognition of his role as leader, explainer, and father of his embattled country—a role he had grown into. Revering the founding fathers, he was joining them in a second generation.

God was more than an occasion for great writing. He was also the prime mover, the first cause. This was a very old role for Him, elaborated by philosophers and theologians whom Lincoln had never read and by authors whom everyone had read ("In the beginning God created the heaven and the earth" [Genesis 1:1]; "All things were made by him; and without him was not any thing made that was made" [John 1:3]). Lincoln, who saw himself bound by his melancholy, and buffeted by eruptions of weather, disease, and (now) slaughter, who saw the world and everyone in it bound in chains of cause and effect, would naturally consider where these chains led, and Who held the remotest ends and for what purpose.

In September 1862 Lincoln wrote out some thoughts on the divine will, perhaps after John Pope's defeat at the Second Battle of Bull Run. The war had entered a stalemate, the first of several; Lincoln had discussed the Emancipation Proclamation with his cabinet, but would not issue it until the Union had won a victory.

He tried to understand what this awful immobility, both military and political, meant. He laid out the alternatives like a geometrical proof. "The will of God prevails." That was axiomatic. "Each party" in this, or any war, "claims to act in accordance with the will of God." That was human nature. But one party "*must* be wrong," since "God can not be *for* and *against* the same thing at the same time." That was elementary logic. And both parties "*may* be" wrong, if God's purpose were different from the purpose of either. That was Lincoln's problem.

What could God's purpose in September 1862 be? He could have prevented the war before it began "by his mere quiet power [acting] on the minds of the now contestants," or He could end it "any day," by letting either side win. "Yet the contest proceeds." Conclusion: "God wills this contest, and wills that it shall not end yet."

His secretaries John Hay and John G. Nicolay, who preserved the fragment, said it was not meant "to be seen of men." But shortly after Lincoln wrote it, he opened his thoughts to a woman.

Eliza Kirkbride was born to a Philadelphia Quaker family in 1801. When she was forty she married Joseph Gurney, a charismatic English

Quaker evangelist and prison reformer; he died after they had been together for six years. Thus it was that as a sixty-one-year-old widow Eliza
Gurney came to the White House in October 1862, with three friends,
to pay "a religious visit" to the president. Photographs of her show a
plain face under straight, pulled-back hair, with intent eyes.

Religious visitors appeared frequently among the hordes of petitioners, complainers, and politicians who descended on Lincoln. Sometimes religious visitors hectored him, asking why he would not free the
slaves tomorrow? On September 13, 1862—in the very week, perhaps,
when he wrote out his thoughts on the divine will—Lincoln had met
with two ministers, a Congregationalist and a Methodist, who presented
an appeal for emancipation from Chicago Christians. In the discussion
that followed, the president allowed himself a touch of humor, perhaps
also of temper: if "God would reveal his will to others, on a point so connected with my duty, it might be supposed he would reveal it directly to
me." Nothing daunted, the ministers replied that God might enlighten
Lincoln by "the suggestions and arguments of other minds." *Just listen
to us, Mr. President, we'll tell you what God wants you to do.*

On September 22, nine days after meeting the helpful ministers,
Lincoln had announced the Preliminary Emancipation Proclamation.
So Eliza Gurney, in October, would not be pressing him about that. Her
purpose was in fact altogether different: she wanted to lead Lincoln to
sustenance and relief.

She addressed an impromptu exhortation to him (Quakers believed
in speaking when the spirit moved them, and they had always believed
that women could speak as truly as men). "There is a river," she said,
"the streams whereof make glad the whole heritage of God. And seeing
how difficult it is to accomplish that which we wish, and how vain is
the help of man, I have earnestly desired that the President might repair day by day . . . to this river of God, which is full of water, even to
the well-spring of Eternal Life, that thus his spirit may be strengthened
and refreshed, and be fitted for the right performance of his various and
arduous duties."

She then became at once more intimate and more exalted: "And now, my dear friend, if so I may be permitted to call thee, may the Lord bless thee and keep thee. . . . He shall cover [the righteous] with His feathers, and under His wings shall they trust. His truth shall be their shield and buckler. A thousand may fall at their side, and ten thousand at their right hand"—practically a description of Antietam, which had been fought five days earlier: over 2,100 Union men killed, over 1,500 Confederates killed—"but it shall not come nigh them, because they have made the Lord their refuge." She ended by kneeling and praying for Lincoln and for America.

Gurney's effusion was a mélange of uplift and biblical imagery (the river of life is from Revelation, God's protecting wings and shield from the 91st Psalm). It had propulsive force, but nothing noteworthy in its shape or its original expressions. Yet Lincoln was moved by it. Why?

Gurney's Quakerism may have touched him. Lincoln had some slight connections to the religion—he believed, on the basis of what he called a "vague tradition" in the family, that his great-grandfather, John Lincoln, had been a Quaker. Quakers were also the only Christian denomination that Thomas Paine ever had a good word for, because they had the plainest services and carried the lightest load of dogma. As a Quaker, Gurney was addressing Lincoln from corners of his past.

Was there something maternal about her? She was only eight years older than he was. Yet she was a widow, which symbolically aged her. Lincoln had a soft spot for widows, from Lucretia Clay to Rebecca Thomas all the way back to his stepmother, Sarah Bush Lincoln, who had been a widow when Thomas Lincoln courted her. But more striking than denominations or gender roles was Gurney's evident sympathy for Lincoln. She wanted to help him, to console him.

He made a reply, which began with a phrase that still smolders. "We are indeed going through a great trial—a fiery trial."

He continued by sharing his thoughts on divine will, but to Gurney he expressed them personally, not with the philosophic detachment of his note to himself. There he had written of "each party" and "the now contestants" as if observing them from on high. To Gurney he spoke of himself, in the heart of his trial. He was, he said, "a humble instrument in the hands of our Heavenly Father." Not God, some airy, overarching being, but our Father, with hands yet. Lincoln went on: "I have sought His aid—but if after endeavoring to do my best in the light which He affords me, I find my efforts fail, I must believe that for some purpose unknown to me, He wills it otherwise." What a tangle of protest and accusation, pain and anger this was, not yet smoothed into acceptance: *I sought to do my best, but I failed; I believe He willed it so.*

Lincoln went on: he had not wanted the war and he wanted it to be over. Yet "it still continues." Therefore "we must believe that He permits it for some wise purpose of His own, mysterious and unknown to us." Lincoln characterized God's purpose in two ways, one comforting, one anything but: it must be wise (since God is wise), but it is opaque.

Lincoln ended with an awkwardly balanced sentence. "We cannot but believe that He who made the world still governs it." He could have said *He who made the world still governs it,* or *We believe that He who made the world still governs it.* Yet he began the sentence with a tricky running start: *We cannot but believe that. . . .* If Lincoln had omitted the word *but,* the sentence would have been completely different: *We cannot believe that He who made the world still governs it.* It would have been a sentence written by Lord Byron for the siege of Ismail, a sentence fit for every corpse-lined trench and burial pit of the war. But Lincoln put the *but* in, which saved his axiom, the axiom of Genesis and the Gospel of John: God rules. This was some consolation. But since His wise purpose was mysterious, unknown, and opaque, it left Lincoln in darkness.

Lincoln's interactions with Gurney continued over the years like some slow-motion conversation. In August 1863, she wrote him. Her approach was as personal as when she had preached before him in the White House. "Esteemed Friend, Abraham Lincoln," she began, " . . . I feel inclined to give thee the assurance of my continued hearty sympathy in all thy heavy burthens [burdens] and responsibilities. . . .

I believe thy conflicts and anxieties have not been few." True enough: she wrote six weeks after Gettysburg and Vicksburg (another thousand had fallen at the side of the righteous, and another ten thousand at their right hand). She ended her letter by commending him and his family "to the preserving care of the unslumbering Shepherd," and signing it, "Respectfully and sincerely, thy assured friend . . . "

A year after that, in September 1864, Lincoln wrote back to her. He began by saying he would never forget her visit in 1862 and her letter of 1863. "I am much indebted to the good Christian people of the country for their constant prayers and consolations; and to no one of them more than to yourself." There is help that is given helpfully, and help that is not (as from the Chicago ministers); Gurney's was the former, which consoled Lincoln.

He returned to the topic of divine will, like a schoolboy to his lesson, still vibrating between his axiom—that God rules—and his perplexity—that he, Abraham Lincoln, did not know for what purpose. Axiom: "The purposes of the Almighty are perfect, and must prevail . . . " Darkness: " . . . though we erring mortals may fail to accurately perceive them in advance." He repeated the pairing, in reverse order. Darkness: "We hoped for a happy termination of this terrible war long before this . . . " Axiom: " . . . but God knows best, and has ruled otherwise." One could almost hear him asking, *Have I learned my lesson yet?* Sarah Bush Lincoln would remember how her stepson set himself to learn something new, repeating it "over to himself again and again, sometimes in one form, then in another."

Lincoln then discussed two of his hopes. One was for understanding: "We shall yet acknowledge [God's] wisdom . . . " The other was for a blessing: "Surely He intends some great good to follow this mighty convulsion . . . " Maybe, maybe not: the fulfillment of the first hope (understanding) would be up to ourselves, the fulfillment of the second (some great good to follow) would be up to God.

Lincoln ended by recalling the prayers Gurney had made for him and for the country two years earlier. They were, he wrote, prayers "to our

Father in Heaven." One thing a mother can try to do, though she doesn't always succeed, is make things right with father.

———

Lincoln began revealing the thoughts about divine will that he had kept to himself and the sympathetic widow in the spring of 1864.

His forum was a private letter meant for publication. In March, three Kentuckians, two politicians, and a newspaper editor had come to the White House to discuss the administration's policy of enlisting black soldiers, which was controversial in their state. Lincoln surveyed the gradual but methodical steps that had led him to the policy, always balancing his convictions, the Constitution, and military necessity. The editor, Albert G. Hodges of the *Frankfort Commonwealth*, asked Lincoln for a copy of his remarks in writing, and in April he obliged, adding a coda—"a word which was not in the verbal conversation." The coda was about the divine will.

It began with Lincoln's axiom: "At the end of three years struggle the nation's condition is not what either party, or any man devised, or expected. God alone can claim it." God rules.

Then Lincoln offered what was for him a new thought. "If God now wills the removal of a great wrong, and wills also that we of the North as well as you of the South, shall pay fairly for our complicity in that wrong, impartial history will find therein new cause to attest and revere the justice and goodness of God."

This was new because it seemed to find a purpose in God's mysterious and unknown movements. Where there had been only darkness (to Lincoln eyes, at any rate), now there might be some light.

God's newly discovered purpose superficially resembled an old hope of Lincoln's—that the North might pay to end slavery and the war. He had floated compensation schemes for years, and he would continue to do so. Buying out slave owners would be cheaper and quicker than beating them on the battlefield. It would be morally right, since "we of the North" were as involved in slavery, through consumption and profit, as planters, slave dealers, or slave catchers.

But the resemblance between Lincoln's new thought and his old plans was only superficial, for the payment he contemplated now was not cash, but blood. He did not go into detail in his letter to Hodges. All he said was that "we of the North . . . shall pay fairly." He was writing Hodges in April 1864; Grant had come east, a new campaign was about to begin, maybe there would be a knockout blow. Surely that would cost the lives of thousands. And if there was no knockout blow, but only more back and forth, then the cost would be thousands and thousands. The Hodges letter anticipated either possibility, and implicitly acknowledged the many thousands already lost ("three years struggle"). Why else would Lincoln have ended it by summoning the august abstractions of his final sentence? He did not need "impartial history" and "the justice and goodness of God" to witness a mere cash deal, even one of several hundred million dollars. History and God the Father give their attention to suffering and death.

There was light in Lincoln's darkness—bloody light.

———

Lincoln finally laid his elaborated thoughts about the war and divine will before the country in his Second Inaugural Address on March 4, 1865. What he had so far only hinted to newspaper readers, and discussed only with the Quaker widow, he would explain to the largest of audiences on the most conspicuous of occasions.

The preceding month had seen the greatest military activity in the Carolinas, Sherman's front, as the major coastal cities fell: Charleston on February 17, Wilmington on February 22. "I have no further use for a newspaper," wrote Mary Chesnut in despair. "I never want to see another one as long as I live." Grant still could not cut Petersburg's last supply lines—a road and a railroad, stretching to the west—though he was able to extend his siege lines in an even wider embrace, thus forcing the weakened defenders to extend their own. These movements were accompanied by a drip of deaths—hundreds, not thousands.

The day of Lincoln's inauguration was rainy. The first ceremony was the swearing-in of Vice President Andrew Johnson, which took place in the Senate chamber. Johnson was worn out by traveling from Tennessee, as well as tipsy (he had had a few drinks to buck himself up). His speech was a mess; Lincoln asked a functionary to make sure that Johnson did not speak again later.

The sun broke through as the dignitaries moved outside for Lincoln's inauguration, which took place at the site of his first inauguration four years earlier, on the East Portico of the Capitol. The chief justice was different—Salmon P. Chase, not Roger Taney. So was the length of Lincoln's remarks. His First Inaugural Address had been among the longest yet given; his second—only seven hundred words—would be among the shortest.

The address consisted of four movements. Lincoln began by saying he would not say anything about his policies or his plans. The war years had generated such a barrage of messages, speeches, announcements, and news stories that he had nothing new to add.

The second movement of the address offered a précis of the causes of the war: four years earlier the rebels had wanted to strengthen and extend slavery; the government (newly confided to Republican hands) wanted to restrict it. Rebels wanted to break up the Union, the government wished to maintain it. Neither would back down, "and the war came."

The third movement presented the conclusions of Lincoln's religious broodings and reasonings, going back to his first note on the divine will, and back, even further, to his chats with Herndon about fatalism and his youthful engagement with Thomas Paine.

He began with an extended statement of men's ignorance and impotence, and God's power. Neither rebels nor government had expected that the war would last so long or be so transformative. Both sides "read the same Bible, and pray to the same God." Yet "the prayers of both could not be answered; that of neither has been answered fully. The Almighty has His own purposes." The axiom: God rules. The darkness: His purposes are not ours.

In the midst of this exposition, Lincoln ventured a criticism of the South, giving voice to his lifelong repugnance for unpaid labor. "It may seem strange that any men should dare to ask a just God's assistance in wringing their bread from the sweat of other men's faces." Speaking from his own years as his father's hired hand, and for the black woman who ought to be able to make her own bread, he had said this, in different ways, dozens of times. Yet now he immediately pulled back. "But let us judge not that we be not judged." This was an admonition of Jesus (Matthew 7:1–2): "Judge not, that ye be not judged. For with what judgment ye judge, ye shall be judged: and with what measure ye mete, it shall be measured to you again." Lincoln, as commander in chief, was willing to kill tens of thousands of rebels; yet as president he was unwilling to judge them.

Why not? He explained by quoting another saying of Jesus (Matthew 18:7), extended by two long, supple sentences of his own. "Woe unto the world because of offences! for it must needs be that offences come; but woe to that man by whom the offence cometh!" (*Needs* here was an old-fashioned adverb meaning "of necessity.") The Lincoln who quoted this Bible verse was Lincoln at his most deterministic, and his most punitive. Offenses—sins, crimes—*will* happen, and those who commit them *will* be punished. It would not matter that the wrongdoer could not have done otherwise; woe to that man.

Jesus was condemning those who destroyed the faith of innocent children; Lincoln was condemning his fellow Americans. "If we shall suppose that American Slavery is one of those offences which, in the providence of God, must needs come, but which, having continued through His appointed time, He now wills to remove, and that He gives to both North and South, this terrible war as the woe due to those by whom the offence came, shall we discern therein any departure from those divine attributes which the believers in a Living God always ascribe to Him? . . . If God wills that [the war] continue, until all the wealth piled by the bond-man's two hundred and fifty years of unrequited toil shall be sunk, and until every drop of blood drawn by the lash shall be paid by another drawn with the sword, as was said three thousand years ago [in Psalm 19:9], so still it must be said, 'the judgments of the Lord are true and righteous altogether.'"

This was the consummation of all Lincoln's plans for monetary compensation, and of his bloodier hint to Albert Hodges. All America had sinned and all America must pay. Most of the lashing in the history of American slavery had been done in the slave states of the South. But there had been northern slavery too, well into the nineteenth century, and the lash had flourished on slave ships captained by northerners (Nathaniel Gordon, the slave trader executed in 1862, was from Portland, Maine). Much of the wealth that bond-men had generated had flowed to northern mill towns, northern brokers and merchants, northern banks. All had sinned, all must pay; woe to those men. Judge not, said Lincoln, quoting Jesus, yet he judged Americans severely.

The Second Inaugural is Lincoln's greatest speech. The Peoria speech and the Cooper Union address were mighty efforts, but as with almost every long oration, there were loose ends. The Gettysburg Address was perfect, but it was a perfect small thing. The Second Inaugural, for all its brevity, was vast—vaster than Lincoln's longest speech, for it encompassed man, history, and God.

Its language was sublime. The King James Bible, which Mrs. Bayne had watched him reading with crossed leg and waving foot, had been so internalized that he switched from Jesus to the psalmist to his own words without a seam.

The Second Inaugural is also the speech that is most deserving of criticism, especially its third movement.

The address as a whole was noteworthy for its air of elevation and evasion. Lincoln spoke as if he were not an actor in the history of his own administration, but an onlooker: a passenger in the basket of an observation balloon, or the dreamer of one of Thomas Cole's allegorical visions. He effaced himself in his very first words: "At this second appearing to take the oath of the presidential office . . . " Not *my second appearing*, but *this*; had *this* just taken the oath of office, not *him*? He even effaced, as far as possible, the combatants. "And the war came." How had it come? He had tried to supply Fort Sumter, South Carolina had bombarded it, and Union and Confederacy had rushed to arms. The war came because Americans had called for it.

One of the crucial Americans calling for war had been President Lincoln. He had been willing to go to war rather than see the Union dissolved by slaveholders, and because of his willingness, Elmer Ellsworth, Edward Baker, William McCullough, the Bixby boys, the young man whose legs were blown off, and hundreds of thousands of others marched out and died, were injured, or witnessed such calamities occurring to comrades and friends. No wonder Lincoln wished to avoid responsibility, for it must needs have been that the war came, but woe to that man by whom it came.

Yet for Lincoln to have taken blame upon himself, in a public address, would have been grandiose. He was an important actor, but not the only one. There had been so many others—maniacs like Preston Brooks and John Brown; genial men like William Seward, warm spirits like the Blairs, intelligent men like Alexander Stephens. Probably Lincoln was right to wrap his address in the cotton wool of impersonality.

The Second Inaugural was equally noteworthy for who was missing from it. For nearly the first time in over a decade, Lincoln gave a major speech without reference to the founding fathers (the "House Divided" speech was another important exception). The men who made the Constitution, the Northwest Ordinance, the Declaration of Independence, and the country, who had forged his intellectual and political sheet anchors and stated his axioms, were gone. They were more dead to this Inaugural Address than they had been in the Lyceum Address, where their passing had at least given rise to melancholy reflections. Now they and their handiwork were only a featureless point in the "two hundred and fifty years of unrequited toil" of slavery. Two hundred and fifty from

1865 equals 1615—the time of the Jamestown Colony, the first of the thirteen colonies and the first to purchase African slaves. That, not the Revolution or its great documents, was the founding moment identified by the Second Inaugural; and the men of the Revolution who had followed in its wake belonged, like their ancestors and their descendants, to the sinful nation.

The last father left standing in the Second Inaugural was God, and what an implacable and unapproachable Father Lincoln made him out to be. In his telling, God exacted a secular equivalent of the substitutionary atonement. Just as in Christian theology God accepts the death of Christ as payment for men's sins, so in Lincoln's theology God now required the deaths of Americans as payment for their sins, and the sins of their fathers and their fathers' fathers.

Transposing such a doctrine into a political context showed how far Lincoln had moved from his young man's infatuation with Paine. Paine had "revolted" at the substitutionary atonement, thinking that it made "God Almighty act like a passionate man that killed his son when he could not revenge himself any other way." Lincoln's God acted like a passionate man who killed thousands of sons, many of them innocent. Men from Vermont or Wisconsin who had never seen, much less owned, a slave, but perhaps had had some sugar with their coffee, or worn a cotton shirt, therefore deserved to die at Bull Run; men from Tennessee or Virginia who, in the new vice president's phrase, had never owned the hair of a nigger, nevertheless deserved to die at Manassas. The moral calculus of the Second Inaugural was outrageous.

Lincoln's discomfort with his own reasoning showed in his buffering rhetoric. The two long sentences of his third movement both began with ifs: "If we shall suppose," "Yet if God wills . . . " An air of hypothesis clung to his argument, even as Lincoln developed it. Nor did he quite claim responsibility for his portrayal of God: it was "the believers in a Living God" who "always ascribe to Him" the "attributes" Lincoln sketched. If you have a problem with my picture of God and His attributes, don't tell me, take it up with those "believers." Perhaps some part of Lincoln still felt, even in 1865, that those attributes were revolting.

There remained, finally, a question of propriety. Why was Lincoln giving a sermon disguised as an Inaugural Address? Clergymen had been giving him advice for years, much of it foolish or unrealistic. But, whether they did it well or badly, they were only doing their jobs the best they could. Lincoln's job was to be president of the United States. Who asked him to be Jesus on a podium?

The best defense for this eloquent, disturbing, wrongheaded speech is that the dead had been killed already; Lincoln wanted to find some meaning in their deaths, he hoped that God knew what it was, and he thought he had found some indication of what God knew. To have continued in the conviction that God's purposes were entirely dark would have been unbearable, after so much slaughter. To have thought that God had no purposes and that there was no meaning in the slaughter would have been worse yet—the final curse, the true damnation. Then it would be time to hide the razors. Better for Lincoln to patch up some theology than leave such a hole in his soul.

The Second Inaugural had a fourth movement, a last paragraph, seventy-five words long: "With malice toward none; with charity for all; with firmness in the right, as God gives us to see the right, let us strive on to finish the work we are in; to bind up the nation's wounds; to care for him who shall have borne the battle, and for his widow, and his orphan—to do all which may achieve and cherish a just, and a lasting peace, among ourselves and with all nations."

The phrase *with all nations* at the end was there for rhetorical fullness (and maybe geopolitical housekeeping: there would be no war with France in Mexico as a time-out from ours). But every other word in this last paragraph was fully freighted.

God made His final appearance neither as the mysterious, passionate Punisher, nor yet as the Helper offered by Eliza Gurney, but as Someone who might show Americans the right. What Lincoln particularly wanted to be shown was how to win and end the war; how to tend to its veterans and its bereaved. Most important, he wanted to be shown how to restore peace "among ourselves." This was the reverse of his message of payment and blood in the preceding paragraph, and like that message it was addressed to the entire country, North and South ("malice toward none . . . charity for all").

The calm, quiet, almost saintly tone of these concluding words superseded, if it did not explain, the dark aria that preceded them. Lincoln's call for magnanimity and hard work was a parade of two-syllable verbs, trochees and iambs: *strive on, finish, bind up, care for, do all, achieve, cherish*. It was as simple as walking, as hard as walking on after so long and with so far yet to go.

The end of the Second Inaugural marked one more stage in Lincoln's thinking about fathers and sons. After letting go of the founding fathers he had faced God the Father directly. He wrestled with Him, as he and his father had wrestled with bullies; as Jacob had wrestled with the angel. Lincoln had a bad bout of it, being thrown again and again. After that painful turmoil, now he and the country had to address the tasks of peace. Now they would have to be men.

Sixteen

1865: VICTORY.
THE TOWERING GENIUS (III)

L INCOLN'S IMMEDIATE TASK AT THE BEGINNING OF HIS SECOND
term was ending the war; how it ended would taint or smooth the
peace.

One fear of the Union—that the remaining Confederate armies in
northern Virginia and the Carolinas, profiting from interior lines of communication, might link up—became less likely as the Union brought
more numbers to bear, and as the Confederates lost strength from casualties and, increasingly, from desertion. In the last week of March the
defenders of Petersburg launched a break-out attack on Fort Stedman,
one of the fortifications in the Union line; when it failed, the fall of
Petersburg (and Richmond) was only a matter of time.

But Lincoln had another military worry: that resistance might collapse without any formal surrender, leaving rebel soldiers to melt back
to their homes and possibly take up guerrilla war. To avoid that disaster,

Lincoln wanted definite surrenders, from the rebel government, if possible, from its commanders, if necessary; he wanted the surrenders approved by himself, not made ad hoc by his commanders in the field. To encourage these results he wanted the beaten enemy treated magnanimously. "I want no one punished," he told his generals. "Treat them liberally all around."

At the end of March Lincoln sailed from Washington to Grant's headquarters at City Point, on the James River. He wanted to make his thinking clear to his commanders and, if possible, witness the surrender of the Confederacy himself. On April 2 Grant finally broke the Confederate lines before him; Petersburg and Richmond fell the next day.

Lincoln went to see the Confederate capital on April 4. He arrived without fanfare, accompanied only by a small bodyguard. When a party of black workmen recognized him, they tried to kiss his feet. "That is not right," Lincoln told them. "You must kneel to God only." What a temptation. Satan only offered Jesus all the kingdoms of the world; these men offered Lincoln their homage. Turning it aside was one of his noblest moments.

Lincoln visited Jefferson Davis's office and the Confederate capitol, but the rebel government had decamped. John Campbell, one of the peace commissioners he had met at Hampton Roads, remained, and Lincoln talked with him about arranging a formal surrender, but nothing came of it. He returned to City Point and sailed back to Washington on the night of April 8. On the trip, he read aloud to his traveling companions Macbeth's lines after the murder of Duncan, when the usurper envies his victim: "Better be with the dead, / . . . Than on the torture of the mind to lie / In restless ecstasy. Duncan is in his grave. / . . . Treason has done his worst [and not even] / Malice domestic . . . / Can touch him further." So Lincoln, in poetry, not theology, this time, still wrestled with the question of his own responsibility, identifying with both Macbeth the destroyer and the dead Duncan, safe at last from mental torture and treason. Uneasy lies the head that wears a crown, or a president's topper.

Lincoln returned to Washington and big news: the Confederate Army of Northern Virginia, which had baffled half a dozen Union commanders and carried the rebellion into Maryland and Pennsylvania, surrendered on April 9 to Grant at Appomattox, a town ninety miles west of Richmond. Following Lincoln's policy, Grant let the surrendering men keep their sidearms and their horses, for spring plowing. Robert E. Lee, their commander, told Grant "with some feeling" that this generosity "would have a happy effect upon his army."

———

If George Washington was the standard by which Lincoln's presidency was to be measured—and Lincoln had invited the comparison himself—then Lincoln's task, even after four years of war, was only half done.

Washington's war, the Revolution, was still, as of 1865, the longest war in American history to date (1775–1783—twice as long as Lincoln's). But soon after the victorious general returned to Mount Vernon it had become clear to him that a new government needed to be made. Washington spent four months at the Constitutional Convention (1787) and a year of discreet politicking to help ratify the document it produced, then two terms as first president (1789–1797), putting the new system into effect. Only after this double exertion did he become, in Henry Lee's phrase, first in peace as well as first in war.

Lincoln had suppressed a rebellion. Now he had to repair the country. During his first term he had shown great skill in keeping the disparate factions of the Republican Party, from ideologues like Salmon P. Chase and Charles Sumner to moderates like William Seward and the Blairs, in harness. His hold on non-Republican unionists was less firm; they contested both his policies and his runs for the presidency. Yet he had managed to be elected and reelected, and to see his party keep its majorities in Congress.

Now Lincoln had to embrace the South, which he had never visited, apart from his youthful trips to New Orleans and his recent trip

to Richmond; where he had never won an electoral vote nor, south of
Kentucky and Virginia, ever won a single vote of any kind.

In this strange third of the country he would have to embrace newly
liberated blacks. If slavery was crippled by the war and in the process
of being abolished by the Thirteenth Amendment (twenty states had
ratified it by the time of the surrender at Appomattox), what then would
be the status of freemen?

Lincoln's early thoughts on the future of blacks in America had been
rather thoughtless. Following Henry Clay, he had considered encouraging them to move away, first to Liberia, then to the Chiriqui coast of
Panama; he had also toyed with the idea of a black American colony
on Île-à-Vache (Cow Island) off the southern coast of Haiti. None of
these plans had come to anything. Blacks hardly figured in his Second
Inaugural Address, where he depicted them as faceless characters in a
morality play—victims of injustice, or occasions for divine wrath. White
Americans in Lincoln's address had at least risen to the dignity of sin-
ning; blacks had simply been sinned against.

But these blinkered views did not, by 1865, express Lincoln's full
view of the place of blacks in American life. The utility and the conduct
of black enlisted men during the war had shown him that they might
deserve, and be capable of exercising, the privileges of citizenship. In
February 1865, Martin Delany, a black abolitionist, was commissioned
as a major, the first black officer in the history of the army. Lincoln sent
him to Stanton with a note: "Do not fail to have an interview with this
most extraordinary and intelligent black man."

In reconstituting the South, Lincoln would also have to embrace
former rebels: men who had killed many Union soldiers, and their families and friends, who had kept up the home front for four bitter years.
Lost-cause nostalgia has made the Confederacy seem more united than
it was: Andrew Johnson was but one of many highlanders in western
Virginia and eastern Tennessee who hated the planter oligarchs who
ran their states. Yet Lincoln had somehow to deal with those who had
accepted disunion, and even labored for it.

He had not accurately judged the pride and desperation of southern bitter-enders before Fort Sumter; afterward, he had vainly expected unionist sentiment in the South to revive. Lincoln's tone-deafness to the force of secessionist feeling had, however, an upside: he did not demonize the enemy. Demagogues, he assumed, had led secessionists astray in their views about the proper position of slavery in the republic; growing up in a slave society had led them astray in their views about human equality ("they are just what we would be in their situation," he had said in his Peoria speech). So why punish them afterward? Some southerners noticed his lack of rancor. At the Hampton Roads Conference, Robert Hunter, another of the three Confederate peace commissioners, asked a potentially awkward question: Did Lincoln consider the Confederacy's leaders to be traitors? Lincoln said that was "about the size of it." "Well, Mr. Lincoln," Hunter replied, "we have about concluded that we shall not be hanged as long as you are president." The man would temper the verdict. Lincoln tried to show his sentiments, making a point of shaking hands with wounded Confederate soldiers when he visited field hospitals in occupied Virginia.

In his first term, Lincoln had been abused as both pro-black (and therefore black himself) and pro-southern ("white trash," in Benjamin Wade's phrase, and an in-law of rebels). In his second term, he would have to find ways of reaching at least some of his symbolic alter egos.

Lincoln laid out his thoughts on the postwar South in a speech to a celebrating crowd on the White House lawn on the evening of April 11, two days after Lee's surrender. Despite the informal circumstances, this was not an impromptu talk but a prepared statement.

Lincoln focused on Louisiana, which had been trying to rejoin the Union since shortly after the fall of New Orleans. In December 1863 he had issued a proclamation offering to recognize any government in a formerly Confederate state where at least 10 percent of the voters in the last prewar election (1860) would take an oath to uphold the Constitution and the Emancipation Proclamation. Lincoln could not guarantee that the representatives of such state governments would be seated in

Congress; that, he pointed out, was up to each house of Congress itself. His plan also excluded voting by free black men, since the necessary 10 percent of voters was to be calculated from presecession voting rolls (which were all white). Louisiana took up Lincoln's offer and elected a new government in February 1864. (Lincoln sent Michael Hahn, the new governor, a private note asking whether "colored people" who were veterans or "very intelligent" might not be allowed to vote, too.) But the same lame-duck session of Congress that passed the Thirteenth Amendment would not recognize the new government of Louisiana. Some of Congress's reluctance was political—Congress wanted to take the lead in readmitting seceded states. Some of it was principled—Radical Republicans felt that Louisiana had not done nearly enough for its black population.

In his speech at the White House, Lincoln compared the Louisiana government to an egg, and asked whether the nation would "sooner have the fowl by hatching the egg" or "by smashing it."

One of his arguments for the Louisiana government was directed at southern whites and their role in the endgame of abolition. If the new Louisiana state government were recognized, it would provide one more vote for ratifying the Thirteenth Amendment (the state had already approved it on February 17). After an amendment received a two-thirds vote in each house of Congress, it then had to be approved by three-quarters of the states before it became part of the Constitution. If the only states that counted in ratifying the Thirteenth Amendment were the twenty-five that had not seceded, the necessary three-quarters (nineteen states) would be more quickly reached. But such a ratification, Lincoln argued, "would be questionable, and sure to be persistently questioned." If, on the other hand, the amendment were ratified by three-quarters "of all the states"—twenty-seven out of thirty-six—it would be safe from doubt or challenge.

As long ago as his days in the Illinois legislature, Lincoln had held that slave owners ought to approve abolition themselves. They were free men, albeit engaged in a wrong; they should not be relieved from their wrongdoing by force or external power. The war had trampled many scruples. Slavery had been shattered by conflict and by Lincoln's proclamations as commander in chief. But requiring all the states, including formerly Confederate ones, to count toward the ratification of the Thirteenth Amendment would restore consent and agency to ex-rebels. Freedom would come, but it should come with their participation.

Another of Lincoln's arguments in favor of the new Louisiana government was directed to blacks. He repeated in public the suggestion he had made privately to Governor Hahn: "I would myself prefer" that colored veterans and "very intelligent" colored men could vote. But how was that goal best reached? By "saving the already advanced steps toward it" (by which he meant a functioning state government that had abolished slavery and approved the Thirteenth Amendment)? Or "by running backward over them"? If the new Louisiana government were recognized, Lincoln argued, "the colored man" would be "inspired with vigilance, and energy, and daring" to win his rights. This figure of Lincoln's imagination was more alive than the inert slaves of Lincoln's Second Inaugural Address; he sounded in fact like the self-made man of old Whig polemics—only he was now to be a self-made man of color.

One of Lincoln's auditors in the crowd on the White House lawn understood the import of these remarks very well. "That means nigger citizenship," said John Wilkes Booth to a friend. "That is the last speech he will ever make."

————

John Wilkes Booth, a month shy of his twenty-seventh birthday, belonged to a famous family of actors. He played dashing heroes, and he looked the part: he had the pale skin and dark curls of Lord Byron (still the nineteenth-century ideal of masculine beauty), with a slim cavalry mustache. The great actor in the family was his older brother Edwin, whose Shakespeare performances were natural, intimate, and profound. John Wilkes Booth was not a great actor, but rather an athletic ranter, good for swordfights and tirades. He was destined to win fame not in drama, but in politics.

The Booth brothers had grown up in Maryland, and their divided sympathies reflected those of the state: Edwin was a unionist, John Wilkes a partisan of slavery and the South. In December 1859 the younger Booth had joined a Richmond militia company so he could travel to Harpers Ferry to witness the execution of John Brown. He hated Brown for both his principles and his deeds, though he admired his aplomb.

As the war progressed, Booth made contact with the lower levels of the Confederate secret service; the eastern shore of Maryland, only a boat ride across the Potomac from Virginia, was sown with agents. In 1864 Booth hatched a plot to kidnap Abraham Lincoln, spirit him to Virginia, and ransom him for the release of Confederate prisoners of war. In November he left a sealed letter to be opened if he should come to grief, justifying his plans.

"I have ever held the South were right," Booth began. It was right because it correctly understood the difference between the races. "The country was formed for the white, not for the black man." Slavery was a blessing for both whites and blacks—"Witness heretofore our wealth and power; witness their elevation and enlightenment above their race elsewhere." The South was doubly right, Booth went on, because it was being bullied and oppressed, and because the founding fathers had given an example of resistance as the remedy in such cases. "To hate tyranny, to love liberty and justice, to strike at wrong and oppression, was the teaching of our fathers."

The villain of the struggle was Lincoln. "The very nomination of Abraham Lincoln four years ago spoke very plainly of war, war, upon Southern rights and institutions. His election proved it." So Booth believed he would be right to make Lincoln "a prisoner." He signed his testament, "A Confederate doing his duty on his own responsibility." Booth meanwhile assembled a team of conspirators to help with his scheme.

The idea of kidnapping Lincoln was harebrained; Jefferson Davis himself had nixed another such plot because it would have likely resulted in killing rather than capturing its object. But Booth's justifications, far from being mad, were the typical reasonings of Confederates and northern peace Democrats: blacks were inferior, the South was a victim, and Lincoln was her oppressor. Booth's disgusted remark on the White House lawn about "nigger citizenship" was in keeping with these views.

The collapse of the Confederacy in April 1865 rendered the kidnapping plot impossible even in theory—To whom would Booth deliver his prisoner, and for what might he be ransomed? It was then that Booth rose (setting morality aside) to greatness.

Assassination was an old tool of statesmanship. It had been used spectacularly in the French wars of religion of the late sixteenth century, in which numerous leaders, including two kings, Henri III and Henri IV, were assassinated by rivals or by zealots. The emergence of modern nation-states and the decline of crusading fervor in the seventeenth century signaled a turn away from assassination. Thereafter wars would be between countries, whose rulers were not to be held personally punishable for their policies. There were no assassinations during the American Revolution; George Washington approved a plot to kidnap Benedict Arnold after his treason, and even managed to insert an agent, a supposed defector, into British-occupied New York to do it, but he wanted Arnold captured, returned, and tried, not murdered (a last-minute change in Arnold's plans put him beyond his would-be captor's reach).

By the nineteenth century assassination seemed to have become the province of the unhinged. In 1812 Britain's prime minister, Spencer Perceval, was shot and killed by a deranged merchant who had once been mistreated while on business in Russia and believed that the British government owed him compensation. Andrew Jackson's would-be assassin in 1835 was a lunatic who believed he was actually the King of England. In the Cooper Union address, Lincoln compared John Brown to assassins, by way of suggesting Brown's insanity: "An enthusiast broods over the oppression of a people till he fancies himself commissioned by

Heaven to liberate them." Brooding enthusiasts belonged on the fringes of reason itself, far beyond the borders of politics.

When Booth transformed his kidnapping plot into an assassination plot, he only returned politics to older methods. He showed thereby an instinct for the crucial point, perhaps related to his lifetime in the theater: Lincoln was the central character, the spring of the action—the inspiration, oracle, and harmonizer of the Union cause. No one had spoken more eloquently, or demonstrated greater political prowess. To strike him even at the end, even after the end, was to strike to the heart.

Booth's new plot reached beyond Lincoln. He assigned two of his minions the jobs of killing Andrew Johnson and William Seward (Seward just then was bedridden from a carriage accident earlier in the month). Lincoln would be joined in death by his vice president and his secretary of state, the senior member of the cabinet. The date for action was April 15. The Lincolns were to attend a performance at Ford's Theater, half a dozen blocks from the White House, of *Our American Cousin*, a popular comedy. Booth's fame as an actor allowed him to scout the theater beforehand, choosing his ingress and his escape route, and to enter it unchallenged during the performance; of course, the famous Mr. Booth could come and go as he liked. In the third act, Booth entered the Lincolns' box and shot the president in the back of the head.

Booth then jumped to the stage, waved a dagger (his backup weapon), and cried *Sic semper tyrannus*—Thus always to tyrants—the motto of the State of Virginia. When Patrick Henry gave his great 1775 speech on the eve of the Revolution, ending with the cry, "Give me liberty, or give me death!" he had mimed driving a dagger into his breast. Now Booth stood fresh from his deed, brandishing an actual dagger. It was political stagecraft of the highest order. (Except for one detail—in Booth's downward leap, one of his spurs had caught on the bunting that hung from the Lincolns' box, causing him to land off balance and break a leg. One eyewitness compared his walk afterward to "the hopping of a bullfrog." This was an error: actors on the stage of history should not hop like bullfrogs.) Booth hopped off-stage to an alley, mounted a horse that he had posted there, and rode off before anyone in the dumbfounded crowd could stop him.

The plot was not a complete success: Johnson's designated assassin lost heart and spent the night roaming about; Seward's managed to break into the secretary of state's house and sickroom and stab him, though not fatally. But Lincoln, who never regained consciousness, died the next morning. Booth eluded pursuit for eleven days, before he was finally hunted down and shot in a barn in Virginia.

On April 17, as Sherman in North Carolina negotiated the surrender of the last major Confederate army, he told Joseph E. Johnston, the Confederate commander, news that he himself had just learned: Lincoln had been assassinated. Johnston, honest soldier, called it a disgrace to the age.

Johnston was honest, but unimaginative. How much more effective than a dozen Chancellorsvilles was Booth's blow. If Booth had hoped, by killing Johnson and Seward, to decapitate the Union government and cause it to waver, even in victory, his comrades had failed him. But Booth himself had done the vital thing. He had killed the man who had won the war; more important, he had killed the man who might have been able to win the peace. Slavery was dead, but much might be saved from the old order of things. Booth had shown the most wicked adherents of his cause how to proceed. Not that they needed any example of violence and lawlessness; the human heart is fertile with such impulses. But he gave them an example of success.

With almost no resources—with no armies, and no political authority, armed only with his beliefs and his will—Booth had nevertheless marked the politics of the nation for the next hundred years. John Brown, a capable guerrilla and terrorist, was muddled by his religious visions. Alexander Stephens, a clear-sighted political philosopher, was an ineffectual officeholder. Here at last in John Wilkes Booth was the towering genius Lincoln had foreseen in 1838.

But morality cannot be set aside. Lincoln did not believe so. "Let us have faith that right makes might," he said at Cooper Union, "and in that faith . . . dare to do our duty as we understand it." "With firmness in the right as God gives us to see the right, let us strive on to finish the work we are in," he prayed at the end of the Second Inaugural Address.

Firmness in the right was never easy to achieve. God never lets us see more than a piece of the picture. Lincoln encountered a lot of people in his life who knew just what should be done right away, and he generally reacted to them with skepticism, if not alarm. Right could be trammeled by old circumstances and arrangements. The founding fathers had found slavery existing among them; they would not name it in their Constitution, but they had secured it there. Right could be limited by countervailing rights. Slave owners were free men and could not simply be ordered to manumit; slaves should not be property, yet they were held as such, which entitled their owners to compensation. So it was necessary to proceed cautiously, legally; to persuade voters and to win elections. The problem of slavery was best solved by the means of politics.

Humor helped, by showing your own and everyone else's limitations; so, in a different way, did poetry, by describing and ministering to life's disappointments; so, most remotely, did God, Who presumably knew what He was doing, even if we did not.

Slavery had to end. That was clearly the right thing; besides, a house divided against itself could not stand. But the end of slavery might not come, in Lincoln's view, until 1893 or 1900, or a hundred years hence. The essential thing until then was to do no new harm, to keep the cancer from spreading.

But the politics of the 1850s, followed by the politics of the war, required the cancer to be cut out. So Lincoln did his duty. There would be charity for all after the bloodletting stopped. And if, thanks to Booth, charity was delayed, it would come one day. The Almighty had His own purposes.

Epilogue:
One Old Man

THE PATTERN OF DIFFICULT SECOND TERMS WAS WELL established by the middle of the nineteenth century, and there is no reason to think that Lincoln, if Booth had failed, would have avoided one.

Second terms were hard because problems sown in first terms came to maturity; because the more talented figures in an administration either retired, burned out, or became locked in intractable feuds; and because other politicians realized that second-term presidents were lame ducks. Though there was no constitutional prohibition then on running for a third term, the precedent of serving no more than two was well established, and the physical and mental toll of eight years was great enough to maintain it.

And yet it is inconceivable that Lincoln would not have done better than his successor. Andrew Johnson's presidency was what his intemperate interview with Charles Francis Adams Jr. suggested it would be; he turned his wrath from southerners to the Radical Republicans who controlled Congress, but wrathful he remained, wasting his almost four years in office in political clashes. Ulysses Grant, who served after Johnson for two terms, from 1869 to 1877, did his best. But Lincoln's great fear at the end of the war—of a neo-Confederate insurgency in the South—became real, and northern voters finally tired of combating it. The election of 1876, like that of 1824, ended with no majority in the Electoral College (or rather, with two, since both parties, Republicans and Democrats, claimed to have won one). The crisis was resolved only by a compromise—giving the White House to the Republicans, and the South to its old masters, rebels no more, but determined to run their section with a firm hand.

Yet slavery had ended (the Thirteenth Amendment received the necessary twenty-seven ratifications by December 1865). Four million bond-men and -women were free. Slavery would not flourish under the American or Confederate flag in Cuba or Central America. And the United States was not two nations but one. Republican government could defend itself against a vast, plausible, but deeply misguided rebellion. America's republican robe, as Lincoln had put it in the Peoria speech, had been washed—if not white, then cleaner.

On February 12, 1878—what would have been Lincoln's sixty-ninth birthday—a joint session of Congress met to receive a gift: a painting of Lincoln reading the Emancipation Proclamation to his cabinet. The picture had been painted in 1864 by Francis Carpenter, a young artist from upstate New York, who had asked Lincoln and members of his cabinet to pose for him. In 1877 a wealthy benefactor bought it, with the intention of donating it to Congress.

There they sit, ranged around a table, the rivals and the ciphers, in their strange beards and their high collars. Seward looks as if his pants and jacket came out of someone else's closet. Lincoln, as befits the occasion, is made to be unusually neat. Carpenter included some political symbolism in his group portrait: from the perspective of the viewer, Chase the Radical's friend stands on the left; Seward and Montgomery Blair are on the right. Lincoln is slightly left of center.

The man who had so admired the founding fathers was now a father of his country, surrounded by the lesser fathers who had helped and hampered him.

By becoming a father, Lincoln risked becoming an icon, as the careless made George Washington and the other founders: a figure in a painting, a face on stamps, money, and monuments, admirable but empty. To understand him, later generations would have to do with him what he had done with the founding fathers—study his actions, study his words. Fortunately, his actions were dramatic and his words meaningful (even though their very beauty is sometimes distracting).

One of the speeches on his birthday in 1878 was given by Rep. James Garfield of Ohio, soon to be president himself (and soon after to be assassinated, not by an ideologue but by a madman). Another was given by Rep. Alexander Stephens of Georgia.

Stephens had had an active political life after the war. He had been arrested in May 1865 for his part in the rebellion and imprisoned for five months. Shortly after his release, Georgia sent him to the Senate, which refused to seat him (Congress's policies toward former Confederate states were much tougher than Lincoln's Louisiana plan). Stephens wrote exculpatory memoirs and histories, and by 1872, Congress having relented, he was elected to the House, where he had last sat in 1859, where he had met Lincoln in 1847.

On February 12, 1878, Stephens had just turned sixty-six—his birthday was the day before Lincoln's—and his body, never robust, was confined to a wheelchair. His oratorical powers were also weakened, by bad faith more than by time. He praised the southern states for helping to put the Thirteenth Amendment into the Constitution—eight of the twenty-seven states to ratify had formerly been in the Confederacy, their assent the fruit of Lincoln's wise policy. But Stephens hedged about slavery's nature and legacy. "It had its faults," he conceded, "and most grievously has the country, North and South . . . answered them." It also, he maintained, gave rise to "the noblest virtues. But let its faults and virtues be buried alike forever." The keen intelligence that had so appealed to Lincoln was almost blunted by trying to have everything all ways.

His memories of Lincoln were tender, but diffuse. "He was warm-hearted; he was generous; he was magnanimous. . . . Every fountain of his heart was ever overflowing with 'the milk of human kindness.'"

But in the midst of this lukewarm bath, half self-protection, half sentiment, the old Stephens for one moment stirred, and spoke a sentence that was half right, half wrong, and entirely riveting.

It came in his discussion of the subject of Carpenter's painting, the Emancipation Proclamation. He made a point similar to one that Lincoln himself had made on various occasions, concerning the power of circumstance. "I claim not to have controlled events," Lincoln wrote in 1864, "but confess plainly that events have controlled me." "The Almighty has His own purposes," he said in 1865. The Emancipation Proclamation, said Stephens, although it grew out of a lifelong principle of Lincoln's, was a product of circumstance, adopted as a war measure, and confirmed only by the Thirteenth Amendment after Lincoln himself was dead.

Stephens then said: "Life is all a mist, and in the dark our fortunes meet us." The true half of that sentence was the second half: "in the dark our fortunes meet us." God, time, chance, and men throw problems, crises, opportunities, blessings, and horrors at us. We may see some coming, but not all. When they come they are obdurate, inescapable, and we face them as best we can.

The false half of Stephens's sentence was the first: "Life is all a mist." Life is all a mist for most of us. We believe a mixture of traditions, lessons, and current opinions: what we have grown up with, what we have been taught, and what we have heard in the street. These are not always the best guides to action. Life had been all a mist for Alexander Stephens—sucked into secession, serving a rebel president with whom he disagreed, then driven to justifying it all afterward.

Lincoln, of all men, wanted not to live in a mist. In his worst moods he believed he was damned; at all times his mind taught him (wrongly probably) that he was doomed, predetermined, caught in a mesh of causes. But he always wanted to see, know, and understand. Herndon noted the comprehensiveness of his curiosity, extending to clocks and omnibuses, but his greatest curiosity was about the great things. He wanted to know what America was, what men were, what God wanted. As he did when he was a boy, he would repeat the lessons of the founding fathers and God the Father until he knew them. What he learned was that all men are created free and equal, and that all men (the people) must understand and defend those truths. Then, because he was a politician, ambitious to lead, he did what he could to clear the mist.

ACKNOWLEDGMENTS

Michael Knox Beran, Andrew Ferguson, Peter Field, and Lewis Lehrman gave me vital early advice. Roger Hertog and Eric Weider gave me generous support.

Theodore J. Crackel, J. Jefferson Looney, and Nicole Seary helped me sort through founders' correspondence, real and bogus. Douglas L. Wilson gave permission to quote William Herndon's 1870 letter on Lincoln and Jefferson. Thanks also to James G. Basker, Linda Bridges, Michael Burlingame, Allen Guelzo, Kale Kaposhilin, Charles Kesler, and Jonathan Leaf.

I would like to thank my editor and publisher, Lara Heimert, my editor Roger LaBrie, and my agent Michael Carlisle. As always, I thank my wife, Jeanne Safer.

Akhil Amar gave me the idea for this book, and the title. I hope he likes it.

NOTES

I have not footnoted the King James Bible or readily available public documents—the Declaration, the Constitution, rebels' ordinances of secession, and the like.

Correspondence of George Washington and Thomas Jefferson that is not found in common anthologies is readily available online; below I give the dates and the recipients.

Introduction

2   **"few millions"** Rowland, I:181.

2   **"out West"** Tocqueville, 86.

3   **"in despair"** Martineau, II:3–17.

5   **"other pillars"** Address to the Young Men's Lyceum of Springfield, Illinois, 1/27/38, SWI:28–36.

5   **"never been before"** Autobiography Written for Campaign, c. 6/60, SWII:167.

6   **"charter of liberty"** 7th Lincoln/Douglas Debate, Alton, Illinois, 10/15/58, SWI:802.

7   **"apple of gold"** Fragment on the Constitution and the Union, c. 1/61, CWIV:169.

7   **"real life"** Weems, 9, 11–13.

7   **"made it?"** 4th Lincoln/Douglas Debate, Charleston, Illinois, 9/18/58, SWI:674.
7   **"fundamentally wrong"** *American Speeches*, 722.
8   **"with Hell"** Chapman, 172.

Chapter One

13   **"mind and memory"** To Jesse Lincoln, 4/1/54, SWI:300.
13   **"living history"** Address to the Young Men's Lyceum, SWI:36.
14   **"prostitution"** HI, 36.
14   **everything** Tarbell, I:17.
15   **"laughing"** HI, 37.
15   **worship God** HI, 40.
16   **"right off"** HI, 503.
16   **"repeat it"** HI, 106–107.
17   **pedagogical tools** HI, 67.
17   **"run together"** HI, 108.
19   **one said twelve** HI, 113, 118.
19   **to love it** HI, 118.
19   **"himself first"** HI, 107.
20   **to rest** HI, 560.
20   **reader he was** Bray, 152, discusses similar behavior when Lincoln was slightly older.
20   **smacked him for it** HI, 39.
20   **"sign his own name"** Autobiography Written for Campaign, SWII:160.
20   **"hug it the tighter"** To Joshua F. Speed, 2/25/42, SWI:91.
21   **quart a day** Wood, 339.
21   **"in his life"** HI, 97.
21   **"tried his manhood"** HI, 96; see also 28, 36.
21   **even better** HI, 454, 37.
22   **"'farting'"** Herz, 398–399.
23   **"yesterday"** HI, 113.
23   **"rams' horns"** HI, 151.
23   **"better than the Bible"** HI, 120.
24   **of his stepbrother** To Thomas Lincoln and John D. Johnston, 12/24/48, SWI:224.
24   **"in any extremity"** To John D. Johnston, 1/12/51, SWI:256.

Chapter Two

26   **steamboat . . . foundered** See Levasseur II:158–164.

26   **"of his age"** Brookhiser (*Washington*), 111.

27   **"country's ruins"** Ibid., 164.

27   **two or three days** The story of Josiah Crawford loaning Weems's *Life* is in HI, 125 and 455. But another old acquaintance remembered the book that Lincoln borrowed as David Ramsay's *Life of George Washington* (HI, 41). Lincoln himself said that he encountered Weems "away back in my childhood, [during] the earliest days of my being able to read," which would have been before he knew Crawford (who arrived in Indiana when Lincoln was seventeen) (Address to the New Jersey Senate, Trenton, 2/21/61, SWII:209).

27   **"not displeased"** Mason L. Weems to Washington (undated), 1795.

28   **not lying all the time** I have forgotten the name of the historian who said this to me, though not his remark.

28   **"industry and honor"** Weems, 13.

28   **"of Latin"** Weems, 54.

28   **"as a wizard"** To Jesse W. Fell, 12/20/59, SWII:107.

29   **"this fall"** Weems, 20.

29   **"a thousand fold"** Weems, 23–25.

30   **"his good!"** Weems, 27–28.

30   **tend the farm?** Weems, 47.

30   **"his own merit"** Weems, 42.

32   ***"frost-bitten"*** Weems, 139–140.

32   **"live with us"** Weems, 137, 143.

32   **"defend her or perish"** Weems, 140.

32   ***"about to fight for"*** Weems, 141.

33   **"was made"** Address to the New Jersey Senate, op. cit., SWII:209–210.

34   **revelation closed** H, 2–3.

Chapter Three

38   **floating driftwood** HI, 12.

39   **both came home** Hanks's testimony is in HI, 457. Lincoln wrote that Hanks turned back at St. Louis (Autobiography for Campaign, SWII:163–164). See also Bray, 15, 232.

40   **"everything all over"** H, 83.

40   **saddled with debt** Donald, 54.
40   **still in use** Thomas, 40.
40   **"Great God Almighty!"** HI, 449.
40   **"I ever saw"** H, 145.
41   **with a romance** See Douglas Wilson, 114–124, and Donald, 608–609.
41   **"quick as a flash"** HI, 534.
41   **"committing suicide often"** HI, 243.
41   **"two weeks I think"** Douglas Wilson, 121.
41   **"raining on her grave"** HI, 557.
41   **"beat on her grave"** HI, 27.
42   **"as he walked"** H, 473.
42   **"never dare"** HI, 205.
42   **"upon yourself"** To Mary Owens, 8/16/37, SWI:21.
42   **"smaller attentions"** HI, 262.
43   **"a fool of myself"** To Mrs. Orville H. Browning, 4/1/38, SWI:39.
       The date of the letter suggests that Lincoln meant it as a joke. But
       the joke falls flat.
43   **"very much chagrined"** To the people of Sangamon County, 3/9/32,
       SWI:5.
44   **the expression was Jefferson's** J, 632–633.
44   **"their esteem"** To the people of Sangamon County, op. cit.
45   **for all the spectators** HI, 451.
45   **"ready servant"** Weems, 316.
46   **"crop of folly"** Martineau, I:269, 273.
47   **"of Illinois"** H, 140.
49   **"in a lump"** To John Stuart, 1/20/40, SWI:66.
49   **"the general wreck"** Guelzo, 92; CWI:200–201.
49   **"like the present"** *American Antislavery Writings*, 269.
50   **"of the District"** Douglas Wilson, 165–166; Protest in the Illinois
       Legislature on Slavery, 3/3/37, SWI:18.

Chapter Four

52   **"more grieved"** P, 415.
52   **Christian antidote** Bray, 23.
52   **in New Salem** One old acquaintance said Lincoln read *Common
       Sense* in New Salem (HI, 172); Herndon wrote that he also read *The
       Age of Reason* (H, 355).

53	**"such sermons"** P, 702.
53	**"enslave mankind"** P, 666.
53	**"exactness is necessary"** P, 766.
53	**"justly deserved it"** P, 801.
54	**"word of God!"** P, 754.
54	**"worn out debauchee"** P, 770–771.
54	**"upon the stroll"** P, 800.
54	**"would she be believed?"** P, 792, 797.
54	**Paine's erotic history** Keane, 49–52, 75–78.
54	**"blasphemy"** P, 750.
54	**"example of murder"** P, 703.
55	**"God to man"** P, 685.
55	**"TO EACH OTHER"** P, 694.
55	**church trustee** Thomas, 12.
55	**"talked about it"** HI, 107.
56	**"grounds of reason"** HI, 472.
56	**"a bastard"** HI, 576.
56	**burned it** Hill's son said his father made Lincoln burn it (HI, 61–62), Herndon said Hill burned it himself (H, 355).
56	**"hundreds of times"** HI, 61.
56	**"an open scoffer"** Handbill Replying to Charges of Infidelity, 7/31/46, SWI:139.
57	**"or explanation"** P, 777.
57	**"and one is three"** P, 697.
57	**"interval of life"** P, 710.
58	**"horses and cattle"** 4th Lincoln/Douglas Debate, Charleston, Illinois, 9/18/58, SWI:677.
58	**"leave her alone"** Speech on the Dred Scott Decision, Springfield, Illinois, 6/26/57, SWI:398.
58	**"upon . . . emetics"** To Erastus Corning and others, 6/12/63, SWII:461.
59	**"MUNIFICENCE"** P, 694.
59	**"still goes on"** P, 674.
59	**"would be hanged"** P, 702.
59	**"think that is"** To Andrew Johnston, 4/18/46, SWI:137.
60	**always had them** See HI, 404.
60	**all the plays** To James Hackett, 8/17/63, SWII:493.
60	**A scholar rediscovered it** See Miller, 1 and 6.

61   **"alive with fun"** The Bear Hunt, before 2/25/47, SWI:148.

61   **Lincoln gave a speech** Address to the Young Men's Lyceum of
      Springfield, Illinois, 1/27/38, SWI:28–36.

63   **portrait of Napoleon** The lines are from *Childe Harold's Pilgrim-
      age*, canto III, stanza 42.

65   **a note of thanks** See CWI:115.

65   **Vicksburg had turned on its gamblers** An account of the whole
      episode is in Foote, 250–262. The bandit behind the supposed plot
      appears in Jorge Luis Borges (*A Universal History of Iniquity*), and
      his cave appears in Mark Twain (*Tom Sawyer*).

66   **panic among masters** Protest in the Illinois Legislature on Slav-
      ery, 3/3/37, SWI:18.

Chapter Five

68   **another story** Boritt, 55.

68   **"*so* interesting"** The Rebecca Letter, 8/27/42, SWI:100.

69   **"for political effect"** To Elias Merryman, 9/19/42, SWI:102.

70   **The Log Cabin Campaign** See Brookhiser (*American History*, Har-
      rison) and Collins.

70   **"Damn such a book"** Guelzo, 93.

70   **"happy condition"** Boritt, 72.

70   **single-issue candidate** Boritt, 175.

71   **"continued in operation"** Address to the People of Illinois, 3/4/43,
      CWI:318.

71   **"he certainly did"** See Douglas Wilson, 216, 353.

72   **"printed on them"** Douglas Wilson, 214.

72   **"on the earth"** To John T. Stuart, 1/20/41, SWI:69.

72   **hid their knives and razors** H, 168–169; HI 475.

72   **"let us hear soon"** Douglas Wilson, 236.

73   **"better than tolerable"** To Mary Speed, 9/27/41, SWI:74–75.

73   **"nervous debility"** To Joshua Speed, c. early 1/42, SWI:77.

73   **"hug it the tighter"** To Joshua Speed, 2/25/42, 90–91.

74   **to fight her battles** Exodus 14:13; 2 Chronicles 20:17; to Joshua
      Speed, 7/4/42, SWI:95.

74   **glad to be married** To Joshua Speed, 10/5/42, SWI:103–104. Lin-
      coln's relationship with Speed, and their relationships with women,
      have been the primary stimulus for the question: Was Lincoln gay?

Tripp argued yes; I reviewed his book (Brookhiser, "Was Lincoln Gay?"), not critically enough.

74 **"the garret or the cellar"** Douglas Wilson, 242.

74 **throw things at him** Strozier, 107.

75 **"he had lived"** HI, 197.

75 **"look in this"** H, 254.

75 **documents and underwear** H, 280.

75 **"his back in a ditch"** HI, 636.

76 **"never very formidable"** H, 210.

76 **"dug up the root"** H, 272.

76 **"as he walked"** H, 473.

76 **"whistle off sadness"** HI, 350.

76 **"reverse the decree"** H, 352; HI, 360. Herndon remembered it as "no prayers of ours can reverse," Mary as "no cares of ours can arrest."

76 **"before the man"** H, 354.

77 **"self-evident demonstration"** P, 736.

77 **the case of Rebecca Thomas** *Lincoln Legal Briefs* nailed down the specifics of the case. Herndon reconstructed Lincoln's speech in H, 274–275; Fehrenbacher and Fehrenbacher are skeptical (*Recollected Words*, 230, 541). But Herndon was there, and he was witnessing a performance in his own profession.

78 **"ruff-scuff generally"** Howe, 35.

78 **"'a gallon of gall'"** Address to the Washington Temperance Society of Springfield, Illinois, SWI:83.

78 **"moral reformation"** Ibid., SWI:90. The real George Washington served wine at his table, treated voters to drinks, and ran a distillery at Mount Vernon.

79 **fun of them** H, 206–207.

79 **"fall dead"** To John J. Hardin, SWI:124.

79 **"the Christian denominations"** Handbill Replying to Charges of Infidelity, 7/31/46, SWI:139. Lincoln's language was careful: he implied that he was no longer a fatalist, but his exact words were that he had "left off . . . arguing thus."

81 **"seemed wonderful"** To Williamson Dursley, 10/3/45, SWI:111.

82 **"spot of soil"** "Spot" Resolutions in the US House of Representatives, 12/22/47, SWI:159.

82 **"Washington would answer"** Speech in the US House of Representatives on the War with Mexico, 1/12/48, SWI:168.

82   **"spotty Lincoln," "spotted fever"** Thomas, 120.
82   **"peace and harmony"** Washington, 972.
83   **"vile dirt!"** *Appendix to the Congressional Globe*, 163.
83   **"I ever heard"** To William Henry Herndon, 2/2/48, SWI:174.
84   **Winthrop's oration** Winthrop, 70–89.
84   **sputter along** One of its lawmakers would be Alexis de Tocque-ville, the man who interviewed Charles Carroll.
85   **"immovable attachment"** See also Washington, 964.
86   **"negro livery stable"** Speech on the Kansas-Nebraska Act at Peo-ria, Illinois, 10/16/54, SWI:313.
86   **"of said District"** Protest in the Illinois Legislature on Slavery, 3/3/37, SWI:18.
86   **"(paradox though it may seem)"** To Williamson Dursley, 10/3/45, SWI:112.
87   **"leading citizens"** Proposal in the US House of Representatives for the Abolition of Slavery in the District of Columbia, 1/10/49, SWI:229.

Chapter Six

90   **"possible to conceive"** Dyer, 222–230.
90   **"supply their places"** Henry Adams, 134.
91   **"knell of the union"** J, 698.
91   **"disgust with the union"** Brookhiser (*Madison*), 243.
92   **rush of the moment** See Dyer, 230.
93   **"Clay and Frelinghuysing"** Schlesinger, 439.
93   **"glorious triumph"** To William H. Herndon, 6/12/48, SWI:185.
93   **"a natural death"** To Williamson Dursley, 10/3/45, SWI:112.
94   **a long Senate speech** *Register of Debates*, 22nd Cong., 1st sess., 1832, 277.
95   **"the opulent"** Madison, 531.
96   **"vigor of his nature"** Hamilton, 663.
96   **"the pistol's mouth," "gallant"** Weems, 288.
97   **"to reflect"** *Abridgement of the Debates*, XVI:391.
98   **" 'successfully compromised' "** H, 292.
99   **delivered a eulogy** Eulogy on Henry Clay, Springfield, Illinois, 7/6/52, SWI:259–272.
99   **"and with Hell"** Chapman, 172.

101   **come back to it repeatedly** 1st Lincoln/Douglas Debate at Ottawa, Illinois, 8/21/58, SWI:527; Speech at Bloomington, 9/4/58, CWIII:89; 5th Lincoln/Douglas Debate at Galesburg, Illinois, SWI:717; Speech at Columbus, 9/16/59, SWII:58.

101   **of every issue** Foner, 20.

Chapter Seven

105   **"as never before"** Autobiography Written for Campaign, c. 6/60, SWII:167.

106   **"miss him very much"** To John D. Johnston, 2/23/50, SWI:244.

106   **"was unanswerable"** HI, 549.

106   **"Knows nothing of Lincoln"** HI, 547.

106   **"he could not be scared"** Eulogy on Zachary Taylor, Chicago, Illinois, 7/25/50, SWI:251.

107   **references to his age** To William H. Herndon, 2/2/48, 7/10/48, SWI:174, 203.

107   **"a little engine that knew no rest"** H, 304.

108   **"as he now is"** Speech to the Scott Club of Springfield, Illinois, 8/14–26/52, SWI:273.

108   **"magnetism"** H, 330.

110   **"interested in it"** Jaffa, 155.

110   **"the whole controversy"** Cutts, 122–123.

112   **When speaking on the stump** Lehrman, 41–43.

112   **"new slavery agitation"** Speech on the Kansas-Nebraska Act at Peoria, Illinois, 10/16/54, SWI:333.

113   **"in the state library"** Lehrman, 44.

113   **"continue to speak"** SWI:334, op. cit.; "is" before "his love of justice" in SWI is a mistake. See CWII:271.

113   **"Lincolnisms"** Lehrman, 44.

113   **"making cheese"** SWI:308, op. cit.

114   **"hogs and Negroes"** Ibid., 325–326.

114   **"wild bears"** Ibid., 326.

114   **"running at large"** Ibid., 327.

115   **"that is despotism"** Ibid., 328.

115   **"ONLY BY NECESSITY"** Ibid., 309, 342, 338.

116   **corrected the error** See letters to John L. Scripps, 6/16/60, and to James O. Putnam, 9/16/60, CWIV:77, 115.

116   **"no slave amongst them"** SWI:309, op. cit.

116   **"slave of another"** Ibid., 328.

117   **"fully, and firmly"** Ibid., 332.

117   **"they would not go"** Ibid., 338.

117   **"rest in peace"** Ibid., 340.

117   **"ancient faith," "old-time men"** Ibid., 328–329.

117   **"bleed to death"** Ibid., 338.

118   **"will not admit of" complete equality** Ibid., 316.

118   **"blood, of the Revolution"** Ibid., 339–340.

Chapter Eight

119   **"events have controlled me"** To Albert G. Hodges, 4/4/64, SWII:586.

120   **buying their votes** Pinsker, 18–19.

120   **"consented to it"** To William H. Henderson, 2/21/55, SWI:357. Shields would go on to serve briefly as a senator from both Minnesota and Missouri, becoming the only man ever to be a US senator from three states.

121   **"backed with wrath"** H, 312–313.

122   **"save every Whig"** To Lyman Trumbull, 6/7/56, SWI:366.

123   **"bound to respect"** Jaffa, 280.

123   **"to disband"** Jaffa, 286.

124   **"is sustained"** Fehrenbacher (*Prelude*), 134.

124   **"amalgamation"** Donald, 201.

124   **"will not admit of" racial equality** Speech on the Kansas-Nebraska Act at Peoria, Illinois, 10/16/54, SWI:316.

124   **"hatred of the negro"** Foner, 109.

124   **"miscegenation"** Foner, 309.

124   **Lincoln answered** Speech on the Dred Scott Decision at Springfield, Illinois, 6/26/57, SWI:390–403.

127   **Douglas responded** Sheahan, 319–320.

128   **"support to Mr. Douglas"** Greeley, 357.

128   **"surrender at once"** To Lyman Trumbull, 12/28/57, SWI:419.

129   **"only choice"** Fehrenbacher (*Prelude*), 67.

129   **Lincoln addressed them** "House Divided" speech, Springfield, Illinois, 6/16/58, SWI:426–434.

129   **"damned fool utterance"** H, 326.

129 **"my natural life"** Fragment on the Struggle Against Slavery, c. 7/58, SWI:438.

130 **"a hundred years"** 4th Lincoln/Douglas Debate, Charleston, Illinois, 9/18/58, SWI:677.

130 **In a draft** Draft of a Speech, c. late 12/57, SWI:413. Governor John Quitman of Mississippi sponsored a revolution in Cuba; William Walker, a southern adventurer, tried to conquer Baja California, Nicaragua, and Honduras.

131 **his published papers** See Moore, X:106–108. Buchanan's letters are quoted to show that he did not meddle in the *Dred Scott* decision, yet they suggest the opposite.

132 **texts of the debates** The standard printed texts of the Lincoln/Douglas debates follow the newspaper accounts that Lincoln put in his scrapbook, with some additions (Lincoln clipped out the crowd reactions). Below I give the reactions that were reported in the newspapers in brackets. I list debates by number (1st, 2nd, 3rd . . .) and their page numbers in SWI.

132 **Republicans kept tabs** Fehrenbacher (*Prelude*), 113.

132 **"any way promoted"** 5th Debate, SWI:709.

133 **"on fire"** Fehrenbacher (*Prelude*), 101.

133 **"the town together"** 1st Debate, SWI:500.

133 **"disgrace to white people"** 2nd Debate, SWI:556–557; 4th Debate, SWI:666.

133 **"almost white"** 4th Debate, SWI:672.

134 **"the superior position"** 1st Debate, SWI:513.

134 **"marrying together"** 1st Debate, SWI:517.

134 **"white people with negroes"** 4th Debate, SWI:637.

134 **was constitutional** 2nd Debate, SWI:538.

134 **"from its limits"** 2nd Debate, SWI:541–542.

134 **"local police regulations"** 2nd Debate, SWI:552.

135 **"every stump in Illinois"** 2nd Debate, SWI:551.

135 **"our fathers made it?"** 1st Debate, SWI:503.

135 **"that day and hour"** 3rd Debate, SWI:598–599. Benjamin Franklin had freed his slaves by 1776; George Wythe did so later.

136 **"at that time"** 6th Debate, SWI:765.

136 **"disapprobation"** 7th Debate, SWI:802.

136 **"for free society"** 7th Debate, SWI:794.

136 **"the course of ultimate extinction?"** 7th Debate, SWI:801.

137   **"existed among us"** 7th Debate, SWI: 802.
137   **"'God was just'"** 5th Debate, SWI:702.
17   **"among possible events"** J, 279.
137   **"oppressed of the whole earth"** 6th Debate, SWI:763.
138   **"same tyrannical principle"** 7th Debate, SWI:810–811.
138   **the newly elected legislature** Fehrenbacher (*Prelude*), 114–120, analyzes the vote.
138   **"I am gone"** To Anson G. Henry, 11/19/58, SWI:831; the next day, To Charles H. Ray, 11/20/59, SWI:832.

Chapter Nine

140   **"damned long-armed ape"** Donald, 186.
140   **"observation and analysis"** H, 478.
140   **"being President"** H, 363.
141   **"to all men and all times"** To Henry L. Pierce and Others, 4/6/59, SWII:19.
142   **"most insidious"** To Steven Galloway, 7/28/59, SWII:27.
142   **Douglas's article** Douglas, 526.
143   **"they clung to freedom"** Speech at Columbus, Ohio, 9/16/59, SWII:46–48.
143   **"hands to labor with"** Speech at Cincinnati, Ohio, 9/17/59, SWII:85.
144   **neither of them was a Christian** Both men esteemed Jesus, Jefferson as a moral teacher, Lincoln as a source of good words, but neither man considered Him his savior.
144   **"a bad tailor at that"** Charles Francis Adams Jr., 59.
144   **"irrepressible conflict"** Brookhiser (*Dynasty*), 127.
145   **"clumsy . . . gaunt"** Donald, 238.
145   **Lincoln's speech** Address at Cooper Institute, New York City, 2/27/60, SWII:111–130.
148   **"since St. Paul"** Holzer (*Cooper Union*), 146.
150   **As he put it at Cooper** Op. cit., 120.

Chapter Ten

151   **"nosing"** Lehrman, 44.
152   **Lincoln glanced over** To Charles C. Nott, 9/6/60, CWIV:113; see also Holzer (*Cooper Union*), 221–226.

153 **caught the error** Charles C. Nott to Lincoln, 8/28/60, CWIV:113.

153 **"confederation of free states"** CWIII:550.

153 **a speech Lyman Trumbull had given** *Congressional Globe*, 36th Cong., 1st sess., 12/8/59, 60.

153 **earlier in the 1850s** Dr. Nicole Seary found nine earlier citations of the bogus Washington letter in northern newspapers, going back to 1855, plus two articles in Democratic newspapers after the Cooper Union speech questioning the letter's authenticity. See Brookhiser, "Abraham Lincoln's Cooper Union Address."

154 **"the abolition of it"** Washington, 594; CWIII:550.

154 **"a good thing"** Speech at Elwood, Kansas, 12/1/59, CWIII: 496.

154 **"where it prevailed"** CWIII:550, quoting Madison (*Debates*), 8/8/87, 392.

154 **"property in men"** CWIII:550, quoting Madison (*Debates*), 8/25/87, 505.

155 **"become the carriers"** Madison (*Debates*), 8/21–22/87, 477, 487.

155 **Rutledge could not be counted** Address at Cooper Institute, New York City, 2/27/60, SWII:117.

155 **"days of Cain"** *Debates and Proceedings*, 2/11/90, 1225, 1229.

156 **"faithful Musselmen"** Franklin, 1160.

157 **"memory of Jefferson"** William Herndon to Ward Lamon, 3/3/70, Ward Hill Lamon Papers, LN2327, Huntington Library.

158 **"contemptible hypocrite"** Hamilton, 977.

158 **"impressions of the moment"** Madison (*Writings*), 860.

158 **published in 1787** There had been a private edition, in English, in Paris in 1785, and a French translation in 1786.

158 **"such a contest"** J, 278–279.

158 **several times** 5th Lincoln/Douglas Debate, Galesburg, Illinois, 10/7/58, SWI:702; Speech at Columbus, 9/16/59, SWII:41.

159 **"a slave's embrace"** Moore, "Epistle of Thomas Hume" (which has "his slave's embrace"); Dickens, *Martin Chuzzlewhit*. See Peterson, 182–183.

159 **Lincoln denied it** To Anson G. Chester, 9/5/60, CWIV:111–112.

159 **slow to defame individuals** In the 4th Lincoln/Douglas debate, at Charleston (SWI:637), Lincoln did make a crack about Richard M. Johnson, Martin Van Buren's vice president, whose common-law wife Julia Chinn was an octoroon. Lincoln called him "Douglas' friend"—an effort to depict Democrats as secretly yearning for that which they denounced.

159   **"the immortal author"** Coles to Jefferson, 7/31/14.

160   **leaked by Coles himself** J. Jefferson Looney, private communication.

160   **"weary in well-doing"** Jefferson to Coles, 8/25/14.

160   **"our fellow Citizens"** Coles to Jefferson, 9/26/14.

161   **The letter, published by Holmes** Jefferson to Holmes, J, 698.

163   **"John Thompson"** J, 178–179.

163   **"Locke, Sidney, etc."** J, 719.

165   **"to be remembered"** J, ii.

165   **"tear [it] to pieces"** Speech on the Kansas-Nebraska Act at Peoria, Illinois, 10/16/54, SWI:339.

165   **"the political community"** *American Speeches*, 703.

166   **"torment"** To Joshua F. Speed, 8/24/55, SWI:360.

166   **"in their situation"** Speech on the Kansas-Nebraska Act, op. cit., SWI:315.

166   **comparing one of his colleagues** *American Speeches*, 558.

167   **could become unbalanced** See Charles Francis Adams Jr., 83: "Even now I can see Sumner's eyes gleaming with something distinctly suggestive of insanity."

168   **"to that instruction"** *American Speeches*, 679.

168   **"truth and manhood"** Thoreau, 282.

168   **condemned him as violent** Speech at Elwood, Kansas, 12/1/59, CWIII:496; Second Speech at Leavenworth, Kansas, 12/5/59, CWIII:503.

169   **"his own execution"** Address at Cooper Institute, New York City, 2/27/60, SWII:123–125.

169   **"he reappeared here"** Thoreau, 273.

Chapter Eleven

172   **"from the four winds"** "House Divided" speech, Springfield, Illinois, 6/16/58, SWI:434.

173   **"in that place"** HI, 162.

173   **"men do care"** Address at Cooper Institute, New York City, 2/27/60, SWII:130

173   **"liberty-loving men"** Speech at Chicago, 7/10/58, SWI:456.

174   **"many better ones"** Donald, 245.

175   **David Herbert Donald doubts** Donald, 249, 637–638.

175	**one of his off-color jokes** The version printed here is in HI, 174. Christopher Brown's recollection is in HI, 438.
178	**"of the past"** Everett, IV:23.
179	**"vote for you"** See SWII:733.
179	**"save the union"** Goodwin, 274.
181	**Chicago post office** Brookhiser (*Dynasty*), 131.
182	**"close corporation"** Goodwin, 314.
182	**"I expect to be there"** Goodwin, 289.
183	**"half a dozen Yankees"** Goodwin, 314.
183	**"hand of peace"** Goodwin, 300.
184	**"superiority"** HI, 332.
185	**"from the union"** Howe, 253.
186	**"heresies"** Eulogy on Henry Clay, Springfield, Illinois, 7/6/52, SWI:269.
186	**"days of Washington"** To Alexander H. Stephens, 12/22/60, SWII:194.
186	**"'pictures of silver'"** See CWIV:160–161.
186	**"whatever"** Address at Cooper Institute, op. cit., SWII:123.
187	**"from the dead"** To William S. Spear, 10/23/60, SWII:182.
187	**"is the rub"** To Alexander H. Stephens, 12/22/60, SWI:194.
187	**"see him no more"** HI, 108.
188	**he examined disturbing dreams** H, 352.
188	**"forsake us now"** Farewell Address, Springfield, Illinois, 2/11/61, SWII:734, given here, is the newspaper account of what Lincoln said. SWII:199 is his written text.
188	**"those men struggled for"** Address to the New Jersey Senate, Trenton, 2/21/61, SWII:209.
189	**"for all future time"** Speech at Independence Hall, Philadelphia, 2/22/61, SWII:212–213.
189	**"to hell"** HI, 709.
190	**Lincoln's address** First Inaugural Address, 3/4/61, SWI:215–224.
191	**"reclaim"** See SWII:735.
191	**"galvanized corpse"** Thomas, 245.
192	**polished Seward's words** See SWII:735.
193	**spoke to a reception** *American Speeches*, 717–731; AS, "Corner-Stone" Speech, Savannah, Georgia, 3/21/61. In later years Stephens tried, not very successfully, to blunt the force of his remarks. See Stephens, 173–175.

194   **"knell of the union"** J, 698.
195   **throughout the Bible** Psalms 118:22, Matthew 21:42, Mark 12:10, Luke 20:17, Acts 4:10, 1 Peter 2:7.
196   **failed to get his way** See Howe, 256–258.
198   **who the president was** Donald, 289–290, gives Seward's memo to Lincoln and Lincoln's reply.
198   **"only provisions"** Donald, 292.
198   **"signifying nothing"** Chesnut, 36. Mary Boykin Chesnut reworked her diary in later years, but she kept the chronological P.O.V.

Chapter Twelve

202   **echo Washington's language** Compare Proclamation Calling Militia and Convening Congress, 4/15/61, SWII:232, and Washington, 872–873.
203   **"of his statesmanship"** Brookhiser (*Dynasty*), 129.
204   **"as fast as it was made"** HI, 331.
204   **"advice about anything," "sent them away"** HI 167, 163.
205   **Lincoln as an ape** Donald, 186, 284, 319, 389, 387.
205   **Mathew Brady** See Holzer (*Cooper Union*), 94–99.
206   **"brow of a hill"** H, 472.
206   **"mental attribute"** Charles Francis Adams Jr., 96.
207   **Lincoln suspended habeas corpus** Chief Justice Taney ruled, in *ex parte Merryman*, that only Congress had the power to suspend habeas corpus. Congress did so in March 1863.
207   **Clement Vallandingham** See Brookhiser (*American History*, Vallandingham); To Erastus Corning and others, 6/12/63, SWII:460–461.
208   **"in the town"** Nasby, 3.
208   **Nasby was hilarious** Donald, 543; Goodwin, 661.
209   **Annual Message to Congress** 12/1/62, SWII:415.
209   **Madison, in the *Federalist*** Madison (*Writings*), 160–167; Washington, 969–970.
210   **"states of it"** To Thurlow Weed, 12/17/60, SWII:192.
210   **"to take Cuba"** To James T. Hale, 1/11/61, SWII:196.
210   **"be restricted"** To Alexander H. Stephens, 12/22/60, SWII:194.
210   **"inflexible"** To Thurlow Weed, op. cit., SWII:192.
211   **"there are of us"** Speech at Cincinnati, 9/17/59, SWII:77.
212   **"than your own"** To Ephraim D. and Phoebe Ellis, 5/25/61, SWII:242.

214   **"a drunken man"** Brookhiser (*Dynasty*), 150.

214   **"mosquitoes"** Speech in the US House of Representatives on the Presidential Question, 7/27/48, SWI:214.

214   **"give us victories"** To Joseph Hooker, 1/26/63, SWII:434.

215   **"please me"** Thomas, 286.

215   **"the better"** Donald, 411.

215   **"bring us success"** Thomas, 289.

215   **"dictatorship"** To Joseph Hooker, op. cit.

216   **"he fights"** Donald, 349.

216   **"whole game"** To Orville H. Browning, 9/22/61, SWII:269.

216   **"poor white trash"** Donald, 317.

216   **"hanged for all this"** Charles Francis Adams Jr., 95.

217   **bait in a trap?** See Donald, 422–423.

217   **"to suffer"** To the Senate and House of Representatives, 5/26/62, CWV:243.

218   **power play** See Goodwin, 486–495.

219   **"circus"** Foner, 272.

249   **"restricted"** To Alexander H. Stephens, 12/22/60, SWII:194.

220   **"strapping negro"** Foner, 186.

220   **"Human Authority"** Stay of Execution for Nathaniel Gordon, 2/4/62, SWII:306.

221   **"twenty five"** Address on Colonization to a Committee of Colored Men, Washington, DC, 8/14/62, SWII:353–357.

222   **"military proclamation"** To Orville H. Browning, 9/22/61, SWII:268.

222   **"Butler's fugitive slave law"** Foner, 171.

223   **calculated . . . estimated** Brookhiser (*Madison*), 232; Ellis, 267–268.

223   **"abrasion"** Appeal to the Border-States Representatives for Compensated Emancipation, 7/12/62, SWII:341.

224   **Delaware** Drafts of Bill for Compensated Emancipation in Delaware, c. late 11/61, SWII:276–278.

224   **another plan** Donald, 365.

225   **"also do that"** To Horace Greeley, 8/22/62, and footnote, CWV:388–389.

225   **"Judassis hed"** Ward, 35.

225   **"to my Maker"** Goodwin, 481–482.

226   **he was crazy** Address at Cooper Institute, New York City, 2/27/60, SWII:125.

226 **"actual armed rebellion"** Final Emancipation Proclamation,
SWII:424–425.
226 **Patrick Henry . . . James Madison** Brookhiser (*Madison*), 231.
227 **John Quincy Adams** Brookhiser (*Dynasty*), 141.
227 **Sumner had asked** Charles Francis Adams Jr., 55–56.
228 **"earnest emphasis"** HI, 197.

Chapter Thirteen

230 **"'pictures of silver'"** The image in the Hebrew original is of jew-
elry; *pictures* could be translated as *carvings*. See Alter, 303.
230 **"bruised or broken"** To Alexander H. Stephens, 12/22/60, footnote, CWIV:161; Fragment on the Constitution and the Union, c.
1/61, CWIV:169.
231 **"freedom of mankind"** To John M. Clay, 8/9/62, SWII:35.
233 **"curse . . . defiance"** Madison (*Debates*), 8/8/87, 392.
234 ***"something* else"** Brookhiser (*Gentleman*), 61–62.
235 **Madison . . . Hamilton** Madison (*Debates*), 6/6/87, 75; 6/18/87,
134; 6/26/87, 190.
235 **None of the delegates** Patrick Henry did question the ramifications
of "We the People" at the Virginia Ratifying Convention. James Madison, as an old man, warned against expending "so much constructive
ingenuity" on the Preamble. See Brookhiser (*Gentleman*), 91–92.
237 **"deliberate decisions"** Special Message to Congress, 7/4/61,
SWII:261.
237 **"common charge?"** Annual Message to Congress, 12/1/62, SWII:408.
238 **"in the world"** Appeal to the Border-State Representatives for
Compensated Emancipation, 7/12/62, SWII:342.
238 **"at stake"** Reply to Chicago Emancipation Memorial, 9/13/62,
SWII:365.
239 **"the occasion"** Response to Serenade, 7/7/63, SWII:475–476.
239 **"top of my head"** Chesnut, 219.
239 **The bodies** For the setting at Gettysburg, see Wills, 19–40.
240 **Everett spoke** Wills reprints his speech, 213–247.
240 **In a letter** To Edward Everett, 11/20/63, SWII:537.
241 **Wills noted** Wills, 174.
243 **portentous phrase** Lowry, 9–15, and Wills, 145–146, give critical
accounts of contemporary opportunists and fearmongers, respectively.

244 **"old American Constitution"** Holzer (*Anthology*), 49.

245 **the Preamble** Lincoln's tripartite invocation of the people echoed nineteenth-century orators, such as Theodore Parker and Daniel Webster (see Wills, 129, 281), but they were intermediate stops on the way back to the Preamble.

245 **"long-continued applause"** Address at Gettysburg, Pennsylvania, 11/19/63, SWII:536; AP account, SWII:748–749.

245 **"no good to them"** Special Message to Congress, op. cit., SWII:260.

Chapter Fourteen

247 **"terrible war"** To Eliza P. Gurney, 9/4/64, SWII:627; Second Inaugural Address, 3/4/65, SWII:687.

248 **"and act"** Grant, 382.

249 **"ever made"** Grant, 477.

249 **"as possible"** To Ulysses S. Grant, 8/17/64, SWII:620.

249 **"public opinion"** Foner, 230.

249 **"of the United States"** Final Emancipation Proclamation, SWII:425.

249 **"no matter"** To James C. Conkling, 8/26/63, SWII:498.

250 **grand painting** See Fischer, 1–4, 21–22, 25, 488.

253 **"hair of a nigger"** Charles Francis Adams Jr., 94–95.

253 **"impossibility"** Donald, 528.

253 **scenarios** See Holzer (*Objects*), for two of Lincoln's preelection vote counts.

254 **"but the negro"** Donald, 537.

255 **Chase yearned** Chase was unemployed at the time, having submitted his resignation once too often. Lincoln accepted it June 30, 1864 (see SWII:603).

255 **"'material aid'"** Thomas, 452.

256 **"privileges and positions"** Speech to the 148th Ohio Regiment, Washington, DC, SWII:626.

257 **"'Here we are again'"** William Herndon to Ward Lamon, 3/3/70, Ward Hill Lamon Papers, LN2327, Huntington Library.

257 **"from a desert," "like a child"** Brooks, 215, 278.

257 **"expect it"** To Fanny McCullough, 12/23/62, SWII:420.

258 **Lydia Bixby** To Mrs. Lydia Bixby, 11/21/64, SWII:644, 755; CWVIII:117.

259 **"shot off"** Brooks, 238.

260   **Lincoln answered** HI, 157.
261   **"this terrible war"** To Eliza P. Gurney, op. cit., SWII:627.
261   **"bleed to death"** Speech on the Kansas-Nebraska Act of Peoria, Illinois, 10/16/54, SWI:338.
261   **a canto** *Don Juan*, canto VIII, stanza 20.
262   **Charles Sumner proposed** The French text (Article 6) reads: *Tous les citoyens étant égaux à ses yeux* . . . (All citizens being equal in its [the law's] eyes . . .). See Foner, 291–292.
264   **"to be in it"** To James M. Ashley, 1/31/65, CWVIII:248.
264   **Davis had embargoed** Howe, 257.
265   **"two countries," "one common country"** Jeffn. Davis to F. P. Blair, 1/12/65, A. Lincoln to F. P. Blair, 1/18/65, SWII:674–675.
265   **without result** Donald, 555–560.
265   **"slave trade"** Donald, 560.

Chapter Fifteen

269   **Paine . . . mocked** P, 683, 722, 676.
269   **favorite phrases** Brooks, 216.
270   **"a good book"** Bayne, 32–33, 184.
271   **"not end yet"** Meditation on the Divine Will, c. early 9/62, SWII:359.
271   **"seen of men"** CWV:404.
272   **"other minds"** Reply to Chicago Emancipation Memorial, 9/13/62, SWII: 361, 363.
273   **"their refuge"** Gurney, 307–312.
273   **"vague tradition"** To Solomon Lincoln, 3/6/48, SWI:177. John Lincoln married a Quaker.
273   **a good word for** See P, 821–822.
274   **"governs it"** Reply to Eliza P. Gurney, 10/26/62, CWV:478.
275   **"assured friend"** Gurney, 313–316.
275   **"in another"** HI, 106–107.
276   **"in Heaven"** To Eliza P. Gurney, 9/4/64, SWII:627.
276   **"goodness of God"** To Albert G. Hodges, 4/4/64, SWII:586.
277   **"as long as I live"** Chesnut, 350.
278   **the address** Second Inaugural Address, 3/4/65, SWII:686–687.
282   **"any other way"** P, 702.

Chapter Sixteen

286 **"liberally all around"** Donald, 574.

286 **"to God only"** Donald, 576.

286 **"touch him further"** *Macbeth*, act III, scene ii. See Chambrun, 35, who quotes no specific lines, but says that Lincoln read the scene.

287 **"upon his army"** Grant, 604.

288 **"intelligent black man"** To Edwin M. Stanton, 2/8/65, CWVIII:273–274. Joseph Louis Cook, who had a black father, was commissioned as a lieutenant colonel in the Continental Army in 1779, but he self-identified as an American Indian.

289 **"their situation"** Speech on the Kansas-Nebraska Act at Peoria, Illinois, 10/16/54, SWII:315.

289 **"as long as you are president"** Thomas, 502.

289 **"white trash"** Donald, 317.

289 **a proclamation** Proclamation of Amnesty and Reconstruction, 12/8/63, SWII:555–558.

290 **"very intelligent"** To Michael Hahn, 3/13/64, SWII:579.

291 **"energy, and daring"** Speech on Reconstruction, Washington, DC, 4/11/65, SWII:699–700.

291 **"he will ever make"** Donald, 588.

292 **"own responsibility"** Francis Wilson, 50–54.

292 **himself had nixed** Donald, 677–678.

294 **"liberate them"** Address at Cooper Institute, New York City, 2/27/60, SWII:125.

294 **"bullfrog"** Donald, 597.

295 **a disgrace to the age** Sherman, II:349. This is Sherman's characterization of what Johnston said. In his own memoirs Johnston said he called it "the greatest possible calamity to the South" (Johnston, 402).

Epilogue

299 **Another was given** *World's Orators*, X:300–305.

BIBLIOGRAPHY

One book that does not appear in this bibliography, but which anyone interested in Lincoln should read, is Richard Weaver's *The Ethics of Rhetoric*, particularly the chapters "Edmund Burke and the Argument from Circumstance" and "Abraham Lincoln and the Argument from Definition."

Abbreviations of Most-Cited Works

CW Lincoln, Abraham. *Collected Works of Abraham Lincoln*. Roy P. Basler, ed. New Brunswick, NJ: Rutgers University Press, 1953.

H   Herndon, William. *Herndon's Life of Lincoln*. With Introduction and Notes by Paul M. Angle. New York: Da Capo Press, 1983.

HI *Herndon's Informants*. Douglas L. Wilson and Rodney O. Davis, eds. Urbana: University of Illinois Press, 1998.

J   Jefferson, Thomas. *The Life and Selected Writings of Thomas Jefferson*. Adrienne Koch and William Peden, eds. New York: Modern Library, 1944.

P   Paine, Thomas. *Collected Writings*. Eric Foner, ed. New York: Library of America, 1995.

SW Lincoln, Abraham. *Speeches and Writings*. Don E. Fehrenbacher, ed. New York: Library of America, 1989.

Abridgement of the Debates of Congress. New York: D. Appleton and Company, 1861.

Adams, Charles Francis, Jr. *An Autobiography.* Boston: Houghton Mifflin, 1916.

Adams, Henry. *History of the United States During the Administrations of James Madison.* New York: Library of America, 1986.

Alter, Robert. *The Wisdom Books.* New York: W. W. Norton, 2010.

American Antislavery Writings: Colonial Beginnings to Emancipation. James G. Basker, ed. New York: Library of America, 2012.

American Speeches: Political Oratory from the Revolution to the Civil War. Ted Widmer, ed. New York: Library of America, 2006.

Appendix to the Congressional Globe for the First Session, Thirtieth Congress. Washington, DC: Blair and Rives, 1848.

Bayne, Julia Taft. *Tad Lincoln's Father.* Boston: Little, Brown, 1931.

Boritt, Gabor S. *Lincoln and the Economics of the American Dream.* Urbana: University of Illinois Press, 1994.

Bray, Robert. *Reading with Lincoln.* Carbondale: Southern Illinois University Press, 2010.

Brookhiser, Richard. "Abraham Lincoln's Cooper Union Address." *For the People, a Newsletter of the Abraham Lincoln Association*, Spring 2014.

————. *America's First Dynasty.* New York: The Free Press, 2002.

————. *Founding Father: Rediscovering George Washington.* New York: The Free Press, 1996.

————. *Gentleman Revolutionary.* New York: The Free Press, 2003.

————. *James Madison.* New York: Basic Books, 2011.

————. "Was Lincoln Gay?" *New York Times Book Review*, January 9, 2005.

————. "We've Been Here Before" (Harrison). *American History*, June 2012.

————. "We've Been Here Before" (Vallandingham). *American History*, August 2013.

Brooks, Noah. *Lincoln Observed.* Michael Burlingame, ed. Baltimore: Johns Hopkins University Press, 1998.

Chambrun, Marquis de. "Personal Recollections of Mr. Lincoln." *Scribner's* 13, no. 1 (1893).

Chapman, John Jay. *William Lloyd Garrison.* New York: Moffat, Yard, 1913.

Chesnut, Mary Boykin. *A Diary from Dixie* . . . Isabella D. Martin and Myrta Lockett Avary, eds. New York: D. Appleton and Company, 1905.

Collins, Gail. *William Henry Harrison*. New York: Times Books, 2012.

Congressional Globe, 36th Cong., 1st sess. Washington, DC: John C. Rives, 1859–1860.

Cutts, J. Madison. *A Brief Treatise upon Constitutional and Party Questions*. New York: D. Appleton and Company, 1866.

Debates and Proceedings in the Congress of the United States. Washington, DC: Gales and Seaton, 1834.

Donald, David Herbert. *Lincoln*. New York: Simon and Schuster, 1995.

Douglas, Stephen. "The Dividing Line Between Federal and Local Authority . . . " *Harper's New Monthly Magazine*, vol. 19, June to November 1859.

Dyer, Oliver. *Great Senators of the United States Forty Years Ago*. New York: Robert Bonner's Sons, 1889.

Ellis, Joseph J. *American Sphinx*. New York: Alfred A. Knopf, 1997.

Everett, Edward. *Orations and Speeches on Various Occasions*. Boston: Little, Brown, 1868.

Fehrenbacher, Don E. *Prelude to Greatness*. Stanford, CA: Stanford University Press, 1962.

Fehrenbacher, Don E., and Virginia Fehrenbacher. *Recollected Words of Abraham Lincoln*. Stanford, CA: Stanford University Press, 1996.

Fischer, David Hackett. *Washington's Crossing*. New York: Oxford University Press, 2004.

Foner, Eric. *The Fiery Trial*. New York: W. W. Norton, 2010.

Foote, Henry S. *Casket of Reminiscences*. Washington, DC: Chronicle, 1874.

Franklin, Benjamin. *Writings*. J. A. Leo Lemay, ed. New York: Library of America, 1987.

Goodwin, Doris Kearns. *Team of Rivals*. New York: Simon and Schuster, 2005.

Grant, Ulysses S. *Personal Memoirs*. New York: Penguin, 1999.

Greeley, Horace. *Recollections of a Busy Life*. New York: J. B. Ford and Company, 1868.

Guelzo, Allen C. *Abraham Lincoln: Redeemer President*. Grand Rapids, MI: William B. Eerdmans, 1999.

Gurney, Eliza P. *Memoir and Correspondence of Eliza P. Gurney*. Richard F. Mott, ed. Philadelphia: J. B. Lippincott, 1884.

Hamilton, Alexander. *Writings*. Joanne Freeman, ed. New York: Library of America, 2001.

Herz, Emanuel. *The Hidden Lincoln*. New York: Blue Ribbon Books, 1940.

Holzer, Harold. *The Civil War in 50 Objects*. New York: Viking, 2013.

———. *The Lincoln Anthology*. New York: Library of America, 1989.

———. *Lincoln at Cooper Union*. New York: Simon and Schuster, 2004.

Howe, Daniel Walker. *The Political Culture of the American Whigs*. Chicago: University of Chicago Press, 1979.

Jaffa, Harry V. *Crisis of the House Divided*. Chicago: University of Chicago Press, 1982.

Johnston, Joseph E. *Narrative of Military Operations*. New York: D. Appleton and Company, 1874.

Keane, John. *Tom Paine*. Boston: Little, Brown, 1995.

Lehrman, Lewis E. *Lincoln at Peoria*. Mechanicsburg, PA: Stackpole Books, 2008.

Levasseur, Auguste. *Lafayette in America*. Philadelphia: Carey and Lea, 1829.

Lincoln Legal Briefs, Quarterly Newsletter of the Lincoln Legal Papers, January–March 1995, no.33.

Lowry, Rich. *Lincoln Unbound*. New York: HarperCollins, 2013.

Madison, James. *Debates in the Federal Convention of 1787*. James McClellan and M. E. Bradford, eds. Richmond, VA: James River Press, 1989.

———. *Writings*. Jack N. Rakove, ed. New York: Library of America, 1999.

Martineau, Harriet. *Retrospect of Western Travel*. London: Saunders and Otley, 1838.

Miller, Richard Lawrence. "Lincoln's 'Suicide' Poem: Has It Been Found?" *For the People, a Newsletter of the Abraham Lincoln Association*, Spring 2004.

Moore, John Bassett, ed. *The Works of James Buchanan*. John Bassett Moore, ed. Philadelphia: J. B. Lippincott, 1910.

Nasby, Petroleum V. *The Nasby Papers*. Indianapolis: C. O. Perrine, 1864.

Peterson, Merrill D. The *Jefferson Image in the American Mind*. New York: Oxford University Press, 1962.

Pinsker, Matthew. "Senator Abraham Lincoln." *Journal of the Abraham Lincoln Association* 14, no. 2 (1993).

Register of Debates in Congress, 22nd Cong., 1st sess. Washington, DC: Gales and Seaton, 1833.

Rowland, Kate Mason. *The Life of Charles Carroll of Carrollton*. New York: G. P. Putnam's Sons, 1898.

Schlesinger, Arthur, Jr. *The Age of Jackson*. Boston: Little, Brown, 1946.

Sheahan, James W. *The Life of Stephen Douglas*. New York: Harper and Brothers, 1860.

Sherman, William T. *Memoirs of General William T. Sherman*. New York: D. Appleton and Company, 1904.

Stephens, Alexander H. *Recollections of Alexander H. Stephens*. Myrta Lockett Avary, ed. Baton Rouge: Louisiana State University Press, 1998.

Strozier, Robert. *Lincoln's Quest for Union*. Philadelphia: Paul Dry Books, 2001.

Tarbell, Ida M. *The Life of Abraham Lincoln*. New York: Lincoln Memorial Association, 1895.

Thomas, Benjamin P. *Abraham Lincoln*. New York: Barnes and Noble Books, 1993.

Thoreau, Henry David. *Great Short Works of Henry David Thoreau*. Wendell Glick, ed. New York: Harper and Row, 1982.

Tocqueville, Alexis de. *Journey to America*. George Lawrence, trans.; J. P. Mayer, ed. New Haven, CT: Yale University Press, 1959.

Tripp, C. A. *The Intimate World of Abraham Lincoln*. New York: Simon and Schuster, 2005.

Ward, Artemus. *Artemus Ward: His Book*. New York: Carleton, 1864.

Washington, George. *Writings*. John Rhodehamel, ed. New York: Library of America, 1997.

Weems, Mason Locke. *Life of Washington*. Cleveland: World Publishing, 1965.

Wills, Garry. *Lincoln at Gettysburg*. New York: Simon and Schuster, 1992.

Wilson, Douglas L. *Honor's Voice*. New York: Vintage Books, 1998.

Wilson, Francis. *John Wilkes Booth*. Boston: Houghton, Mifflin, 1929.

Winthrop, Robert C. *Addresses and Speeches on Various Occasions*. Boston: Little, Brown, 1852.

Wood, Gordon S. *Empire of Liberty*. New York: Oxford University Press, 2009.

The World's Orators. Guy Carlton Lee, ed. New York: G. P. Putnam's Sons, 1901.

INDEX

Richard Brookhiser is a senior editor of *National Review* and the author of eleven books, including *James Madison*, *Alexander Hamilton, American*, and *Founding Father: Rediscovering George Washington*. He lives in New York City.